THE NEW CAMBRID

GENERAL EDITOR: Brian C

ASSOCIATE GENERAL EDITOR: A. R. Braunmuller

From the publication of the first volumes in 1984 the General Editor of the New Cambridge Shakespeare was Philip Brockbank and the Associate General Editors were Brian Gibbons and Robin Hood. From 1990 to 1994 the General Editor was Brian Gibbons and the Associate General Editors were A. R. Braunmuller and Robin Hood.

THE FIRST QUARTO OF KING RICHARD III

Shakespeare's *Richard III* presents difficult textual problems. There are some two thousand verbal differences between the text of the first quarto (1597) and the version in the First Folio (1623). Although the narrative of the two plays is virtually identical, each has lines which are not found in the other, parts of the play are arranged differently, and the quarto deploys fewer characters.

In the past editors have based an analysis of the quarto text on its conjectural relationship with the Folio. In this edition Peter Davison examines every quarto reading to establish a presumption of originality. He proposes that Shakespeare's company, the Lord Chamberlain's Men, used a memorially reconstructed text of *Richard III* during a touring production of the play, and that text provided the manuscript for the 1597 quarto. A lengthy Introduction sets out the problem and the proposed solution. The text of the quarto is accompanied by a Collation of variant readings and substantial Textual Notes.

An important element of this edition is the history of what happened to the text on tour. Using examples of touring practice of the past four hundred years, the Introduction shows how the actors' involvement helped to produce the text we have. Much new information is adduced about touring in Shakespeare's time, the doubling of parts, and how tours were financed. The result is a breakthrough in textual studies.

THE NEW CAMBRIDGE SHAKESPEARE

Romeo and Juliet, edited by G. Blakemore Evans
The Taming of the Shrew, edited by Ann Thompson
Othello, edited by Norman Sanders
King Richard II, edited by Andrew Gurr
A Midsummer Night's Dream, edited by R. A. Foakes
Hamlet, edited by Philip Edwards
Twelfth Night, edited by Elizabeth Story Donno
All's Well That Ends Well, edited by Russell Fraser
The Merchant of Venice, edited by M. M. Mahood
Much Ado About Nothing, edited by F. H. Mares
The Comedy of Errors, edited by T. S. Dorsch
Julius Caesar, edited by Marvin Spevack
The Second Part of King Henry IV, edited by Giorgio Melchiori
King John, edited by L. A. Beaurline
King Henry VIII, edited by John Margeson
Antony and Cleopatra, edited by David Bevington
The Two Gentlemen of Verona, edited by Kurt Schlueter
Measure for Measure, edited by Brian Gibbons
The First Part of King Henry VI, edited by Michael Hattaway
The Second Part of King Henry VI, edited by Michael Hattaway
The Third Part of King Henry VI, edited by Michael Hattaway
The Poems, edited by John Roe
King Henry V, edited by Andrew Gurr
The Tragedy of King Lear, edited by Jay L. Halio
Titus Andronicus, edited by Alan Hughes

THE EARLY QUARTOS

The First Quarto of King Lear, edited by Jay L. Halio
The First Quarto of King Richard III, edited by Peter Davison

THE FIRST QUARTO OF KING RICHARD III

Edited by
PETER DAVISON

Professor of English, Media, and Cultural Studies,
De Montfort University, Leicester

CAMBRIDGE UNIVERSITY PRESS
Cambridge, New York, Melbourne, Madrid, Cape Town, Singapore, São Paulo

Cambridge University Press
The Edinburgh Building, Cambridge CB2 8RU, UK

Published in the United States of America by Cambridge University Press, New York

www.cambridge.org
Information on this title: www.cambridge.org/9780521418188

First published 1996
This digitally printed version 2007

A catalogue record for this publication is available from the British Library

Library of Congress Cataloguing in Publication data

Shakespeare, William, 1564–1616.
[King Richard III]
The first quarto of King Richard III / edited by Peter Davison.
  p. cm. – (The New Cambridge Shakespeare)
ISBN 0 521 41818 6 (hardback)
1. Richard III, King of England, 1452–1485 – Drama. 2. Great
Britain – Kings and rulers – Drama. I. Davison, Peter Hobley.
II. Title. III. Series: Shakespeare, William, 1564–1616. Works. 1984
Cambridge University Press.
PR2750.B21 1996
882.3′3–dc20 95-40628 CIP

ISBN 978-0-521-41818-8 hardback
ISBN 978-0-521-04207-9 paperback

THE NEW CAMBRIDGE SHAKESPEARE
THE EARLY QUARTOS

There is no avoiding edited Shakespeare, the question is only what kind of editing. A Shakespeare play first assumed material form as the author's bundle of manuscript sheets. The company of players required a manuscript fair copy of the play (apart from the individual actors' parts). Into the fair copy were entered playhouse changes, and the bookholder used it during each performance. However, none of Shakespeare's plays survives in contemporary manuscript form. There is one passage in the manuscript of *Sir Thomas More* by Hand D which has been ascribed to Shakespeare himself, but this attribution remains in serious dispute. In short, there is no direct access to Shakespeare's play-manuscripts – there is only print, and this implies editing, since the first printed versions of Shakespeare were mediated by compositors and proof-readers at least, and sometimes also by revisers, bookholders, editors, censors, and scribes. The first printers used either the author's or a playhouse manuscript or some combination of the two, although for several plays they used a scribal transcript by Ralph Crane, who is known to have habitually effaced and altered his copy.

There are certain quartos which are abbreviated, apparently because they are re-ported texts or derive from playhouse adaptation. These early quartos are not chosen as copy-texts for modern critical editions and are not readily available, though indis-pensable to advanced students of Shakespeare and of textual bibliography. Alongside the standard volumes in the New Cambridge Shakespeare, editions of selected quarto texts are to be published in critical, modern-spelling form, including early quartos of *King Lear*, *Hamlet*, *Richard III*, and *Othello*.

While the advanced textual scholar must work either with the rare, actual copies of the earliest printed editions, or with photo-facsimiles of them, there is more general interest in these texts and hence a need to present them in a form that makes them more generally accessible, a form that provides the most up-to-date and expert schol-arship and engages with the key issues of how these texts differ from other quarto versions and from the First Folio, and to what effect. These are the precise aims of New Cambridge Shakespeare quartos.

Each volume presents, with the text and Collation, an introductory essay about the quarto text, its printing, and the nature of its differences from the other early printed versions. There is discussion of scholarly hypotheses about its nature and provenance, including its theatrical provenance, where that issue is appropriate. The accompany-ing notes address textual, theatrical, and staging questions, following the spacious and handsome format of the New Cambridge Shakespeare.

BRIAN GIBBONS
General Editor

CONTENTS

FIGURES

PREFACE

This edition of the first quarto of *Richard III* complements the forthcoming Folio-based edition independently prepared in the New Cambridge Shakespeare. Readers should turn to that edition for an account of sources, stage history after 1597, and critical interpretation. The Introduction and Textual Notes to this edition are limited to problems posed by the quarto.

The Introduction and Textual Notes attempt to distinguish the nature of the kinds of verbal differences between Q and F and from this to establish, in the context of what can be gleaned of the play's stage history up to 1597 (when the Lord Chamberlain's Men visited six towns in southern England), the kinds of authority represented in the quarto. It cannot be stressed too strongly that trying to establish how a variant has arisen is speculative. Nevertheless, although different people will explain variants differently, it is believed that, in their totality, the explanations given here, read in the context of the play's theatrical provenance, provide a sound basis for suggesting how the quarto came to be the text it is.

Spelling and punctuation have been modernised in conformity with the style of the New Cambridge Shakespeare. A full Collation of verbal variants is provided; variations in punctuation are noted only if they affect meaning; variant lineation is rarely described. Only a minimum of editorial emendations has been made and those chiefly stem from what is perceived to be the work of scribes or compositors. The text is otherwise deliberately faithful to the quarto. It would not be difficult on the basis of what is shown here to prepare a version that could be performed by a small company of actors much in the manner that it is suggested was done by the Lord Chamberlain's Men at the end of the sixteenth century. Because of the importance given to touring to explain how the quarto was generated, more attention has been paid to the exigencies of touring than would otherwise have been necessary.

Anyone attempting to produce a new edition of one of Shakespeare's plays is indebted to scholars and critics without number. I have tried to acknowledge all specific debts in the usual manner but I should like here to thank two institutions and several people for more general help. I must first express my gratitude to the British Academy and the Folger Shakespeare Library for enabling me to spend three months at the Folger in 1982. It was then that I made an analysis of Q1 and prepared the doubling pattern reproduced here when engaged on a projected edition of *Richard III* based on the Folio text.

I should like to acknowledge the help I have had, in many more ways than those specifically mentioned, from Antony Hammond's excellent Arden edition. I occasionally disagree with Professor Hammond, especially over the use of clowns, but that in no way calls into question the valuable help given me by his edition. I wish to thank Professor Molly Mahood for some specific points but, more generally, for her kind encouragement at a particularly depressing time. As I now live in a small town, I have been dependent on the local public library in obtaining books through inter-library loan. I should like to thank Marlborough Public Library, and especially the librarian, Margaret Miller, and those who have lent books, for their patience and efficiency. I am very grateful to the Bibliographical Society for giving me an opportunity to discuss the problem of editing the first quarto of *Richard III* in my Presidential Address in 1994.

I had the pleasure of trying out drafts of parts of this edition with lively groups of American students at Summer Schools organised by Georgetown and De Montfort Universities in 1993 and 1994 and with students of De Montfort in 1994–5. I greatly appreciated their participation. Finally, I should like to thank the General Editor, Brian Gibbons, and the copy-editor, Margaret Berrill, for their meticulous checking: they saved me from many errors. I am very grateful to them.

P.D.
De Montfort University, Leicester

ABBREVIATIONS AND CONVENTIONS

Works listed below are those which have been important in the preparation of this edition; where abbreviations are used in the footnotes and Textual Notes, these are given. Details of other works to which reference is made are included in the footnotes and the Textual Notes. This list is not intended to be a full reading list.

Abbott	E. A. Abbott, *A Shakespearian Grammar*, 1879
Arden	*King Richard III*, ed. Antony Hammond, 1981 (Arden)
Baker	Sir Richard Baker, *Theatrum Redivivum, or The Theatre Vindicated*, 1662; facsimile edn, 1972
Barroll	Leeds Barroll, *Politics, Plague, and Shakespeare's Theater: The Stuart Years*, 1991
Binns	J. W. Binns, 'Women or transvestites on the Elizabethan stage? An Oxford controversy', *Sixteenth Century Journal*, 2 (1974), 95–120
Binns, 'Gentili'	J. W. Binns, 'Alberico Gentili in defense of poetry and acting', *Studies in the Renaissance*, 19 (1972), 224–72
Boddy	G. W. Boddy, 'Players of interludes in North Yorkshire in the early seventeenth century', *North Yorkshire County Record Office Journal*, 3 (1976), 95–130
Boswell-Stone	W. G. Boswell-Stone, *Shakespeare's Holinshed: The Chronicle and the History Plays Compared*, 1896
Bradley	David Bradley, *From Text to Performance in the Elizabethan Theatre: Preparing the Play for the Stage*, 1992
Bullough	G. Bullough, ed., *Narrative and Dramatic Sources in Shakespeare*, vol. III, 1960
Capell	*Mr William Shakespeare his Comedies, Histories, and Tragedies*, ed. Edward Capell, 10 vols., 1767–8
Chambers	E. K. Chambers, *William Shakespeare: A Study of Facts and Problems*, 2 vols., 1930
Chambers, *Stage*	E. K. Chambers, *The Elizabethan Stage*, 4 vols., 1923.
Cibber	Colley Cibber, *Richard III, Altered from Shakespeare*, [1700], 1757, 1769
Collier	*The Works of William Shakespeare*, ed. John Payne Collier, 8 vols., 1842–4
Cook	Ann Jennalie Cook, *The Privileged Playgoers of Shakespeare's London, 1576–1642*, 1981
Cunnington	B. Howard Cunnington, *Records of the County of Wilts*, 1932
Davison	Peter Davison, 'Bibliography: Teaching, research and publication; reflections on editing the first quarto of *Richard III*', *The Library*, VI, 17 (1995), 1–31

* In the Collation, an asterisk before a line reference indicates an editorial emendation.

Davison, 'Evidence' Peter Davison, 'The selection and presentation of bibliographic evidence', *Analytical and Enumerative Bibliography*, 1 (1977), 101–36

Dawson Giles E. Dawson, ed., Malone Society, *Collections VII*, 1965

F1, F *Mr William Shakespeares Comedies, Histories, and Tragedies*, 1623 (First Folio)

F2 *Mr William Shakespeares Comedies, Histories, and Tragedies*, 1632 (Second Folio)

F3 *Mr William Shakespeares Comedies, Histories, and Tragedies*, 1663–4 (Third Folio)

F4 *Mr William Shakespeares Comedies, Histories, and Tragedies*, 1685 (Fourth Folio)

Fair Maid *The Fair Maid of the Exchange* (1607), ed. Peter Davison (Malone Society), 1963

Fenton Doris Fenton, *The Extra-Dramatic Moment in Elizabethan Plays before 1616*, 1930

Foster Donald Foster, 'SHAXICON 2.0', (1994; privately supplied); for earlier version, see *Shakespeare Newsletter*, Summer, Fall, Winter, 1991

Furness *Richard III*, ed. H. H. Furness, 1908 (New Variorum)

George David George, 'Jacobean actors and the Great Hall at Gawthorpe, Lancashire', *Theatre Notebook*, 37 (1983), 109–21

Green-Room *Authentic Memoirs of the Green-Room*, Anonymous, 2 vols., 2nd edn, 1806

Greg, *Bibliography* W. W. Greg, *A Bibliography of the English Printed Drama*, 4 vols., 1939–70

Greg, *Editorial Problem* W. W. Greg, *The Editorial Problem in Shakespeare*, 1954

Greg, *Facsimile* *Richard III*, ed. W. W. Greg (*Shakespeare Quarto Facsimile*, 12), 1959

Greg, *First Folio* W. W. Greg, *The Shakespeare First Folio: Its Bibliographical and Textual History*, 1955

Greg, *Licensers* W. W. Greg, *Licensers of the Press, &c. to 1660*, 1962

1H4 *The First Part of King Henry the Fourth*

2H4 *The Second Part of King Henry the Fourth*

H5 *King Henry the Fifth*

3H6 *The Third Part of King Henry the Sixth*

Halle Edward Halle, *The Union of the Two Noble and Illustre Famelies of Lancastre & Yorke*, 2nd edn, 1550; facsimile edn, 1970

Hammond Antony Hammond, ed., *Richard III* (Arden)

Hankey *Richard III* (Plays in Performance), ed. Julie Hankey, 1981

Harland *The Home and Farm Accounts of the Shuttleworths of Gawthorpe Hall in the County of Lancaster at Smithills and Gawthorpe, September 1582–1621*, ed. John Harland, 4 vols., 1856–8

Henslowe *Henslowe's Diary*, ed. R. A. Foakes and R. T. Rickert, 1961

Hinman Charlton Hinman, *The Printing and Proof-Reading of the First Folio of Shakespeare*, 2 vols., 1963

Holinshed Raphael Holinshed, *The Firste . . . Volume of the Chronicles of Englande*, 2nd edn, 1587

Holloway David Holloway, *Playing the Empire: The Acts of the Holloway Touring Theatre Company*, 1979

Honigmann E. A. J. Honigmann, 'The text of *Richard III*', *Theatre Research*, 7 (1965), 48–55

Honigmann, *Stability*	E. A. J. Honigmann, *The Stability of Shakespeare's Text*, 1965
Johnson	*The Plays of William Shakespeare*, ed. Samuel Johnson, 8 vols., 1765
Kane	*Piers Plowman: The A Version*, ed. George Kane, 1960
King	T. J. King, *Casting Shakespeare's Plays: London Actors and their Roles, 1590–1642*, 1992
King Leir	*The True Chronicle of King Leir* (1605), ed. W. W. Greg (Malone Society), 1907
Lear	*King Lear*
Malone	*The Plays and Poems of William Shakespeare*, ed. Edmund Malone, 1790
More	Sir Thomas More, *The History of King Richard the Third*, ed. Richard S. Sylvester, *The Complete Works of St Thomas More*, vol. II, 1963
Murray	J. T. Murray, *English Dramatic Companies, 1558–1642*, 2 vols., 1910
MV	*The Merchant of Venice*
NCS	*Richard III*, ed. John Dover Wilson, 1954 (the original New Cambridge Shakespeare)
Odell	G. C. Odell, *Shakespeare from Betterton to Irving*, 2 vols., 1920
OED	*The Oxford English Dictionary*, 2nd edn, 1991.
om.	omitted
Patrick	D. L. Patrick, *The Textual History of Richard III*, 1936
Popular Appeal	Peter Davison, *Popular Appeal in English Drama to 1850*, 1982
Prosser	Eleanor Prosser, *Shakespeare's Anonymous Editors: Scribe and Compositor in the Folio Text of '2 Henry IV'*, 1981
Prynne	William Prynne, *Histrio-Mastix*, 1633; facsimile edn, 2 vols., 1972
Q1, Q	*The Tragedy of King Richard the third*, 1597 (first quarto)
Q2	*The Tragedie of King Richard the third*, 1598 (second quarto)
Q3	*The Tragedie of King Richard the third*, 1602 (third quarto)
Q4	*The Tragedie of King Richard the third*, 1605 (fourth quarto)
Q5	*The Tragedie of King Richard the third*, 1612 (fifth quarto)
Q6	*The Tragedie of King Richard the Third*, 1622 (sixth quarto)
Q7	*The Tragedie of King Richard the Third*, 1629 (seventh quarto)
Q8	*The Tragedie of King Richard the Third*, 1634 (eighth quarto)
Rainolds	*Th'overthrow of Stage-Playes*, 1599; facsimile edn, with Introduction by J. Binns, 1972
Rhodes	*Plays and Poems of Richard Brinsley Sheridan*, ed. R. Crompton Rhodes, 3 vols., 1928
Riverside	*The Riverside Shakespeare*, gen. ed. G. Blakemore Evans, 1974
Schoenbaum	Samuel Schoenbaum, *Shakespeare: A Documentary Life*, 1975
Schoenbaum, *Records*	Samuel Schoenbaum, *William Shakespeare: Records and Images*, 1981
SD	stage direction
SH	speech heading
Shr.	*The Taming of the Shrew*
Smidt	Kristian Smidt, *The Tragedy of King Richard the Third: Parallel Texts of the First Quarto and the First Folio with Variants of the Early Quartos*, 1969
Smidt, *Imposters*	Kristian Smidt, *Iniurious Imposters and Richard III*, 1964
Smidt, *Reassessment*	Kristian Smidt, *Memorial Transmission and Quarto Copy in Richard III: A Reassessment*, 1970
Spedding	J. Spedding, 'On the quarto and Folio of *Richard III*', *Shakespeare Society Transactions*, 1875–6

Spevack	Marvin Spevack, *The Harvard Concordance to Shakespeare*, 1973
Spevack, *Thesaurus*	Marvin Spevack, *A Shakespeare Thesaurus*, 1993
Sprague	A. C. Sprague, *The Doubling of Parts in Shakespeare's Plays*, 1966
Stevenson	Janet H. Stevenson, *Marlborough and Preshute*, 1990
Stone	Lawrence Stone, 'Companies of players entertained by the Earl of Cumberland and Lord Clifford, 1607–39', Malone Society, *Collections V*, 1959 (1960), 17–28
Streitberger	W. R. Streitberger, *Jacobean and Caroline Revels Accounts, 1603–1642* (Malone Society, *Collections XIII*), 1986
Sweet	Henry Sweet, *A Short Historical Grammar*, 1892
Tanselle	G. Thomas Tanselle, 'Editing without a copy-text', *Studies in Bibliography*, 47 (1994), 1–22
Tarlton	*Tarltons Iests*, 1613
Taylor	Gary Taylor, 'We happy few: the 1600 Abridgement', in S. Wells and Gary Taylor, *Modernizing Shakespeare's Spelling, with Three Studies in the Text of 'Henry V'*, 1979
Textual Companion	Stanley Wells and Gary Taylor, with William Montgomery and John Jowett, *William Shakespeare: A Textual Companion*, 1987
Theatrum Redivivum	*Theatrum Redivivum*, comp. Peter Davison, 17 vols. (facsimiles), 1972
Thomson	George Thomson, 'Marxism and textual criticism', *Wissenschaftliche Zeitschrift der Humboldt-Universität zu Berlin*, Gen-Sprachw. R., 12 (1963), 43–52
Thomson, 'Method'	George Thomson, 'Scientific method in textual criticism', *Eirene*, 1 (1960) 51–60
Thomson, 'Simplex'	George Thomson, 'Simplex ordo', *Classical Quarterly*, 15 (1965), 161–75
True Tragedy	*The True Tragedy of Richard the Third 1594*, ed. W. W. Greg (Malone Society), 1929
Turner	Robert Y. Turner, *Shakespeare's Apprenticeship*, 1974
Two Bouquets	Herbert and Eleanor Farjeon, *The Two Bouquets* [1936]; stage manager's annotated vocal score (in possession of the editor)
Urkowitz	Stephen Urkowitz, 'Reconsidering the relationship of quarto and Folio texts of *Richard III*', *English Literary Renaissance*, 16 (1986), 442–66
Walton	J. K. Walton, *The Copy for the First Folio of Richard III*, 1955
Wandering Patentee	Tate Wilkinson, *The Wandering Patentee: A History of the Yorkshire Theatres, from 1770 to the Present Time*, 4 vols., 1795; facsimile edn, 2 vols., 1973
Waylen	James Waylen, *A History Military and Municipal of . . . Marlborough*, 1854
Wells	*William Shakespeare, The Complete Works: Original-Spelling Edition*, gen. eds. Stanley Wells and Gary Taylor, 1986
Winter	W. Winter, *Shakespeare on the Stage*, 1911
Wiv.	*The Merry Wives of Windsor*
Wright	Louis B. Wright, 'Variety entertainment by Elizabethan strolling players', *JEGP*, 26 (1927), 294–303
Zimmerman	Susan Zimmerman, 'The use of headlines: Peter Short's Shakespearian quartos *1 Henry IV* and *Richard III*', *The Library*, VI, 7 (1985), 217–55

INTRODUCTION

There are basically two versions of *Richard III*: one, the first quarto, published in 1597; the other as part of the First Folio of 1623. They show some two thousand verbal differences – roughly, 10 per cent of the words of the play. The 1597 text omits lengthy passages found in the Folio, but it includes an important section not found in 1623. Sixty years ago D. L. Patrick suggested that the 1597 version was based on a memorial reconstruction by the actors.[1] The manuscript lying behind the Folio is thought to be Shakespeare's foul papers collated with one of the reprints of the first quarto.[2] There is no evidence to suggest that a prompt-book for the London theatre was available for either Q1 or F.

This edition is limited in its intentions; it seeks only to explore the nature of the quarto version of *Richard III* printed in 1597 and the circumstances that led to its production. It is not designed to establish what the author, or Shakespeare's company, the Lord Chamberlain's Men, 'intended' to be 'the' *Richard III*, and although comparison is constantly made with the Folio text of 1623 (the version, by and large, preferred by most editors), it is not with the purpose of preparing a critical edition of *Richard III*. Thus, although the layout and accidentals (e.g., the spelling, capitalisation, and punctuation) have been modernised, only such textual emendations have been made where error can reasonably be attributed to a scribe or compositor; editorial additions are shown within square brackets and, in the Collation, an asterisk marks all changes from Q1. The analysis of the quarto inevitably throws light on the Folio and it would be a relatively simple matter to produce from this edition a 'corrected version' of Q1 that would be as close as conjecture allows to a version of Q1 as performed in Shakespeare's day. Such a version would be closely akin to editions based on the Folio but distinct from them. The quarto of *Richard III* is fascinating in its own right for it

---

[1] D. L. Patrick, *The Textual History of Richard III* (Stanford, 1936); see also p. 5, n. 1; as 'Patrick' hereafter. David Bradley maintains 'that the evidence so far produced for memorial reconstruction is unconvincing and vulnerable in fact and logic', *From Text to Performance in the Elizabethan Theatre: Preparing the Play for the Stage* (Cambridge, 1992), p. 10; as 'Bradley' hereafter. Bradley does not discuss *Richard III*, for which I hope to demonstrate he is wrong. *A Textual Companion* to the Oxford Shakespeare, ed. Stanley Wells, Gary Taylor, *et al.* (Oxford, 1987), believes 'Patrick's hypothesis holds the field, and has held it, virtually uncontested, for half a century' (p. 228); and that Q can, 'because of other variants, be played by a smaller cast with less equipment than the Folio' (p. 228). Earlier, Taylor maintained that 'Q1 is the proper copy-text for *Richard III*' (*The Library*, VI, 3 (1981), 35), a position with which I agree.

[2] 'Considering the evidence as a whole, it is difficult to avoid the conclusion that behind F there lies not a prompt-book but foul papers', W. W. Greg, *The Shakespeare First Folio: Its Bibliographical and Textual History* (Oxford, 1955), p. 195; so too, Antony Hammond, the Arden *Richard III* (London, 1981), pp. 43–4. The balance of opinion favours Q6 as the quarto collated with the manuscript (Greg, p. 196; Hammond, pp. 32–3) but J. K. Walton has argued for Q3 in *The Quarto Copy for the First Folio of Shakespeare* (Dublin, 1971); see Hammond, pp. 33–41. Although I do not always agree with Hammond, I should like to stress that I have found his edition particularly helpful. Hereafter I refer to him simply as 'Hammond' and the edition as 'Arden'.

can tell the inquiring reader a great deal about how this play was performed. It makes an important contribution to a world of drama that tends to be disregarded and even looked down upon as inferior: the touring drama. But that is to anticipate.

Theories of the genesis of Q1

Editors tend to consider Q1 a deformed version of the Folio text and, up to a point, they are correct. Theories as to Q1's origin have been many, but since D. L. Patrick in 1936 published *The Textual History of Richard III*, the starting point has been, in the main, that the text of Q1 was 'collaboratively prepared by the company in order to replace a missing prompt-book'.[1] Greg assumed that the company that prepared this text was the Chamberlain's Men but A. S. Cairncross[2] and Karl P. Wentersdorf[3] have linked Q1 with the 'bad' quartos of *2* and *3 Henry VI, The First Part of the Contention*, and *The True Tragedie of Richard Duke of York*; they have argued that these were all produced by Pembroke's Men when they toured the provinces in 1592. Forty years ago, Sir Walter Greg, in a study of ' "Bad" quartos outside Shakespeare', in particular Peele's *Battle of Alcazar* and Greene's *Orlando Furioso* (both first published in 1594), remarked that 'two facts emerged: one that there really existed a class of shortened texts (originating, it is commonly supposed, with reduced companies forced to tour the provinces) the other that not all shortened texts were of the same character'.[4] Andrew Gurr does not believe that the argument that these 'bad' quartos derived from shortened texts used by touring companies will withstand close inspection[5] and David Bradley thinks there is 'nothing much . . . to indicate that the provinces were regularly treated to maimed or truncated performances'.[6] Although Q1 in verbal detail differs greatly from F1 and is some 140 lines shorter, I am sure that when *Richard III* was toured it was presented virtually complete and with no intention of offering a text radically cut down from that regularly given in London. I shall try to show its characteristics can be explained by the circumstances attendant upon the production of the play in London and on tour. Antony Hammond has argued cogently for the association of Q1 with the Chamberlain's Men on the grounds of the 'enormous qualitative difference between Q1 of *Richard III*' and the *Henry VI* 'bad' quartos and because the Chamberlain's Men would not tamely have allowed the publication of such a piracy with their name on the title-page.[7] I share that view. To his arguments can be added the particular circumstances of the licensing of Q1 for printing in 1597, to which reference will be made later.

[1] Sir Walter Greg, reviewing Patrick's book, *The Library*, IV, 19 (1938), 118–20, quoted by Hammond, p. 10.
[2] 'Pembroke's Men and some Shakespearian piracies', *Shakespeare Quarterly*, 11 (1960), 335–49.
[3] 'The repertory and size of Pembroke's Company', *Theatre Annual*, 33 (1977), 71–85; '*Richard III* (Q1) and the Pembroke "bad" quartos', *English Language Notes*, 14 (1977), 257–64.
[4] W. W. Greg, *The Editorial Problem in Shakespeare* (Oxford, 1954), p. 56.
[5] Information kindly provided by Professor Gurr, who let me see the typescript of a chapter on 'Travelling companies', ch. 3, *Playing Companies* (Oxford, 1995).
[6] Bradley, p. 74.
[7] Arden, p. 11.

Important alternatives to the Patrick–Greg conclusion have been put forward by Kristian Smidt and Stephen Urkowitz. Smidt, in two studies,[1] has argued that Q1 is a revision, not a memorially constructed text. Revision was probably involved but that does not necessarily invalidate reporting, and Smidt later slightly modified his approach and in the Preface to his enormously useful parallel text (published a year earlier than his studies) he seemed to admit the possibility of memorial transmission.[2] Urkowitz has argued that Patrick's case for memorial reconstruction has been too readily accepted. Patrick, he concludes:

> offers no secure evidence indicating that the underlying source of the Quarto text was a memorial reconstruction; nor do we know, reliably, when or by whom the Folio text was generated. We may have two texts representing an author's work in progress, or we may have one 'authorized' text and another generated by professional players intimately familiar with the authorized version in performance, or we may have two texts influenced, benignly or malignantly, by Shakespeare's fellows in the playhouse or even by theatrical professionals associated with other companies.

He offers 'a model of *Richard III* as a work in progress, an early state in the Quarto, a later state in the Folio'. In one aspect of this, all can agree: we do not know reliably the nature and relationship of the manuscripts underlying Q1 and F, nor can we be absolutely certain of their provenance. Urkowitz demonstrates that if an editor is determined to see F's manuscript as preceding Q1's, differences in reading offered by Patrick (or by me) can be made to support that progression, but that if the order of manuscripts is reversed, then alternative explanations can be offered for Patrick's differences, some of which are at least as convincing.[3]

There is another troubling aspect to the Patrick–Greg position. Q does not strike one as a wholly satisfactory prompt-book; it has some vague directions and it lacks a number of exits. However, if the text is a memorial transcript of what the actors recalled doing and saying it may be that prompt-book precision was less important, especially if, as is likely, the bookkeeper prepared a Plot as a guide to entrances, exits, etc. As Hammond summarises it, 'it is worth underlining that Greg himself saw nothing inherently impossible in the supposition that Q1 was a reconstructed prompt-book'.[4]

It would be less than honest to pretend that anyone can come to *Richard III* with a wholly fresh, unencumbered mind over half-a-century after Patrick and the discussions he prompted. The Patrick–Greg reported-text conclusion may by and large be

---

[1] *Iniurious Imposters and Richard III* (Oslo, 1964); *Memorial Transmission and Quarto Copy in Richard III: A Reassessment* (Oslo, 1970).
[2] See Smidt's *Reassessment* and *The Tragedy of King Richard the Third: Parallel Texts of the First Quarto and the First Folio with Variants of the Early Quartos* (Oslo, 1969): 'It is generally admitted that the Q text of *Richard III*, whether or not it is memorially contaminated, exhibits a degree of completeness and coherence which relates it not too distantly to an authorial text. And in any case a text reported from memory may transmit variants produced by the author, or at least accepted by him, after his fair copy first left his hands' (p. 8).
[3] Stephen Urkowitz, 'Reconsidering the relationship of quarto and Folio texts of *Richard III*', *English Literary Renaissance*, 16 (1986), 442–66; the references are to pp. 465 and 466; as 'Urkowitz' hereafter.
[4] Arden, p. 12.

correct; Smidt was surely right to argue for revision and possibly quite pervasive revision; Urkowitz cannot be dismissed out of hand. The problem may be resolved by a fresh re-examination of the variants to see whether the theory of reporting can be sustained; to point to what revision may have taken place; and to try to distinguish between revisions that may have been made in London and those, if any, for a tour (possibly a tour earlier than that of the year in which Q1 was published). The problem of Q1 must be regarded as still unresolved. Urkowitz's approach is salutary and a proper warning not to take the accepted order as absolutely determined.

Q1 and F

Five editions of *Richard III* are known to have been published in Shakespeare's lifetime. These were all quartos, the first in 1597 (Q1), then Q2 (1598), Q3 (1602), Q4 (1605), and Q5 (1612). A sixth edition (Q6) appeared in 1622, the year before the publication of the First Folio edition of all Shakespeare's plays (F), which had been got together by two of Shakespeare's colleagues, John Heminges and Henry Condell. Before the theatres were closed in 1642, two more quartos were published, Q7 in 1629 and Q8 in 1634. In published form therefore, as well as on the stage, *Richard III* was a very popular play. The Folio was reprinted in 1632 (F2), 1663–4 (F3) and 1685 (F4). All the quartos are dependent upon Q1 and the folios on F1 so that Q1 and F1 are the prime authorities. F1 was influenced by later quartos as, for example, the Collations for 3.1.1–165, where Q is the prime authority for F, make plain. For example, 3.1.123 shows the Q3 compositor erroneously repeating 'as'; the Q4 compositor corrects but the F compositor, working here from Q3, endeavours to make sense of the repetition by adding commas after each 'as', so that young York appears to stutter. (See also below, p. 26.) The title-page of Q1 reads:

[Ornament 23 × 75 mm.] THE TRAGEDY OF / King Richard the third. / Containing, / His treacherous Plots against his brother Clarence: / the pittiefull murther of his iunocent nephewes: / his tyrannicall vsurpation: with the whole course / of his detested life, and most deserued death. / As it hath beene lately Acted by the / Right honourable the Lord Chamber- / laine his seruants. / [ornament 19 × 51 mm.] / AT LONDON / ¶ Printed by Valentine Sims, for Andrew Wise, / dwelling in Paules Chuch-yard, at the / Signe of the Angell. / 1597.

This edition is based on the British Library copy, Huth 47; this is the copy W. W. Greg used for his *Shakespeare Quarto Facsimile*, No. 12, 1959.

Although the narrative lines of Q1 and F1 are virtually identical, the differences between Q1 and F1 (hereafter referred to as Q and F unless a later quarto or Folio is specifically referred to) are legion. Thus, Q deploys fewer characters, characters lose their names, they are combined, become mutes, and take over the lines of others. Parts of Q are arranged differently from F – for example, the Ghosts appear out of chrono-logical order in Q – and whereas throughout F Richard is so described in speech heads, in Q he is referred to as Gloucester until he is crowned and then, from 4.2, as King. Among other differences of varying significance are the naming of the Pursuivant in Q as Hastings, so that Hastings meets Hastings. A full account of these changes is given below. Many of the two thousand or so verbal differences between Q and F are slight and seemingly insignificant, yet, cumulatively, they build up Q's nature and origins; some even give an insight into the way the play was performed in the sixteenth century, for example, the 'improvements' several actors made to their parts (the additions of 'Well', 'Tut, tut', 'Come, come' etc.).

Yet, despite all these differences, the two versions of *Richard III* are far more closely akin than are *The First part of the Contention betwixt the two famous Houses of Yorke and Lancaster* (Q1) and *The true Tragedie of Richard Duke of Yorke, and the death of good King Henrie the Sixt, with the whole contention betweene the two Houses [of] Lancaster and Yorke* (O) to the Folio texts of 2 and 3 *Henry VI*, or of Q1 *Hamlet* to Q2 and F. Given that many stage directors take a pretty free hand with the text of Shakespeare, even a reasonably well-informed theatregoer might be forgiven for thinking that, if he or she attended a production of Q1, amended (as would be any 'good' text in order to eliminate errors), it was a production of the play based on the Folio text. The only line that might appear to be missing would be Richard's command when Buckingham is taken: 'Off with his head! So much for Buckingham', following 4.4.444. And that, of course, is not by Shakespeare but by Cibber (and still to be heard as late as the mid-1950s, e.g. in Olivier's film version).

This edition

I propose these hypotheses: (1) that Shakespeare's company, the Chamberlain's Men, lost a combined prompt-book used for its London and touring performances of *Richard III* on one of the visits it made to the provinces in 1596 and 1597 and had no alternative available; (2) that the actors recalled their parts and one or more scribes took them down to produce a memorially reconstructed text; and (3) that this memorially reconstructed text provided the manuscript for the 1597 quarto.

I have endeavoured to start afresh by comparing anew what is demonstrably differ-ent: the variant readings of Q and F, aware that there is an ever-present danger of falling prey to circular arguments. In studying the variant readings, I have adapted techniques developed by George Thomson for Aeschylus and George Kane in editing *Piers Plowman, A.*[1] As Kane puts it: 'The sole authority is the variants themselves, and among them, authority, that is originality, will probably be determined most often by the identification of the variant likeliest to have given rise to the others.'[2] They argue that variant readings in manuscript copies may arise from deliberate alteration (e.g., in

---

[1] George Thomson, 'Marxism and textual criticism', *Wissenschaftliche Zeitschrift der Humboldt-Universität zu Berlin*, Ges.-Sprachw. R., 12 (1963), 43–52; 'Simplex ordo', *Classical Quarterly*, 15 (1965), 161–75; and 'Scientific method in textual criticism', *Eirene* 1 (1960), 51–60; George Kane, *Piers Plowman: The A Version* (London, 1960); see especially ch. 4, 'Editorial resources and methods', pp. 115–72; as 'Kane' hereafter. I was fortunately able to teach a course in editorial method with George Thomson and other colleagues at the University of Birmingham for three years and I learned much from him. Patrick devotes his chapter 4 to 'Errors of memory – shifting', suggesting that the many transpositions could not all be attributed to the several compositors who set the play but were 'tricks of the actor's memory' (p. 35); and chapter 5 to 'Errors of memory – substitutions'. Both chapters give many examples of these characteristics.

[2] Kane, p. 115.

the case of *Richard III*, revision for performances in London or on tour), or mechanical error, e.g.: anticipation, repetition, inversion and transposition, exaggeration, substitution, approximation, and telescoping. For Kane and Thomson, this technique is
especially applicable when no hierarchy can be established and recension is not practicable. A hierarchy of quartos and Folios can readily be established for *Richard III*, so
I have used Thomson's and Kane's approach for a different purpose: to try to work out
how the readings of QI came to be as they are. But, as Kane emphasises: 'presumption
of originality is never strictly equivalent to proof, and varies greatly in strength. [. . .]
The authority of the text reconstructed by these means must vary with the character
of the evidence available; it cannot be uniform any more than it can be exactly
determinable. In the last analysis all decisions about originality are provisional only.'[1]

Recently, G. Thomas Tanselle discussed 'Editing without a copy-text', taking as his
starting point a re-assessment of the implications of Fredson Bowers's work on radiating texts. What he proposes is directly relevant to editing *Richard III*:

> Every choice made among variants in radiating texts is an active and critical choice; no reading
> is settled on by default, for there is no text that offers a fall-back position. When the variants in
> radiating texts seem 'indifferent,' an editor may of course choose a reading from the text that
> supplies the largest number of other readings; but the decision is still an active one, in which one
> of the factors taken into account is the apparent general reliability of a particular text. The
> process remains one of building up a new text rather than making changes in an old one. If this
> idea – that critical editing is constructive rather than emendatory – were also applied to texts in
> linear genealogies, the rôle of judgment might more clearly be seen as dominant, and any
> practical guideline (such as Greg's rationale), might be better recognized as an aid to judgment,
> not a brake on it. [. . .] What I am proposing . . . might be called 'constructive critical editing'
> to distinguish it from an approach that emphasizes emendation. To see critical editing as an
> activity of rebuilding rather than repairing forces the judgment to play its central rôle in
> recovering the past.[2]

The virtue of examining each Q/F variant individually and then applying a constructive rather than an emendatory critical approach to *Richard III* is that no overall
hypothesis defines the text because the variants themselves are the source of authority
and the validity of each must be considered separately. As Kane says of his *Piers
Plowman*, all decisions made about the variants of *Richard III* cannot be exactly
determinable and must be provisional. Only in assessing the Q/F variants, using
neither text as copy-text, lies hope of a convincing edition of the play. The present
study is, of course, concerned only with Q's rôle in preparing a 'constructive critical
edition' of *Richard III*.

QI was set in two printing houses. One compositor in Valentine Simmes's house set
to the end of G; Alan Craven has examined his work. Two compositors in Peter Short's
house set from H to the end; they set by formes and their work has been identified by
MacD. P. Jackson. Both houses and all three compositors are well represented in all
groups with more than a few variants. Susan Zimmerman has argued against establish-

---

[1] Kane, pp. 148, 149.
[2] G. Thomas Tanselle, 'Editing without a copy-text', *Studies in Bibliography*, 47 (1994), 19, 22. For
Bowers's study, see 'Editorial apparatus for radiating texts', *The Library*, V, 29 (1974), 330–7.

ing correlations between compositor and press-work in general and in particular in Peter Short's house. However, Q1 was set in two printing houses and Ms Zimmerman suggests that there is 'strong prima-facie evidence for two compositors in [the Short section] of *Richard III* which cannot be refuted by any other single test of equal weight'.[1] The many variants are a result of revision when the play was presented in London and on tour, and also attributable to the work of one or more scribes, three compositors, and, if memorial reconstruction took place, the actors. The editor's task is to distinguish between these. The knowledge that characteristics found throughout the play in a particular rôle (e.g. Buckingham's) appear in settings in two printing houses by three compositors demonstrates that they cannot derive from an individual compositor's laxness or idiosyncrasy.

The ensuing lists deal first with readings attributable to scribes and compositors; then the kinds of variant attributable to recall by actors are summarised; these are followed by examples of actors' 'improvements' – ad-libs – and changes which reflect production (often for touring purposes); finally, revision (which may be authorial) is considered. It can be argued, for instance, that it is not Q that inverts F, but F that inverts Q. But given the loss of force of many substitutions, and in the light of the argument advanced as a whole, I believe Q must appear to be the less authorial text. Whenever some such expression as 'Q's variants' is used, it should be assumed that this means Q1 as compared to F1. The origins of many variants cannot be firmly distinguished; some variants could be attributable to scribe, compositor, actor, or even the author. Examples include Q's 'her' for F's 'my' at 1.2.222; Q's 'perilous' for F's 'parlous', 2.4.35; the aural error in Q, 'Graces pleasure' for F's 'gracious pleasure', 3.4.17; and Q's 'dead' for F's 'deare', 4.1.64. As Kane put it in the passage quoted above (reading 'interpretation adduced here' for his 'text reconstructed'): 'The authority of the text reconstructed . . . must vary with the character of the evidence available; it cannot be uniform any more than it can be exactly determinable. In the last analysis all decisions . . . are provisional only.' Some particularly doubtful instances are double entered and marked with a question mark, but Kane's caveat is always applicable. As the accuracy of the compositors is clearly important, the list below gives a generous, widely drawn record of such demonstrable errors. The other lists refer to the Textual Notes; these notes list other examples of similar categories of variants to be found in that scene in the Collation or Textual Notes. The intensity of variants in the individual scenes is highlighted by such grouping.

SCRIBAL CHANGE

The bookkeeper would have acted as the scribe but he may have been assisted, perhaps by the author if time pressed. The expansion of elided forms in Q, though not wholly consistent, is almost certainly the work of a scribe. Examples include 1.3.180 ('ever' for

---

[1] For a summary of the work of the compositors, see Arden, pp. 23–30. For Susan Zimmerman, 'The use of headlines: Peter Short's Shakespearian quartos *1 Henry IV* and *Richard III*', *The Library*, VI, 7 (1985), 217–55, especially pp. 238 and 241. See also P. Davison, 'The selection and presentation of bibliographic evidence', *Analytical and Enumerative Bibliography*, 1 (Spring 1977), 101–36.

F's 'ere'); 1.3.276 ('I will' for F's 'Ile') – but compare Q's 'Ile' for F's 'I will' at 283; 'I pray thee' for F's 'I prythee' (e.g. 1.4.66 and 101), but Q and F both have 'I pray you' at 3.1.110 and 3.4.61. A scribe may have been responsible for punctiliously correcting 'who' to 'whom' on a number of occasions (see 1.3.54n); and see 1.3.98n for 'yea'/'I'. Lineation errors were inevitable in producing a memorial text, e.g. 2.1.132. It may have been the scribe or the actor who corrected what is found in F at 3.4.84, 'rowse our Helmes' to 'raze his helm'. The scribe may be responsible for Tyrrel being given the first name Francis (instead of James) at 4.3.0 SD. Some of the errors attributed to compositors may stem from the scribe(s), e.g. 1.3.66, 2.2.56, 4.3.19, 5.3.11.

COMPOSITORIAL ERROR

Q1's shortening to 'lo' at 1.2.1 was not because there was a lack of space in the line for two or three more letters. The later quartos took 'lo' to be an abbreviation for 'lord', which makes sense, though F's 'load' is more imaginative (and is selected here) and Anne later refers to 'your holy load' (line 27). The use of the shortened form is strange; as it lacks a full point it may be that the compositor was interrupted and simply failed to complete the word and that the proof-reader either did not notice or let it pass as if it were an abbreviated form. Q1's 'squakt' at 1.4.51 looks like an example of what Kane describes as a scribe's distracted attempt to make out a word resulting in 'a meaning-less group of letters of shape similar to the supplanted word',[1] but here the work of a compositor; 'squawked' did not enter the language for another two-and-a-half centu-ries; 2.1.24–5 may be an omission arising from *homoeoarchy*, but could be an authorial revision; the error at 2.3.39, 'bread' for 'dread', is certainly compositorial, probably a result of faulty dissing; the speech head in Q at 3.5.50, *Dut.* for *Buc.*, is impossible in this scene because the Duchess does not appear, and must be a compositorial misread-ing; the repeated speech head at 3.7.40, *Glo.*, is also likely to be compositorial, though it may stem from a repeated use of the indication made by the scribe when he started a fresh leaf; '*ʃoule-fac't*' for 'foul-faced' at 3.7.211 may be a result of faulty reading or dissing, confusing long '*ʃ*' and 'f'; there is a rash of compositorial errors in 4.1 (corrected in the text but not included in the Collation because given here) starting with 'the' for 'thy' at 4.1.34: 'ftom' for 'from', 44; 'hatch' for 'hatcht' and 'thc' for 'the', 49; 'thar' for 'that', 53; 'were' for 'Were', 55; 'rhy' for 'thy', 59; and 'Richatds' for 'Richards', 65 (and see 3.3.10); 4.4.328 (omission of 'by'). The effect of setting by formes in Peter Short's printing house and the need for copy-fitting may be the cause of the reading discussed at 3.7.182n. Q2 may have been printed from a copy of Q1 that had been corrected in the course of printing but which has not survived. See notes to 1.1.101–2, 2.1.5, and 5.3.10 (where copy must have been consulted).

For further certain and possible compositorial (or scribal) errors, see also Textual Notes or Collation at: 1.2.100; 1.3.3, 5, 48, 255, 299; 1.4.32, 69, 122, 142, 199, 224; 2.2.56, 59, 105; 2.4.12, 22, 30, 68; 3.1.78 (Q2); 3.2.9, 82, 85 ?; 3.3.0 SD, 2, 10, 21; 3.4.17, 42, 57, 87; 3.5.0 SD, 31, 50; 3.7.40; 4.2.71, 87; 4.3.19, 25, 31; 4.4.38, 54, 69, 92, 129 (where the omission of trumpets and drums in the stage direction looks like a simple

---

[1] Kane, p. 132.

failure by the compositor to complete the line), 174, 214, 228, 266?, 273, 297, 305, 328, 374; 5.1.10 ?, 26; 5.2.24; and 5.3.11, 142, 158, 226, 263.

Sometimes Q's compositor is correct and the F compositor wrong: at 2.1.54 the F compositor evidently read a crossed double 'l' in 'unwillingly' and produced 'vnwittingly'; and at 2.3.44, Q's 'Ensuing' is correct – F's 'Pursuing' is revealed to be an error by its preceding catchword: 'Ensuing'; and see Textual Note at 4.4.122, where F has 'intestine' for Q's 'intestate'.

The following groups illustrate characteristics that can reasonably be attributed to actors recalling their parts, although the possibility that such variants may be the work of the compositor can never be as demonstrably ruled out as at Q2, 4.2.69, where instead of 'two enemies', the compositor, setting from Q1, anticipated 'deep enemies' of the next line and set that. Although individual examples from these groups may be the work of a compositor (or scribe), the sheer quantity, crossing the work of two printing houses and three compositors, indicates another source – the actors. Anticipation (such as that in Q2 noted here), or repetition, inversion etc., are far, far rarer in the dependent quartos. These references are to the Textual Notes (where further examples within these scenes will be found).

ANTICIPATION

1.2.11, 104, 224; 1.3.77, 269, 328; 1.4.13, 114; 2.1.9, 32, 76; 2.2.40–1, 116; 2.3.6; 2.4.26; 3.2.24, 26; 3.7.33; 4.2.49–50 ?; 4.3.27; 4.4.34, 238, 266.

COLLOQUIAL SUBSTITUTION

2.3.1 (possibly of the actor's own form of greeting); 2.3.17; 4.3.35.

EXAGGERATION

Q's 'Ten thousand men', for F's 'A thousand men', 1.4.24, could easily be taken to be the kind of careless exaggeration typical of medieval scribes and in memorial reconstruction. Thus George Kane, *Piers Plowman: The A Version* (1960):

the most striking of the variations originating from the scribe's association of himself with what he copied are those designed to increase the emphasis of statements [. . .] Such variation took place because scribes were enthusiastic for the poem, and consciously or unconsciously, if sometimes without intelligence or taste, strained to participate in the experience that it recorded, as well as to contribute to its purpose.[1]

Kane gives many examples of numerical exaggeration: e.g., fifteen becoming four score (III. 38), and eleven becoming fifteen which, in turn, became thirty in different manuscripts at V. 141. However, here, editors regularly take F to be in error; Arden, for example, argues that F's 'thousand' is compositorial repetition of that word in the preceding line and that 'Ten' is logically correct: if there are a thousand wrecks there must be many more men to be gnawed upon – though that implies that dreams are

---

[1] Kane, pp. 138–9.

logical. F may not be someone's error, however, but Shakespeare's first thoughts and 'Ten thousand' his revision. What is plain is that such variants can be argued for and against, and supported and denied, in contrary ways. See also notes to 1.2.14; 1.3.41; 1.4.54, 179; 2.2.77, 78, 113; 4.2.121. But compare Q1's 'nearer' for F's 'nearest' at 4.4.375.

INCREASED ALLITERATION
1.4.242; 2.1.43; 2.2.8; 4.1.87.

INVERSION AND TRANSPOSITION
1.2.167–9; 1.3.109, 227 (possibly an authorial change), 287; 1.4.3, 136; 2.1.7; 2.2.6; 2.3.26; 2.4.20, 25; 3.1.167; 3.2.14; 3.3.15, 16; 3.4.26; 3.5.3, 48–9; 3.6.8; 3.7.54; 4.1.45; 4.2.23, 30–1, 78; 4.3.1, 2; 4.4.21, 29–31, 58, 62, 282–3, 292–5, 324–5, 417; 4.5.16–18; 5.3.38–41, 143–50.

OMISSION
1.1.101–2; 1.2.15–16, 23–4 ?, 154–5; 1.3.304, 315; 1.4.26–7, 34, 65–6, 99–100, 146–7, 231–2, 237–8; 2.1.1, 24–5, 64; 2.2.15–16, 87, 109; 2.3.9; 2.4.69; 3.1.169–72; 3.2.0 SD, 15; 3.3.13–14; 3.4.78–80, 103–4; 3.5.7, 100; 3.7.32, 92–3, 131; 4.1.1–2, 9; 4.2.1–2; 4.3.35; 4.4.22, 29–31, 48–9, 95–8, 141, 153, 164, 170, 171–2, 210–11, 260–1, 305, 317–18, 345–6 ?; 4.5.15; 5.3.4–5.

REPETITION
1.3.278; 1.4.133, 199; 2.2.66; 3.2.77; 3.5.23, 102; 3.7.216; 4.1.22–3 (of 1.1.84 and 103), 70 (of 1.2.25), 82 (of 58); 4.2.81–2 (of 3.1.186), 98; 4.4.106; 5.3.34, 159–60.

SIGNIFICANT ADDITIONS
3.3.1; 3.5.25; 3.7.200, 207; 4.2.98–117; see also 'Ensemble playing' below.

SUBSTITUTION (INCLUDING APPROXIMATION, PARAPHRASE, AND TELESCOPING)
Listings of Textual Notes and Collations are given at these references: 1.1.50; 1.2.26; 1.3.6; 1.4.3; 2.1.18; 2.2.7; 2.3.5; 2.4.1–2; 3.1.182; 3.2.5; 3.3.11; 3.4.1; 3.5.16; 3.6.6; 3.7.1; 4.1.10; 4.2.4; 4.3.4; 4.4.4; 4.5.2; 5.1.2; 5.2.11; 5.3.1.

WEAKENING
Only the clearest weakening changes are listed: many substitutions in the section above might be regarded as weaker than the words replaced: 1.2.25–6, 156; 1.3.5, 193; 1.4.191; 2.1.76, 101; 2.4.55; 3.7.219–20, 222; 4.4.229, 266.

The variety, quantity, and pervasiveness of these variants, found in the work of all three compositors, point to memorial reconstruction by the actors. That it was the various actors and not a single presiding genius, like John Bernard who recalled *The School for Scandal* in 1777 (see p. 12 below), is indicated by the wide variation in accuracy of those playing the different rôles.

There is an external piece of evidence that may point to the unusual nature of the manuscript underlying the quarto of 1597, though it cannot show that the manuscript had been memorially reconstructed. On 20 October 1597 Andrew Wise entered *Richard III* in the Stationers' Register and this became the quarto that is conjectured to be based on a memorial construct. Only three other extant plays were printed for the first time in 1597: *Richard II*, sold to Wise by the company in August; *Romeo and Juliet*, which was not entered in the Register and was printed irregularly by John Danter; and John Lyly's *The Woman in the Moon*, which had been entered two years earlier. Of these only one was specifically licensed: *Richard III*.[1] Even though all plays required a licence to be printed, it seems that very frequently a licence to perform, given by the Revels Office, was accepted as a licence to print. Eight of Shakespeare's plays were specifically licensed for printing; of these, four were licensed by representatives of the Revels Office, i.e. those who also licensed for performance. The four licensed for printing were *Richard III*; *1 Henry IV* (by Dix, 25 February 1598); *A Midsummer Night's Dream* (by Rodes, 8 October 1600); and *Hamlet* (by Pasfield, 26 July 1602).[2]

What was so special about *Richard III* that it required licensing? I suggest that the company's copy bearing the licence to perform, given by the Master of the Revels, had been lost when the original combined London and touring prompt-book was lost. As the company would probably not have risked touring long without a licensed copy, it is likely that the loss occurred on the 1597 tour. As the licenser, William Barlowe, had only licensed for the first time on 27 November 1596 (Thomas Beard's *Theater of Godes Iudgementes*), it can reasonably be assumed that it was the manuscript of the quarto he saw. This Barlowe was a protégé of Archbishop Whitgift, a keen licenser, and Bishop Bancroft, a zealous Puritan, who had been involved in tracking down the Marprelate printers, so he might have been expected to be energetic. As *Richard III* was the first of only two plays that he licensed (the second being Marlowe's *Dr Faustus* four years later), and only the fourth work that he licensed, he might also have been over-cautious.[3]

Theories of sixteenth-century memorial reconstruction are themselves constructs, but we do know of later texts memorially reconstructed. Tate Wilkinson recounts that he wrote from memory what he cheekily called 'Wilkinson's Duenna', first performed on 9 April 1776.[4] In his *Memoirs*, he describes how he 'vamped up a version of

[1] See W. W. Greg, *A Bibliography of the English Printed Drama*, I (London, 1939; rptd 1970), items 141–4.
[2] Greg, *Bibliography*, items 144, 170, 197. The first edition of *Hamlet* was pirated and the entry (and licensing) may have been connected with the wish to assert copyright. Greg remarks that the first edition of *Hamlet*, the bad quarto, 'appeared in contravention rather than in pursuance of this entry'. Licensing of *1 Henry IV* may have a connexion with the fuss made by the Cobhams over Oldcastle/Falstaff. I know of no explanation for licensing *A Midsummer Night's Dream*.
[3] W. W. Greg, *Licensers of the Press, &c. to 1660* (Bibliographical Society, Oxford, 1962), pp. 9–10.
[4] Tate Wilkinson, *The Wandering Patentee: A History of the Yorkshire Theatres, from 1770 to the Present Time* (4 vols., York, 1795); facsimile reprint, Scolar Press (London and Ilkley, 1973), I, 219. See also *An Index to the Wandering Patentee*, compiled by C. Beecher Hogan (The Society for Theatre Research, London, 1973); as '*Wandering Patentee*' hereafter. Wilkinson refers to this version as '*my* Duenna' at I, 247, 251, and 304, himself italicising 'my' at 247 and 304.

Sheridan's *Duenna*': 'I locked myself up in my room, set down first the jokes I remembered, then I laid a book of the songs before me, and with magazines kept the regulation of the scenes, and by the help of a numerous collection of obsolete Spanish plays I produced an excellent opera.'[1]

Another text of *The Duenna* was printed in *The European Magazine*, May 1783. One editor of Sheridan, R. Crompton Rhodes, describes this as 'reproduced from memory'. Rhodes reproduces in parallel columns 'The genuine text' of 3.4 and that printed in the magazine; these versions are given here as figure 1, with my annotations. This pirated version shows, in exaggerated form, the memorial characteristics I have identified in the first quarto of *Richard III*: inversion, exaggeration, approximation, substitution, excision, and addition; also one of the stage directions that points to what took place on stage.[2] In 1777, *The School for Scandal* was first performed at Drury Lane. This suffered the same fate as *The Duenna*, for in that same year, 1777, John Bernard constructed a text from 'parts and from recollection' for the theatre in Exeter.[3]

Memorial reconstruction

The application of 'Thomson–Kane' to the first quarto of *Richard III* proves remarkably illuminating especially when considered in the context of touring, even though that lays one open to the dangers of circular argument. The process enables a 'history of the text'[4] to be conjecturally established. It is possible to show how this text was a product of memorial reconstruction and to suggest in what ways it was modified, perhaps by Shakespeare himself, for a touring company requiring fewer actors than for a regular London production. It is impossible to know the size of the company and what I suggest is but a guess and, it must be stressed, runs counter to prevailing wisdom. Antony Hammond, having examined various arguments for the sizes of companies that might have played Q1 and F, suggested that the fifty-two speaking and three named mute rôles of F might, 'in practice', have required about twenty actors with some mute help from the stage-keepers; and that Q1 might have been performed by seventeen or eighteen actors.[5] David Bradley has argued persuasively for rather large touring companies, challenging what he describes as 'probably an unshakeable myth of theatrical history' that company-size was reduced for touring. He does not specifically discuss *Richard III* nor *The Fair Maid of the Exchange*, but in proposing twelve men and eight boys for the former and twelve men and three boys for the second, he allows his theories to overrule the practicalities – even the actualities – of touring. Although he notes that *The Fair Maid of the Exchange* was offered for

[1] Greg, *Editorial Problem*, p. 74. What is believed to be 'Wilkinson's Duenna' was published as *The Governess* (Dublin, 1777).

[2] R. Crompton Rhodes, *Plays and Poems* (3 vols., Oxford, 1928), I, 263–8.

[3] Rhodes, I, 255, II, 162. Greg refers to this memorial reconstruction in *Editorial Problem*, p. 60.

[4] Ian Willison, 'Remarks on the history of the book in Britain as a field of study within the humanities', *Library Chronicle of the University of Texas at Austin*, 21 (1991), 107, n. 10.

[5] Arden, pp. 62 and 65.

THE GENUINE TEXT	SETTING CHANGED	THE EUROPEAN MAGAZINE
A Room in the Priory.		*Scene a Convent.*
FATHER PAUL, FATHER FRANCIS, FATHER AUGUSTINE, *and other* FRIARS, *discovered at a table drinking.*	SHORTER SD *Augustine* OMITTED	*Discovers* FATHER PAUL, BROTHER FRANCIS, &c. &c. *at a Table drinking.*
Paul. Brother Francis, toss the bottle about, and give me your toast.	toss > Push TRANSPOSITION me > us	*Father Paul.* Push the bottle about, brother Francis, and give us your toast.
Francis. [Have we drank the Abbess of St. Ursuline?]	[APPROXIMATION]	*Brother Francis.* [The abbess of St. Dunstinane.]
Paul. Yes, yes; she was the last.		*F. P.* That was our last.
Francis. Then I'll give you the blue-ey'd nun of St. Catherine's.		*B. F.* Then here's to the little blue eyed nun of St. Catharine's.
Paul. With all my heart. –	*Paul* > *Omnes* OMITTED	*Omnes.* With all our hearts.
[*Drinks.*] Pray brother Augustine, were there any benefactions left in my absence?		– [*drink*] *F. P.* Has any benefaction been left to the convent in my absence?
	[ADDITION]	[*B. F.* Yes. *F. P.* What were they?]
Aug. Don Juan Corduba has left a hundred ducats to remember him in our masses.	D-J-Corduba > Francisco us ADDED ducats > pistoles	*B. F.* Francisco the merchant, has left us a a hundred pistoles to remember him in our masses.
Paul. Has he? let them be paid to our wine-merchant, and we'll remember him in our cups, which will do just as well.	Has he OMITTED cups > glasses APPROXIMATION [ADDITION]	*F. P.* Let that be paid to our wine merchant; we'll remember him in our glasses, it will do every jot as well. [*Omnes.* Ha! ha! ha!]
Anything more?		*F. P.* Any thing more?
Aug. Yes; Baptista, the rich miser, who died last week, has bequeath'd us a thousand pistoles, and the silver lamp he used in his own chamber, to burn before the image of St. Anthony.	EXAGGERATION 1000 pistoles > 100 ducats the > a that ADDED TRANSPOSED EXAGGERATION	*B. F.* Yes; Baptista, the rich old miser, who died last week, has left us a hundred ducats, and a silver lamp that he used to burn in his own chamber, to be continually burning before the image of St. Anthony.
Paul. 'Twas well meant; but we'll employ his money better – Baptista's bounty [shall light the living, not the dead – St. Anthony is not afraid to be left] in the dark, though he was. –	money > bounty bounty > cash [APPROXIMATION]	*F. P.* 'Twas well meant, but we'll employ his bounty better: let it be converted to cash, [and paid to our wax chandler – we'll have light – St. Anthony was never afraid to sleep] in the dark, though he was – [*Knocking*
[*A knocking.*] See who's there. [FRANCIS *goes to the door and opens it.*]	OMISSION EXPANDED SD	*at the door; the table, &c. drawn behind a curtain. Brother Francis unlocks the door.*]

1 Parallel passages from Sheridan's *The Duenna*.

performance by eleven actors, he does not examine the implications of the doubling plot (printed on A2^r), nor note that it does not work, nor consider reasons for that.[1] The Chamberlain's Men might, indeed, have had special reason for touring with smaller than full-size companies in 1596 and 1597. In 1591 or 1592, five of the Chamberlain's sharers – Kemp, Pope, Heminges, Phillips, and Bryan – were members of the combined Admiral's–Strange's Company that petitioned to be allowed to return to London from the provinces because 'our Companie is greate, and thearbie our chardge intollerable, in travellinge the Countrie'.[2] That experience would still have seemed pertinent five years later, especially in the light of the crisis the company faced when the London theatres were, it seemed, to be closed down permanently. T. J. King has proposed nineteen men and seven boys for the sixty-four parts he lists for Q and the same complement for the seventy-two he records for F.[3]

I suggest that Q1 could have been performed on tour by ten men and two boys. My doubling pattern, reproduced as figure 2, resolves what are said to be the quarto's specifically theatrical cruxes. For example, the elimination of Dorset from 2.2 is believed by Hammond (in his note to lines 89–100), with other 'patently interrelated' cuts in this scene, to 'have served some specific theatrical purpose'; he also suggests that the substitution of Dorset for the Messenger in 2.4 is 'quite clearly [a] change [that] must have been made to accommodate a theatrical need which we cannot now determine'; and, referring to Catesby and Ratcliffe, he suggests that 'If one replaces the other, it can thus only be for a specific theatrical or dramatic reason.'[4] These changes arise from the tight doubling schedule demanded by a small touring company. There would also have been men whose primary function was not acting (the book-keeper, the wardrobe-keeper, stage-keepers) who could take on small rôles. As Bradley has shown, hireling actors might undertake the tasks of gatherers on tour (and he gives Richard Errington as an example)[5] and they could well have been taken on tour to work mainly behind the stage but, being able to stand in as actors if the need arose, preferred to the London stagehands. There is nothing sacrosanct about the number twelve – that it is speculative cannot be stressed too strongly – but the omission of

[1] Bradley, p. 58, and ch. 3 *passim*, pp. 58–74. I argued nearly forty years ago that *The Fair Maid of the Exchange* as we have it had been revised in nine places and that the doubling plot might originally have worked; University of London MA thesis, 1957: this served as the basis for the Malone Society edition of the play (Oxford, 1963). Barnard doubles with Mistress Flower but the former exits at 1756 and the latter simultaneously enters; both are on stage at 2456. There is a very tight change-over at 604 when Bobbington exits; Berry, with whom he doubles, enters three lines later. Gary Taylor in 'We happy few: the 1600 Abridgement' shows how eleven actors could present the '1600 Abridgement of *Henry V*'; he uses the table in *Fair Maid* as evidence without mentioning that the scheme will not work (Stanley Wells and Gary Taylor, *Modernizing Shakespeare's Spelling, with Three Studies in the Text of 'Henry V'* (Oxford, 1979), pp. 72 and 109, n. 2). Taylor's argument has been challenged by T. J. King, *Casting Shakespeare's Plays: London Actors and their Rôles, 1590–1642* (Cambridge, 1992), p. 73; as 'King' hereafter.
[2] E. K. Chambers, *The Elizabethan Stage* (4 vols., Oxford, 1923), I, 12 and IV, 311–12; quoted by Bradley, pp. 69–70.
[3] King, pp. 80, 162–7, and 254.
[4] Arden, pp. 15–16.
[5] Bradley, p. 69.

several of the *dramatis personae* and the re-ordering of the ghosts in Q1 suggests a small rather than a large touring company.[1]

Who would comprise the membership of this touring company? The Lord Chamberlain's Men was a sharing company and it so happens that we know from the cast list of Jonson's *Every Man in his Humour* of the following year, 1598, the names of the principal actors of that company, and we know who were the sharers. These provide ten names for the main actors. We cannot be sure they would all tour and Professor Park Honan (who is working on a biography of Shakespeare) believes that Shakespeare would take this opportunity to visit 'his native Countrey', as John Aubrey put it in his 'Brief Life'. However, when the London theatres were closed, touring was the most obvious way for actors to earn a living, and at times of lengthy closure (and after the *Isle of Dogs* scandal, seemingly permanent closure) it would be the more important players, and especially those with a financial stake in the company, who would be given the opportunity of touring rather than, as often nowadays, stuffing a production with substitutes. Burbage undoubtedly played Richard. Hammond thinks 'that *Richard III* has no part for a clown, and Kemp therefore, though available, would presumably not have been used in its performance'.[2] I think that both the company's clowns would have toured. Kemp would have played the First Executioner (in the serio-comic style that derives from executioners of Christ in the mystery plays), Ratcliffe, and Tyrrel; and Cowley the Second Executioner and Catesby. And Shakespeare?

Here one enters the realm of pure speculation but it is not a trivial exercise for, as Steven Urkowitz has argued, anyone proposing that Q1 is a memorial reconstruction must attempt to show what rôles Shakespeare played.[3] Few parts have been convincingly assigned to Shakespeare until very recently. John Davies of Hereford wrote in 1610 that Shakespeare 'plaid some Kingly parts in sport'; in 1991 Professor Donald Foster began publishing the initial results of an electronic Shakespeare lexicon that attempted to identify what rôles Shakespeare played and the years in which he acted them, based on a higher-than-expected recurrence in later plays of words rare in Shakespeare that he had earlier learned. The recently revised (but still interim) results, called 'SHAXICON 2.0', has produced an 'Abstract of Shakespeare's career' which shows all Shakespeare's rôles from 1591 to 1613 inclusive. Professor Foster is at pains to stress the current limitations to what could prove a most valuable tool:

---

[1] For logistical convenience, plays requiring less than a full company of actors would, one imagines, also be toured, and I shall refer later to what happens if vital members of a company are absent. One reason for such a reduction is that it would be more likely to make a tour financially viable. Even today, tours are undertaken of small towns by, for example, Welsh National Opera (and opera presents far trickier problems on tour than does drama), with reduced-size companies: singers doubling, a chamber orchestra, and no chorus. This is partly to save money; partly because of the smallness of performance places, which affects stage size and box-office take. Peter Knapp established Travelling Opera on a similar basis in 1986. This gives 120 performances a year in forty auditoria attracting audiences of 80,000. (Brian Hunt, 'An aria in your area', *Daily Telegraph*, 12 November 1994, Arts Supplement, p. 16.) I shall consider the 'practicalities and actualities' of the 1597 tour later, and also give grounds for believing that adult males might on occasion have played women's rôles.

[2] Arden, p. 65.
[3] Urkowitz, p. 464.

It must not be supposed that SHAXICON offers an unerring and unequivocal record of Shakespeare's activities as a writer and actor. SHAXICON cannot solve all our problems with respect to Shakespeare's texts, and it may in fact raise as many questions as it answers. However, when used judiciously, SHAXICON can shed considerable light on problems of authorship, dating, staging, and textual transmission . . . where evidence of authorship, date, or stage production is lacking, SHAXICON must be used with caution . . . The most severe limitation of SHAXICON in its present form is that I have not yet developed a scale of statistical significance that can be used readily by literary scholars . . . What is needed is a consistent scale against which all of the designated Shakespeare rôles can be measured. Similarly, a sliding scale of reliability must be devised for the dates assigned by SHAXICON. . . . In such matters as date, textual authority, and casting, certainty is beyond hoping for . . .

Foster believes on the basis of his present researches that *Richard III* was performed in 1593, 1594, 1596 (when it was 'possibly . . . recopied or slightly revised'), 1599, 1606, 1607, 1608, and possibly 1612. He thinks Shakespeare played Clarence and the Scrivener until 1599; that in 1606 and 1607 he played Clarence and the Third Citizen and possibly dropped the Scrivener; and that he was probably not included in 1612. Clarence is pretty accurately recalled in Q, 1.1, but much less so in 1.4; the Scrivener and Third Citizen are inaccurately recalled. As well as *Richard III*, Foster lists Shakespeare as playing Clifford in *3 Henry VI* and King Henry in *1 Henry IV* in 1596; in 1597 he lists him as playing King Ferdinand in *Love's Labour's Lost*, Boyet in a major revision of that play, Gaunt in *Richard II* (a part one might have thought designed for John Sincklo), the Host in *The Merry Wives of Windsor*, and Leonato in *Much Ado About Nothing*. He stresses that assignment of a part to Shakespeare, such as Adam, is not a fact but an inference: 'In such matters as date, textual authority, and casting, certainty is beyond hoping for.'[1] His dating for *Titus Andronicus*, for example, is unreliable (see p. 48).

It had earlier seemed to me that, if Shakespeare, in his capacity as author, was gifted in the accurate recall of his lines, the accuracy of two parts might suggest that he played Hastings and Richmond. These double conveniently and would offer Shakespeare 'a Kingly part', but, at present, the computer throws cold water on that. I have, whilst SHAXICON's allocations are not yet certain, thought this still worth mentioning on occasion. I have proposed that adult actors should play Queen Margaret and the Duchess of York and that the two boys would double Dorset and Grey (though their rôles could, at a pinch, be allocated to adult males). This is controversial and again

---

[1] John Davies, *The Scourge of Folly*; reproduced in S. Schoenbaum, *William Shakespeare: A Documentary Life* (Oxford, 1975), p. 148. Donald Foster outlined his earlier researches in *Shakespeare Newsletter*, Summer, Fall, and Winter 1991. I am deeply grateful to him for a copy of a later account of his work, 'SHAXICON 2.0', and to Professor Park Honan of the University of Leeds, who made a copy available to me and for his summary of Foster's 'Abstract of Shakespeare's career' (28 September 1994); these documents were copiously annotated by Professor Honan. The passages quoted are from 'SHAXICON 2.0', pp. 3, 4, and 5. Foster suggests that plays were usually kept in the repertoire for two years and then rested for four years, after which they might be revived; also that if plays were revised, 'the usual time to do so was just prior to the second winter-season at court in the standard two-year repertory' (p. 10). He believes that the theory of memorial reconstruction is mistaken but seems to refer only to *2H6*, *3H6*, and *H5* (pp. 10–11).

2 A conjectural doubling plot for *Richard III*, Q1

	1.1	1.2	1.3	1.4	2.1	2.2	2.3	2.4	3.1	3.2	3.3	3.4	3.5	3.6	3.7	4.1	4.2	4.3	4.4	4.5	5.1	5.2	5.3 1–114	5.3 115–173	5.3 174–end	5.4	5.5
1. Richard [Burbage]	•	•	•	•	•	•		•	•			•	•		•	•	•	•	•				•	•	•	•	
2. Duchess of York		Att				•	1 Cit		•		Mess				Cit (M)	•			•				Norf	Gh Hast	Norf		Lord (M)
3. Hastings / Richmond	H		H		H	H				H	Halb (M)	H			Bp (M)		Lord (M)		1 Mess			Rmnd	Rmnd	Rmnd	Rmnd		Rmnd
4.	Brak	Att (M)	Riv	Brak	Riv			Card	Card		Riv				BP (M)	Lieut	Lord (M)		2 Mess	Ursk		3 Lord	Blnt	Gh Riv	Blnt		Lord (M)
5. 1. Exec / Ratcliffe [Kemp]	Gd (M)	Halb (M)	1 Exec	1 Exec		Rat					Rat						Tyrl	Tyrl			Rat		Rat	Gh Grey	Rat		Lord (M)
6. 2. Exec / Catesby [Cowley]	Gd (M)	Halb (M)	2 Exec	2 Exec					Cate	Cate		Cate	Cate		Cate		Cate	Cate	Cate				Cate	Gh V'n		Cate	Lord (M)
7.		Berk (M)	Qu Marg		Kg Edw					Prst (M)			Ld Mayr		Ld Mayr		Lord (M)		Qu Marg		Gd (M)		Sol/Ld (M) (Rmnd)	Gh Hy 6	1 Lord (Rmnd)		Lord (M)
8. Queen Elizabeth		Att (M)	•		•	•				Purs		Ely		Scr	Cit (M)	•			•			2 Lord	Sol/Ld (M) (Rmnd)	Gh Pr Ed	2 Lord (Rmnd)		Sol (M)
9. Buckingham			•		•	•			•	•		•	•		•	•	•				•			Gh Buck	Mess		Sol (M)
10. Clarence / Derby	Clar	Att (M)	Dby	Clar	Dby	Dby			Att (M)	Dby	Grey	Dby			Cit (M)†	Dby	Dby		Dby	Dby		1 Lord	Dby	Gh Clar			Dby
Boy 1		Tres (M)	Dors		Dors	Boy	3 Cit	Dors	Yg Pr Edw		V'n (M)					Dors	Page		4 Mess†				Sol (M) (Kg)	Gh Yg Pr Edw	1 Lor (M) (Kg)		Sol (M)
Boy 2		Anne	Grey		Grey	Girl		Yg Duke York	Yg Duke York	Grey		Grey			Cit (off)	Anne			3 Mess				Sol (M) (Kg)	Ghs Anne & Yg Yk	2 Lor (M) (Kg)		Sol (M)

(M) = Mute

Minor characters could be played by any of several actors.

• = appearance of character named in column 2.

* Leaves at 202 SD

runs counter to received wisdom. Bradley maintains that 'boys will not normally double with men. To which we may add that men will not normally play female rôles,' and T. J. King comes to the same conclusion.[1] I find it difficult to believe that men did not act character rôles such as Queen Margaret, Juliet's Nurse, and Mistress Quickly, and it seems to me improbable that when a boy ceased to be 'a boy-actor' and became a hireling, that he would immediately and automatically cease to play a rôle to which he had become accustomed, such as the Duchess of York, especially if the exigencies of touring required that. Bradley does not exclude something along these lines: 'Any too hard-and-fast rule may, however, be out of place. We know that boys bred up as apprentices with the King's Men did stay with the company as men and there may have been a period for each when the sex of the rôles assigned to them was uncertain', and he gives one or two examples.[2]

Rankins, Rainolds, Gager, Gentili, and Prynne make it perfectly plain that men as well as boys played female rôles. Though they refer frequently to classical drama, that is because 'authority' to them was the Bible, the Christian Fathers, and Roman Law. Despite the university context in which they wrote, tucked away are references to performances at the Theatre, the Curtain, and to Frenchwomen playing a French play at the Blackfriars in 1629. Rainolds and Prynne carefully distinguished – good scholars that they were – between men and boys acting the rôles of women and Prynne concludes that 'men-Actors in womens attire, are not altogether so bad as women Stage-players'.[3] Sir Richard Baker in his *Theatrum Redivivum, or The Theatre Vindicated*, confutes Prynne's claim that there were no authorities supporting men dressing as women and acting female rôles. He implies that, because Prynne was so widely read, he had dissembled. Baker cites Luther and 'the learned *Jesuite Lorinuse*' in support of the sexes wearing each other's clothes, the latter maintaining, '*For representing a Person in Comedie, or Tragedie; or for avoiding of danger, or such like Cases, a woman may lawfully put on a man's apparel; and a man a woman's.*' Baker bluntly states: 'Thus these men allow *that* in *Plays*.' In his discussion of this matter, Baker refers both to men and to boys wearing women's garments, and to men more frequently than to boys.[4] *Henslowe's Diary* (though it is plagued with uncertainties) seems to show that Robert Shawe was lent money to buy tinsel for Borne's 'womones gowne' on 1 December 1597.[5] 'The diuision of the partes' of *Cambises*, published in 1569, a play well known

[1] Bradley, p. 41. T. J. King is as certain from the evidence of eight Elizabethan playhouse documents (four plots and four prompt-books) that boy-actors did not play adult male rôles nor did adult males play female rôles (p. 6).

[2] Bradley, p. 19.

[3] John Rainolds, *Th'overthrow of Stage-Playes* (London, 1599), pp. 11, 14–15, 111, 136–7; William Prynne, *Histrio-Mastix* (London, 1633), pp. 201, 212, 214, and 215 (which has the reference to women acting). He was certainly not referring only to university drama. See also J. W. Binns, 'Women or transvestites on the Elizabethan stage?: An Oxford controversy', *Sixteenth Century Journal*, 2 (1974), 95–120.

[4] Sir Richard Baker, *Theatrum Redivivum, or, The Theatre Vindicated*, C1ʳ–C2ʳ and B8ʳ–C1ʳ respectively. Though not first published until 1662, it was written much earlier. Baker died, aged about 77, in 1645. He refers to 'honest *Tarlton*' and to Edward Alleyn and Richard Burbage as 'the best *Actours* of our Time' (D1ᵛ).

[5] *Henslowe's Diary*, ed. R. A. Foakes and R. T. Rickert (Cambridge, 1961), p. 85; as 'Henslowe' hereafter.

1:	Gloucester/Richard III. BURBAGE?
2:	Duchess of York; Attendant, 1.2; 1 Citizen, 2.3; Messenger, 3.2; Halberdier (Mute), 3.3; Citizen (Mute), 3.7; Norfolk; Ghost of Hastings; Lord (Mute), 5.5.
3:	Hastings; Richmond; Bishop (Mute), 3.7; Lord (Mute), 4.2; 1 Messenger, 4.4.
4:	Brakenbury; Attendant (Mute), 1.2; Rivers; Cardinal; Bishop (Mute), 3.7; Lieutenant, 4.1; Lords (Mute), 4.2, 5.5; 2 Messenger, 4.4; Urswick; 3 Lord, 5.2; Blunt; Ghost of Rivers.
5:	Guard (Mute), 1.1; Halberdier, 1.2; 1 Executioner; Ratcliffe; 2 Citizen, 2.3; Attendant (Mute), 3.1; Citizen (Mute), 3.7; Tyrrel; Ghost of Grey; Lord (Mute), 5.5. KEMP?
6:	Guard (Mute), 1.1; Halberdier (Mute), 1.2; 2 Executioner; Catesby; Ghost of Vaughan; Lord (Mute), 5.5. COWLEY?
7:	Berkeley (Mute), 1.2; Queen Margaret; King Edward IV; 3 Citizen, 2.3; Lord Mayor; Priest (Mute), 3.2; Lords (Mute), 4.2, 5.5; Guard (Mute), 5.1; Soldier (Mute), 5.3; 1 Lord, 5.3; Ghost of Henry VI.
8:	Attendant (Mute), 1.2; Queen Elizabeth; Pursuivant; Ely; Scrivener; Citizen (Mute), 3.7; 2 Lord, 5.2, 5.3; Soldier (Mute), 5.3, 5.5; Ghost of Prince Edward.
9:	Buckingham; Ghost of Buckingham; Messenger, 5.3; Soldier (Mute), 5.5.
10:	Clarence; Attendant (Mute), 1.2, 3.1; Derby; Citizen (Mute), 3.7; 1 Lord, 5.2; Ghost of Clarence.
Boy 1:	Tressel (Mute), 1.2; Dorset; Boy (Clarence's Son), 2.2; Young Prince Edward; Vaughan (Mute), 3.3; Citizen (Mute), 3.7; Page, 4.2; 4 Messenger, 4.4; Soldier and Lord (Mutes), 5.3, 5.3; Ghost of Young Prince Edward.
Boy 2:	Lady Anne; Grey (or perhaps by actor 2); Girl (Clarence's Daughter), 2.2; Young Duke of York; Citizen (voice off), 3.7; 3 Messenger, 4.4; Soldier and Lord (Mutes), 5.3, 5.5; Ghost of Anne; Ghost of Young Duke of York.

3 Conjectural disposition of rôles for touring version of *Richard III*, with ten men and two boys

to Shakespeare (as *1H4* 2.4.387 demonstrates), has one man doubling male rôles (including Ruf) and Venus, and another man doubling five female rôles and also Otian, the male successor to Sisamnes. Bradley does not mention this doubling of male and female rôles but, to the eight men stipulated for performance of this play according to the 1569 edition, adds four boys, presumably to bring the play into line with his theory.[1] A later play, *The Fair Maid of the Exchange*, published in 1607 but probably written in 1597, has a plot showing how eleven actors might present it; the same actor plays Barnard, an adult male; Ursula, a young woman; Mistress Flower, an older woman; and the Boy, a pert apprentice. 'The Actors Names' printed in the 1623 edition of *The Duchess of Malfi*, show that the same actor, Robert Pallant, played Cariola, the Doctor, and 'Court Officers' (A2ʳ).

Doubling has a long tradition. It is most often used to reduce the number of actors required but it can also serve to make a dramatic point. John Bale's *Kyng Johan* (1538), by doubling the Pope with Usurped Power, and Cardinal Pandulphus with Private Wealth, does more than limit the number of actors. Four hundred years later, T. S. Eliot in *Murder in the Cathedral*, deliberately (as he explained in the 1937 edition) doubled the Four Tempters with the Four Knights who, respectively, tempt and murder Becket. In Steven Berkoff's *Decadence* (1981), dramatic purpose is served by a single pair of actors playing an upper- and a lower-class couple. Doubling may also

---

[1] Bradley, p. 230. On p. 80 he categorises *Cambises* among plays for eight-cast companies 'presumed to have been acted by adult companies'.

be used to accord with the demands of convention. Da Ponte says he was 'compelled to reduce the sixteen original characters [of Beaumarchais's *Marriage of Figaro*] to eleven, two of which can be played by a single actor' for Mozart's opera. When the opera was first given in Vienna in 1786, Michael Kelly sang Don Basilio and Don Curzio, and Francesco Bassanio, Dr Bartolo and Antonio.[1] However, economy was and is the chief reason for doubling. In 1994, Third Party Productions presented Shakespeare's *Richard III* with six actors: 1: Richard; 2: Clarence, Buckingham; 3: King Edward, Rivers, Ely, Tyrrel, Stanley, Second Murderer; 4: Queen Elizabeth; 5: Queen Margaret, Lady Anne, Catesby; 6: Hastings, Richmond, Lord Mayor, First Murderer. Although the text was 'reformed' more thoroughly than that of Q, this was no trivial production and was described by the press as a 'swift and vital production', its many characters doubled 'comfortably' by its six players and so successfully, artistically and financially, as to be able to repeat its tour in 1995 with *The Comedy of Errors* and to be able to afford a slightly larger company.[2]

Reformation, the adaptation of texts of plays for Court performance, was one of the duties of the Master of the Revels in Shakespeare's time. Year after year there appears in the Revels Accounts a statement on these lines: 'Edmond Tylney [. . .] for his owne attendaunce and iiij^{er} men from the laste of October 1605 vntyll Ashwednesday following aswell for rehearsalle and makeing choyse of playes and Comodies and reforming them as for his other attendaunce for Maskes and devises p^{r}sented before the king and Queenes Maties'.[3]

What is immediately apparent from a study of the whole of both texts is how close are speeches in Q to those in F for certain characters and how 'consistently different' are those of others, suggesting that 'reformation' by a single hand, of the kind Tylney refers to, is not at the root of the differences in language. The speeches of Richard, Hastings, and Richmond are very similar in Q and F; Buckingham in Q, except in 2.1, often only approximates to Buckingham in F; the same is true of minor characters – Citizens and (with one exception) Messengers. Because two printing houses and three compositors set the plays, this variation cannot be put down to compositorial idiosyncrasy. Buckingham, for example, appears in work set by both houses. Textual variation must, therefore, go back to the compositors' copy. The kinds of substitution are those to which we are all accustomed when recalling quotations or a part in a play and they are a characteristic I have become very familiar with in editing Orwell, who had a capacious memory and who quoted verse and prose from memory, but not always word-perfectly.

---

[1] From da Ponte's introductory remarks, quoted by Alfred Einstein, *Mozart, His Character, His Work*, translated by Arthur Mendel and Nathan Broder (London, 1946), p. 430. Einstein refers to Kelly playing both Basilio and Don Curzio on p. 431.

[2] Doubling pattern from the programme; reviews from *Plays and Players*, February 1994, and *Time Out*, 20–7 April 1994. I am indebted to Nicholas Collett, co-producer and company secretary, for this information.

[3] *Jacobean and Caroline Revels Accounts, 1603–1642*, ed. W. R. Streitberger, Malone Society, *Collections XIII* (Oxford, 1986), p. 18. Many such references to reforming could be cited. See also the glossary, p. 180.

Marvin Spevack's recent *Shakespeare Thesaurus* attempts to classify the whole of
Shakespeare's vocabulary in order to reveal Shakespeare's idiolect: the linguistic
system peculiar to Shakespeare. A preliminary examination of the thesaurus shows
that although, as one would expect, many Q/F variants fall into the same sub-group –
for example, heart/soul, scorned/flouted, soul/man, speak/say, bad/ill, fear/doubt,
fares/doth, there is a large number which do not: zeal/love, grant/hear, foul/deep,
guile/vice, hugged/pitied, this/here, pretty/young, blind/bold. I hesitate to use
these distinguishing characteristics, because there are weaknesses in the thesaurus,
especially the failure to classify accurately English, Welsh, Scottish, and Irish names,
and there are curious omissions. Nevertheless, a large number of significant variants
do show a different idiolect from Shakespeare's as classified by Spevack. Thus, a *trial*
examination of nouns, adjectives, verbs, and adverbs used by Hastings in Q1 shows
twice as many substitutes drawn from what Spevack identifies as Shakespeare's
idiolect, compared to Buckingham, where the reverse obtains.[1] If Spevack's thesis can
(when modified) be sustained, this would suggest that Q could not be solely authorial
and would lend support to my analysis of the variants.

ACTORS' 'IMPROVEMENTS'

There are occasional indications in *Richard III* for actors to ad-lib (indications for
which are found in many plays),[2] hence '&c' at 1.3.229. Such expressions as 'Tut, tut'
appear at the same point in Q and F (e.g. 4.2.21), indicating that Shakespeare had
written this phrase into F and that it had been accurately recalled by the actor for Q, but
Q shows many more such expressions than does F. Some actors seem to have been
particularly prone to 'improve' their parts with, 'Well', 'Come, come', and the like.
Shakespeare complained of clowns ad-libbing in a speech given to Hamlet in that play
– 'let those that play your clowns speak no more than is set down for them' (3.2.38–40)
– but, ironically, in Q1 of *Hamlet*, it is Burbage who ad-libs, and at length.[3] Louis B.
Wright quotes from Röchell's chronicle of Münster for 1599 which describes an
English touring company playing there, in English, but 'They were accompanied by a
clown, who, when a new act had to commence *and when they had to change costume*,
made many antics and pranks in German *during the performance*, by which he amused
the audience' (my italics). Wright is surely correct in suggesting that this experience
led to such popular entertainment being introduced into plays toured in England and,

---

[1] Marvin Spevack, *A Shakespeare Thesaurus* (Hildesheim, 1993). Thus, the Captains of *Henry V* are all
listed as English, as are, for example, Sir Hugh Evans, Ross, Douglas, and Glendower. Examples of
omissions from groups that I find strange include 'report' and 'unfold' which ought both to appear in the
groups headed 'make known' and 'disclose' (24.25 and 24.28 respectively); and 'downfall' and 'ruin' which
should both appear in the groups headed 'destruction' and 'descend' (20.21 and 34.08), instead of only one
of them in each group. The word 'those', which Spevack lists as occurring 614 times in his *Concordance*,
is omitted. These examples suggest weaknesses, but, modified, the thesaurus could prove a very valuable
tool. See my review in *The Year in Reference, 1994* (London, 1995), pp. 161–3.
[2] See Doris Fenton, *The Extra-Dramatic Moment in Elizabethan Plays before 1616* (Philadelphia, 1930),
especially p. 19, n. 28; she gives specific examples of the use of 'etc.' for this purpose.
[3] See P. Davison, *Popular Appeal in English Drama to 1850* (London, 1982), pp. 41–3; as *Popular Appeal*
hereafter.

perhaps, in London also.¹ Despite suggestions that ad-libbing was uncharacteristic of Burbage,² he frequently improves his part, but he is not alone. The Buckingham and the two Executioners 'improved' their parts as did Clarence, Elizabeth, Brakenbury, Hastings, Ely, the Scrivener, the Page, and, possibly, Catesby and Derby, on occasion. Allowing for doubling, six to eight of the twelve of my suggested company seem to have 'improved' their parts, and that is hardly surprising. Other characteristics that are thrown up are clues to stage business, such as Clarence's little son saying in Q1 at 2.2.23 that Richard had 'hugged me in his arm'; ensemble playing – the way actors interjected words into the speeches of others (a 'naturalistic' acting technique); pronunciation ('Granam' for 'Grandam'); and the taking over by certain characters of other rôles.

Most of the 'improvements' to Richard's part are slight but clear: 1.2.141, 175; 3.7.19, 47, 200, 204; 4.2.98, 119; 4.4.257, 279, 369, 380, 404, 427–8; and 5.3.2. In Q, Richard throws a line at the much-bemused Lord Mayor at 3.5.25, not found in F. This could be an authorial addition, but given Burbage's propensity for 'improvement', it could be his work. At 4.2.81–2 there is a more elaborate improvement. Instead of Tyrrel leaving the stage with 'I will dispatch it straight', as in F, in Q he approximates to that line with ''Tis done, my gracious lord', whereupon Richard asks, 'Shall we hear from thee, Tyrrel, ere we sleep?', to which Tyrrel replies, 'You shall, my lord.' Richard's question is asked of Catesby at 3.1.186 and Tyrrel replies as did Catesby then. The repetition is almost certainly an addition by the actors and might have been Burbage's work. Tyrrel and Catesby would probably have been played by different actors on tour and 4.3.43 SDn suggests that the actor playing Ratcliffe played Tyrrel. Nevertheless, it would not have been impossible for Catesby to have made a quick change after exiting at 4.2.58 and re-entered as Tyrrel after 64; and in 4.3 he would have had eight lines to make a similar switch. This *seems* an unnecessary complication but if the same actor did play Catesby and Tyrrel this improvement might have been his and Burbage's work. Catesby seems to improve his part at 3.7.79 by repeating Buckingham's last two words, 'My lord'; in F, Buckingham has 'your Grace'.

The subtle dramatic modification of their rôles by the two murderers who kill Clarence in 1.4 demonstrates how *Richard III* was developed through performance. At their entry they are called murderers in Q and F but the Q speech heads describe them as executioners. Some of their lines are significantly different in Q as compared to F, but it is noticeable how closely the actors recall their lines when, as Hamlet put it, 'some necessary question of the play be then to be considered' (3.2.42–3). There can be little doubt that what Shakespeare drafted appears in F and that Q prints what was performed by the two actors – the two clowns, Kemp and Cowley (identified as playing Dogberry and Verges in *Much Ado About Nothing*, Q1, 1600). Hammond maintains that the play had no part for a clown and that Kemp 'would presumably not

---

¹ Louis B. Wright, 'Variety entertainment by Elizabethan strolling players', *Journal of English and Germanic Philology*, 26 (1927), 300–1, 303. 'Stroller' for an itinerant actor entered the printed language in 1608: 'Strowlers, a proper name giuen to Country-players, that . . . trotte from towne to towne vpon the hard hoofe', Thomas Dekker, *Lanthorne and Candle-light*, G1 (*OED*).

² Arden, note to 4.4.456.

have been used in its performance',[1] but this is surely incorrect. Would the company omit one of its sharers? Would Shakespeare be allowed to omit Kemp? What we have in Q is not merely 'the survival of gag'[2] but indications of how the actors worked up their rôles. Here (in a manner that Hamlet would have favoured) this is carefully controlled, unlike the development of the clowns' rôles in *Dr Faustus*.[3] Like the Torturers, or Knights, who crucify Christ in the mystery plays in the Wakefield and York versions, the two Executioners lace their task with black humour. The tradition is found closer to Shakespeare in *The History of King Leir* (1588–94) where 'The Messenger or murtherer' enters 'with two daggers in his hands' (lines 1453–4) to kill Leir and Perillus as they sleep. There are not only occasional similarities of dialogue (see 1.4.90n and 92–3n) but, more significant, a common use of low comedy. Thus, when Leir asks if he comes from France, the Messenger responds:

From France? zoones, do I looke like a Frenchman? Sure I haue not mine owne face on; some body hath chang'd faces with me, I know not of it: But I am sure, my apparell is all English. Sirra, what meanest thou to aske that question? I could spoyle the fashion of this face for anger. A French face!

(1572–76)

A slight but significant change in Q is that the First Executioner, Kemp, the senior partner of the duo, is given the first line when the clowns enter in 1.4, so marking their ranking. In the main the clowns then retain the lines given them in F, but see 78n, 136n, 222–3n, and 224n. A more significant change, though again it appears slight, is the use of the 'clown-word' 'gear' in 'Come shall we to this gear' at 1.4.131 for F's more prosaic 'Come, shall we fall to worke?' Just as 'I came hither on my legs' at 78 is reminiscent of the Vice's catch-line in *Mankind*, so is 'gear' associated with the Vice. Ambidexter uses it at least three times in *Cambises* (694, 753, 995); it appears in *King Darius*; the Devil, Hypocrisy, and Fellowship use it in *Lusty Juventus* (325, 655, and 835); as does Nichol Newfangle in *Like Will to Like* (595). In addition to its use here, Shakespeare uses 'gear' only ten times, once by Launcelot Gobbo with something of the Vice-like implications: 'if Fortune be a woman, she's a good wench for this gear' (*MV*, 2.2.166–7). See also Textual Notes to 100, 105, 124–5, and 128; also 1.3.346–8 and 346.

Possible improvements in the parts of other actors listed in the Textual Notes and the Collation are:

Clarence:	1.4.20, 40, 189, 201.
Hastings:	2.1.27?; 3.4.31; and see 'Ensemble playing' below.
Buckingham:	3.4.10; 3.5.5; 3.7.38, 199; the last may not be an improvement but the survival of the swearword, 'Zounds', eliminated from F as a result of the Statute to Restrain Abuses, 1606 (3 Jac. I., c.21); see also 1.4.165–6 and 5.3.205.

[1] Arden, p. 65.
[2] Arden, note to 1.4.88 ff.
[3] *Popular Appeal*, pp. 44–7.

Catesby:	3.2.58 (and see 'Ensemble playing' below), 3.7.79.
Ely:	3.4.33 (and see 'Ensemble playing' below).
Derby:	3.4.60.
Scrivener:	3.6.10.
Elizabeth:	4.1.13.
Lieutenant (Brakenbury):	4.1.14.
Page:	4.2.35.

See 1.3.229n for the direction that Margaret should continue cursing; also 1.3.92n.

PRONUNCIATION AND PHRASING

Q may give pointers to how words were pronounced. The most interesting instance is Q's 'Granam' for 'F's 'Grandam' (see 2.2.1n). The only exception to this pattern is Q's 'Grandam' at 2.4.10. This may stem from actor, scribe, or compositor. See also Textual Notes to 1.3.98, 101, 117, 315; 1.4.56; and 5.3.179.

ENSEMBLE PLAYING

At various points the differences in Q as compared to F suggest the ensemble playing practised by the Chamberlain's Men. At 3.2.58, F has a single line, 'Well *Catesby*, ere a fort-night make me older'; in Q, Catesby breaks into this:

> [HASTINGS] I tell thee, Catesby –
> CATESBY   What, my lord?
> HASTINGS Ere a fortnight make me elder,

Catesby employs the same technique at 4.2.49, interjecting 'my lord'. At 3.4.30–4, the change is more extensive. Richard, having claimed Hastings knows and loves him well, goes on to ask the Bishop of Ely for strawberries from his garden in Holborn. In F, Richard has two successive lines in the middle of a five-line speech: 'His Lordship knowes me well, and loues me well. / My Lord of Ely, when I was last in Holborne', but these in Q are developed in another good example of ensemble playing by Hastings's addition and Ely's interjection:

> [GLOUCESTER] His lordship knows me well, and loves me well.
> HASTINGS I thank your Grace.
> GLOUCESTER My Lord of Ely –
> ELY My Lord?
> GLOUCESTER When I was last in Holborn

See also Textual Notes to 1.3.92; 1.4.124–5; 4.2.98; and 4.4.286, which is an example of Q as a more sophisticated text than F and a pointer to Q not being an early version of *Richard III*.

STAGE BUSINESS

Dialogue occasionally gives a clue to stage business. At 2.2.3 in F, Clarence's daughter asks the Duchess of York why she weeps so oft; in Q, Clarence's son has this speech (and his next speech is given to his sister); he asks her, 'Why do you wring your hands.' What he recalls may have been prompted by his remembrance of the Duchess's actions. Later, at 23, instead of the fairly bland, 'And pittied me', he has in Q, 'And hugged me in his arm'. This, in the context of the play, is a particularly vivid image. Richard is described as hugging with one arm only and that is logical if Burbage played a 'withered-arm Richard' (the ground for his trumped-up charge against Hastings, 3.4.70–1). The play does not call for Clarence's son to be hugged by Richard. Such an action may have taken place in 3.1, and at 1.4.220 Clarence describes the way Richard had 'hugged me in his arms' (using the plural form) and that might betoken the way Richard bade his brother farewell at 1.1.114–16. Although it is dangerous to make much of a missing 's', were this simply a compositorial error it would be so jarring that it might be expected to be picked up in proof-reading. See also Textual Notes, 1.2.191, 194; 1.3.242; and 4.4.427–8.

METRICAL VARIATION

It is evident that actors, when recalling their parts, did not hesitate to create irregular lines if it suited them and it is plain that they were not constrained by theoretical metrical rules. For notes on metre, regular and irregular, see 1.1.71; 1.3.101, 304; 1.4.56, 114, 179; 2.1.1; 2.2.55, 113; 2.4.65, 69; 3.1.169–72, 184; 3.2.5 ff., 15, 26, 76; 3.4.10, 59, 78–80; 3.5.5; 3.7.31, 207; 4.2.47–8; 4.3.27; 4.4.286.

RÔLES UNFAMILIAR TO ACTORS

Where it would seem that an actor has taken on an additional rôle but had not become thoroughly familiar with it, the new rôle is often less well recalled. The variants in the lines given the children in 2.2, especially Edward's, may not result from poor memories but stem from these parts having only recently been taken over by the boy-actors in the course of re-assignment of doublings. The children's second and third speeches have been exchanged in Q and Margaret's line after 15 in F, 'And so will I', is omitted from Q. Uncertainty is also apparent in the eight lines taken over by Brakenbury from the Keeper in 1.4 on tour. The Keeper's few lines are rather less well recalled than Brackenbury's own, with approximations at 8, 61, and 62 and substitutions at 33 and 39. Unsurprisingly the minor parts of Citizens and the Scrivener are poorly recalled: see 2.3 and 3.6. The entry in 2.3 in F demands two doors but Q simply has '*Enter two* CITIZENS'; that simplification may have arisen because facilities on tour in a very small town might have made such an entry more complicated than necessary. The ensuing dialogue is very irregularly reported in its first few lines and there is some reallocation of parts, especially at the opening (which may indicate how the play was presented in London as well as on tour). The substitution in the opening line of the scene, 'Neighbour, well met', for F's 'Good morrow Neighbour', may be the actor's own mode of greeting. These rôles would probably have been taken by hireling actors in London but may have fallen to the lot of sharers on tour. This, and the habit, still found, of paying less attention in rehearsal to such minor scenes, may account for the relatively weak recall of this and similar scenes. The Messengers at the end of 4.4, excepting the first, are particularly inaccurate.

The actor playing Tyrrel shows considerable uncertainty in his speech that opens 4.3. In lines 1 and 2, 'deed' and 'act' are transposed and there are inversions in 5 and 11. There is a series of substitutions: 6, 'Although' for F's 'Albeit'; 7, 'Melting' for

'Melted'; and 'kind' for 'milde'; 8, 'stories' for 'Story'; 9, 'Lo' for 'O'; and 'those tender' for 'the gentle'; 13, 'Which' for 'And'; 15, 'once' for 'one'; 17, 'Whilst' for 'When'; 19, 'ever he' for 'ere she' ('ever' probably being a scribal expansion; the 'he' making Nature male instead of, as in F, female); 20, 'Thus' for 'Hence'; 22, 'bring' for 'beare'; 23, 'hail' for 'health' and 'leige' for 'Lord'. These are not the sort of changes a clown might make to embroider his part. The sense of the original is closely followed; it is simply that it is reported in the manner of someone unfamiliar with the detail, so also for the few lines he has in 4.2.

In general, the actors playing Richard, Margaret, Hastings, and Richmond recall their parts very well, although there are errors. Derby is fairly accurate; Buckingham, King Edward, Rivers, and the Bishop of Ely are unreliable.

UNRELIABILITY OF F

The text of F is not the concern of this edition but there are at least half-a-dozen places where readings in F, if the relationship of F and Q were reversed, would have been said to be faulty versions of Q. These might prove a salutary warning not to take without quibble the allocations above; see Textual Notes and Collation at: 1.2.126, 138, 190, 199; 1.3.6, 159, 337; 1.4.177, 212; 2.1.54; 2.2.70, 83–4, 111, 123; 2.3.44; 3.2.87–9; 4.4.36, 122, 282–3?, 314; 5.3.55, 209–11.

Some variants were introduced into F from quartos later than Q1, e.g.: 1.1.65, 124; 1.2.224; 1.4.12, 21, 22, 214; 2.2.86; 2.4.1; 3.1.40, 43, 63, 78, 87, 96, 97, 120, 123, 141; 3.7.16, 117; 4.3.25; 4.4.112 (2), 243, 249, 340; 5.3.122, 144, 177, 193; 5.5.7, 32.

Reorganisation of staging and cast

Q suggests the way the staging was reorganised and the alterations made to the *dramatis personae*. Some of these would go back to the pre-touring London production, but it is Q that provides this information. The most important variation is the 'addition' to Q of the Rougemont passage, 4.2.98–117. Professor Molly Mahood has suggested to me that this passage was introduced early in the play's history in order to lengthen the time between Tyrrel's agreeing to murder the princes and his reporting that they were dead. The Rougemont passage is not long (about half the forty lines between Tyrrel's exit and re-entry) but the introduction of such striking new matter makes dramatic time. The source is not Halle (Shakespeare's chief historical source for *Richard III*) but, exceptionally, the second edition of Holinshed, 1587. See Arden, pp. 334–5 and also note to 3.4.0 SD. Many of the following changes can be related to reorganisation of the play for touring. They are listed under two heads: 'Production and staging'; and 'Reduction in size of company (and reorganisation of *dramatis personae*)'. There is some deliberate duplication of references.

PRODUCTION AND STAGING

See Textual Notes or Collation at: 1.2.191; 1.3.242, 317; 1.4.0 SD (and see 4.1.22–3), 69–76, 77, 78, 86, 136, 222–3, 224, 225, 237–8; 2.1.137; 2.3.0 SD and see reallocation of speeches recorded in Collation; 3.2.0 SD, 3 SD, 92 SD; 3.3.0 SD; 3.4.0 SD; 3.5.11, 15 (and compare 3.7.89 SD), 16, 25; 3.7.46, 50, 50 SD; 4.2.0 SD, 30–1, 49–50; 4.4.421 SD, 427–8; 5.3.0 SD, 18 SD, 38–41, 219 SD.

Despite the complications of mounting 5.3, with its several actions, many characters, and two on-stage tents, a touring company of ten men and two boys could cope with its demands. Back-stage workers could supplement those on stage to 'bulk out the scene', but the pattern of doubling in figure 2 shows that they are not essential and none are there allocated. Entries have been modified by indicating, within square brackets, the number of mutes available as attendant soldiers and lords from the acting troupe proper.

REDUCTION IN SIZE OF COMPANY (AND REORGANISATION OF
DRAMATIS PERSONAE)

The reduction of characters in Q is discussed below and the Textual Notes indicate where changes have been made. Not all such combinations and omissions were necessarily for purposes of touring. D. L. Patrick suggested that by combining the rôles of the Archbishops of Canterbury and York (the former also being a Cardinal) into a single character, there would be economy in the provision of episcopal costumes, a suggestion Hammond finds plausible.[1] These costumes would have been elaborate and, unless given to the company, very expensive. If York were retained, three very bulky costumes would be required for him, Canterbury, and Ely. Even if the company could run to three copes, mitres, etc., the opportunity might well have been taken to reduce the baggage on tour by combining the rôles of York and Canterbury. Curiously, More, and later Holinshed, telescoped the rôles of the two prelates but Shakespeare's source, Halle, distinguishes between Dr Rotherham (York and the Chancellor), and Cardinal Bourchier (Canterbury).

Crowd scenes with a very small cast present obvious problems. Some mute bystanders could be provided at a pinch from stage staff but the doubling pattern has been plotted to avoid the necessity of calling on such men. There is no entry in Q at 3.7.50 for citizens, but obviously the Mayor is required at this point. All those not having speaking rôles in this scene could play mute citizens, that is, those who play the Duchess of York, Queen Elizabeth, Dorset, Anne, Derby, and Ratcliffe, as the play is doubled for this edition. Later, one of these is given a line off (see 202n). The first four of these actors must enter at the start of 4.1; that would be made practicable if they did not return to the stage when Gloucester relents at 204 (see 200 SDn). Obviously, if one or two back-stage staff could stand in, a more effective crowd could be presented. At 5.3.267, the doubling pattern again allows for two lords (or soldiers) to match Richmond's pair of lords; three would be a practicable possibility at each point without drawing on back-stage men. Neither Richard nor Richmond need address their orations to a tiny force on stage but rather should directly address the audience, as Richmond patently does at 5.5.23–41, demanding from the theatre audience a final 'Amen' in the Morality tradition (as, for example, in Barnabas's address to the audi-

[1] Arden, p. 16.

ence at the end of *A Nice Wanton*, 1550). Balanced staging would suffice to symbolise the rival contenders for the throne.

See Textual Notes 1.2.34; 1.3.317, 346–8, 350; 2.1.44, 137; 2.2.32 SD; 2.4.0 SD, 21, 37 SD (and see consequential change at 2.4.51, 'lady' for 'Lord'); 3.1.150 SD; 3.2.106–8; 3.3.0 SD; 3.4.0 SD (and omission of Lovell from 3.4, 3.5, and 4.2), 6, 78–80; 3.5.15; 3.7.200 SD, 202 SH; 4.2.0 SD; 4.3.43 SD; 4.4.370; 5.2.0 SD; 5.3.2, 18 SD, 143–50; 5.4.0 SD.

Some of the features described above can be seen in figure 4. This presents the opening of 3.5, the texts of Q1 and F1 having been adjusted to make comparison easier. The annotations point to some of the differences. The scene can be played on one or two stage levels (the Arden edition prefers the latter arrangement)[1] but Richard's order to Catesby to 'ouerlooke the wals' must, in Q, be addressed to Buckingham; Catesby has yet to enter in Q because he has replaced Ratcliffe as Hastings's executioner. This, in effect, ensures that the action is on one level, however F might be interpreted. This is not because two levels were impossible on tour (they are required in 3.7) but because rapid access from one level to another might be difficult in touring venues. In F, Ratcliffe and Lovell bring in Hastings's head. Ratcliffe's replacement by Catesby may have had nothing to do with touring but have been made for the London production when it was realised Ratcliffe was at Pomfret overseeing the executions of Rivers, Grey, and Vaughan. Lovell is eliminated. Others in F cut from Q include the Keeper, the Sheriff, Surrey, Oxford, and Herbert. The Archbishop and Cardinal become a single prelate (discussed above). Their lines are either cut or allocated to others. Clarence's daughter is omitted from 4.1 in Q and the reference to 'neece Plantagenet' at 4.1.1, which in F refers to her, becomes, with the omission from Q of the second line of F, a reference to Anne – a particularly neat adaptation for touring. Brakenbury takes over the Keeper's rôle in 1.4 (discussed above), and, almost certainly, the rôle of the Lieutenant (of the Tower) in 4.1. All the speech heads in Q and F indicate that it is the Lieutenant who speaks and the others refer to him as such. Many editors follow Capell's identification of Brakenbury as the Lieutenant.[2] That the same actor played both parts on tour is confirmed by the actor's repetition at 22 of 1.1.84 and 103, 'I do beseech your Grace(s) (both) to pardon me.' It is possible that, especially on tour, an attempt was made to suggest that this was an additional character, so seeming to bulk out the company's resources and for that reason, the description 'Lieutenant' has been retained. Dorset takes over the Messenger's rôle in 2.4 (and Q is adjusted at 51 so that Dorset refers to his mother, as 'lady', instead of, as in F, addressing the relevant prelate (the Archbishop of York in F, the Cardinal in Q) as 'lord'. Ratcliffe takes over from the Sheriff in 5.1; neither is given an entry but each is given appropriate speech headings and, in F, there is an entry for 'Halberds' to accompany Buckingham to his execution. Catesby takes over from Surrey in 5.3. (see 2n). In Q, the Priest becomes a mute in 3.2; Sir William Brandon is given an entry in F at 5.3.18 SD and is directly referred to at 22 in F (but is mute); in Q he has no entry

---

[1] Arden, note to 3.5.17 SD.
[2] Arden, p. 5.

and instead of being told directly by Richmond that he shall bear his standard, Richmond asks, 'Where is Sir William Brandon?' and, because he is not present, says, 'He shall bear my standard': again, a neat adaptation for a smaller-cast company. Dorset and Rivers are excised from 2.2 of Q and, apart from his two lines as a ghost (which anyone could speak), Vaughan becomes a mute. That Vaughan should be silent at his execution, losing the only line he has in F (3.3.7), is surely evidence for a sharp reduction in the number of actors available on tour. Had the man standing mutely for Vaughan been capable of a single line, surely he would have been allowed it? He would hardly have forgotten to recall something appropriate to such an occasion.

Such compression suggests that the company had been considerably reduced in size from that which had presented the play in London. The most intriguing result of the doubling pattern I have suggested for a company of this size is that it explains why only in Q1 (and its reprint, Q2) the ghosts appear out of the chronological order of their deaths. Hammond believes that this re-ordering in Q1 'arose through some confusion in the reporting process'.[1] This seems correct if one is editing F. The order in Q, however, arises not from confusion but as a result of doubling. Further, if the company had been any larger, doubling would not have been so tight and it would not have been necessary for the ghosts of the two young princes to appear before the ghost of Hastings. (See also pp. 49–50.)

Q1 is, allowing for 'London cuts' and the Rougemont addition, virtually a full-length version of the play. One possibility that has been suggested is that it was put together by the actors as a reading text.[2] However, the many compressions and the re-ordering of the ghosts implies performance. If the Q3 compositor could work out the reason for the order of the ghosts, the actors would surely have been able to do so.

REVISION FOR LONDON PRODUCTION

I have concentrated on changes that point to modification for touring and on verbal substitutions indicative of actors' recall, but revision by Shakespeare for production in London is also to be found in Q1. Acceptance of such revisions should lead to the omission of some 140 lines from F.[3]

To what extent revision may have been for the London production (and thus later than the text as represented by F) and to what extent it was specifically for touring, cannot always be determined. Did Shakespeare plan *Richard III* with two prelates initially and increase their number to three? Or did he start with three and cut them to two? And if the latter, was that for the London or for the touring productions? A reduction in casting for touring seems to me by far the most likely development, if only because, if the reverse were the case and the cast amplified, so little is made of the

[1] Arden, note to 5.3.147–51.
[2] I am indebted to Professor Park Honan for putting the possibility of a reading text to me.
[3] I wished to omit these lines from a projected edition of *Richard III* in 1983, but the publishers insisted on their restoration in order to make the text acceptable for study for public examinations. Three years later, Oxford published *William Shakespeare, Complete Works, Original-Spelling Edition*, ed. Stanley Wells, Gary Taylor, *et al.*; this excluded these passages from the text proper, but printed them in an appendix (pp. 250–1). For my review article of this edition and its *Textual Companion*, which refers particularly to *Richard III*, see *The Library*, VI, 10 (1988), 255–67.

| QUARTO 1: 1597 | AUTHORIAL / ANNOTATION | FOLIO: 1623 |

QUARTO 1: 1597

Enter Duke of Glocester and Buckingham in armonr.

Glo. Come Cosen, canst thou quake and change thy colour?
Murther thy breath in middle of a word,
And then beginne againe, and stop againe,
As if thou wert distraught and mad with terror.
Buc. Tut feare not me.
I can counterfait the deepe Tragedian:
Speake, and looke backe, and prie on euery side:
Intending deepe suspition, gastly lookes
Are at my seruice like inforced smiles,
And both are ready in their offices
To grace my stratagems.   *Enter Macor.*
Glo. Here comes the Maior.
Buc. Let me alone to entertaine him. Lo: Maior,
Glo. Looke to the drawbridge there.
Buc. The reason we haue sent for you.
Glo. Catesby ouerlooke the wals.
Buck Harke, I heare a drumme.
Glo. Looke backe, defend thee, here are enemies.
Buc. God and our innocence defend vs.   *Enter Catesby*
Glo. [O, O, be quiet, it is Catesby.]   *with Hast. head.*
Cat. Here is the head of that ignoble traitor,
That daungerous and vnsuspected Hastings.
Glo. So deare I lou'd the man, that I must weepe:
I tooke him for the plainest harmelesse man,
That breathed vpon this earth a christian,
Looke ye my Lo: Maior.

AUTHORIAL / STAGE DIRECTION?

n for *u*
AUTHORIAL
STAGE DIRECTION?

INVERSION

wert > were
ANTICIPATES l.92

OMITTED from Q

Maior ENTERS
ALONE in Q

Buc. 'IMPROVES'
LINE ORDER

(a)
(d)
(c)
(b)

RELIC from F
heare ADDED

Catesby for Ratcliffe
[Q ADAPTED]

Lovell OMITTED

Richard
'IMPROVES'

FOLIO: 1623

Enter Richard, and Buckingham, in rotten Armour, maruellous ill-fauoured.

Richard. Come Cousin,
Canst thou quake, and change thy colour,
Murther thy breath in middle of a word,
And then againe begin, and stop againe,
As if thou were distraught, and mad with terror?
Buck. Tut, I can counterfeit the deepe Tragedian,
Speake, and looke backe, and prie on euery side,
Tremble and start at wagging of a Straw:
Intending deepe suspition, gastly Lookes
Are at my seruice, like enforced Smiles;
And both are readie in their Offices,
At any time to grace my Stratagemes.
But what, is Catesby gone?
Rich. He is, and see he brings the Maior along.
  Enter the Maior, and Catesby.
Buck. Lord Maior.
(a) Rich. Looke to the Draw-Bridge there.
(b) Buck. Hearke, a Drumme.
(c) Rich. Catesby, o're-looke the Walls.
(d) Buck. Lord Maior, the reason we haue sent.
Rich. Looke back, defend thee, here are Enemies.
Buck. God and our Innocencie defend, and guard vs.
  Enter Louell and Ratcliffe, with Hastings Head.
[Rich. Be patient, they are friends: Ratcliffe, and Louell.]
Louell. Here is the Head of that ignoble Traytor,
The dangerous and vnsuspected Hastings.
Rich. So deare I lou'd the man, that I must weepe:

I tooke him for the plainest harmlesse Creature,
That breath'd vpon the Earth, a Christian.
Made him my Booke, wherein my Soule recorded
The Historie of all her secret thoughts.
So smooth he dawb'd his Vice with shew of Vertue,
That his apparant open Guilt omitted,
I meane, his Conuersation with *Shores* Wife,
He liu'd from all attainder of suspects.
Buck. Well, well, he was the couertst sheltred Traytor
That euer liu'd.
Would you imagine, or almost beleeue,
Wert not, that by great preseruation
We liue to tell it, that the subtill Traytor
This day had plotted, in the Councell-House,
To murther me, and my good Lord of Gloster.
Maior. Had he done so?
Rich. What? thinke you we are Turkes, or Infidels?
Or that we would, against the forme of Law,
Proceed thus rashly in the Villaines death,
But that the extreame perill of the case,
The Peace of England, and our Persons safetie,
Enforc'd vs to this Execution.
Maior. Now faire befall you, he deseru'd his death,
And your good Graces both haue well proceeded,
To warne false Traytors from the like Attempts.
[*Buck.* I neuer look'd for better at his hands,
After he once fell in with Mistresse *Shore*:]
Yet had we not determin'd he should dye,
Vntill your Lordship came to see his end,
Which now the louing haste of these our friends,
Something against our meanings, haue preuented;

COMP MISREAD liu'd
suspect > suspects

haue ADDED

F's that OMITTED
you? > that
Had TRANSPOSED

APPROXIMATION

you my > your
Lords > Graces
[TRANSFERRED]
Dut. COMP ERROR
INVERSION
death > end
longing > louing
meaning > meanings

Made him my booke, wherein my soule recorded,
The history of all her secret thoughts:
So smoothe he daubd his vice with shew of vertue,
That his apparant open guilt omitted:
I meane his conuersation with *Shores* wife,
He laid from all attainder of suspect.
Buck. Well well, he was the couertst sheltred traitor
That euer liu'd, would you haue imagined,
Or almost beleeue, wert not . by great preseruation
We liue to tell it you? The subtile traitor
Had this day plotted in the councell house,
To murder me, and my good Lord of Glocester.
Maior. What, had he so?
Glo. What thinke you we are Turkes or Infidels,
Or that we would against the forme of lawe,
Procede thus rashly to the villaines death,
But that the extreame perill of the case,
The peace of England, and our persons safety
Inforst vs to this execution.
Ma. Now faire befall you, he deserued his death,

And you my good Lords both, haue well proceeded,
To warne false traitours from the like attempts:
[I neuer lookt for better at his hands,
After he once fell in with Mistresse *Shore*.]
Dut. Yet had not we determined he should die,
Vntill your Lordship came to see his death,
Which now the longing haste of these our friends,
Somewhat against our meaning haue preuented,

'additional' characters in F. But that does not mean that authorial revision did not occur – surely an inevitable procedure especially for one of Shakespeare's earlier plays. Clarence's five lines in F, not found in Q, between 1.4.231 and 232 are interpreted by some editors as a 'botched insertion' into F rather than an authorial cut:

> Which of you, if you were a Princes Sonne,
> Being pent from Liberty, as I am now,
> If two such murtherers as your selues came to you,
> Would not intreat for life, as you would begge
> Were you in my distresse.

But the ordering of speeches earlier (see 77n and 78n), the joint speeches at 209 and 215 (both given to the First Murderer in F), and the patterning of 'thou' and 'you', show a very careful dramatic re-ordering that must betoken authorial revision. Clarence appeals not solely to the supposedly less savage Second Executioner, but turns desperately from one to the other (and see below). Both are vicious; both hesitate – or, perhaps, toy with their victim. That the man who does not strike the blow should then show revulsion (240–2) is typical of many a brute criminal. What one has here, in the lines not found in Q, and Q's other modifications, is a later, authorially refined text, more sophisticated than F, that must surely go back to the initial production of the play in London.

In addition to Rivers's and Dorset's lines cut from 2.2, and the former's exchanges with Buckingham and Richard, there are a number of small omissions (some of which may be accidental), seventeen lines from 3.7 at various points after 92, and significant omissions from 4.4: fourteen lines between 210–11 and fifty-five lines between 260–1, all sixty-nine spoken in F by Elizabeth and Richard. Of the lines omitted from 3.7, six at five places are omitted from Buckingham's part and ten by Richard following 'your condition' at 133. This last looks like a deliberate cut; the two omitted after 92 are probably missed by oversight as could be the three separate lines after 112, 118 (and see 178n), and 122, but as these pile on repetitious detail Buckingham's speeches may have been trimmed deliberately. The omission of 182 is probably a compositorial error (see note thereto). With respect to the differences in 4.4, it must be theoretically possible that, if Q were an earlier version, Shakespeare added to the length of this already lengthy scene of what was to be his second longest play (and F's 4.4 is almost one-third of the length of the whole of *The Comedy of Errors*), giving Richard an extra speech of forty-six lines, and a further twenty-three lines shared by Elizabeth and Richard at various points, but it is far more likely that these are lines cut from F. These cuts, or rather, these authorial revisions, would probably have been made when the play was produced in London. There is a remote possibility that the fifty-five lines (including Richard's long speech) following Q's 260 were written on a lost page of manuscript; if the manuscript of *Sir Thomas More* is a safe guide, fifty-five lines could be got onto one side – but what was on the other side? It is noticeable that there is no disjunction in the sense.

Q transfers two of Buckingham's derogatory lines about Hastings to the Lord Mayor at 3.5.48–9: 'I never looked for better at his hands / After he once fell in with Mistress

Shore.' In Q, Buckingham's speech thus begins with 'Yet had not we determined', but the speech heading is *Dut.* for *Buc.*, an impossible assignment because the Duchess is not present in the scene. Hammond believes the lines are correctly assigned in F, quoting the New Shakespeare's explanation that the first of these lines looks back to 'attempts' in 47 and, spoken by Buckingham, is said by one of those threatened. Arden continues, 'The displacement of the speech-prefix . . . and its erroneous printing there, imply a damaged or illegible margin.'[1] There is, I believe, an alternative way of interpreting this transfer. I agree that the false speech head is a product of illegibility, but I think that might have been caused by these two lines being marked for transfer from Buckingham to the Lord Mayor. They are very petty for so aristocratic a character as Buckingham and suit well a smug Mayor safely daring in such circumstances to criticise a once-powerful noble. With these lines, the Mayor is given a distinctive character. Q may, therefore, represent authorial revision (and probably not for the touring version).

A possible authorial revision at 1.4.9 has been interpreted as an accidental omission. In Q, Clarence makes one line of F's two: 'Me thoughts that I had broken from the Tower, / And was embark'd to crosse to Burgundy', reducing these to 'Methoughts I was embarked for Burgundy.' A conventional way of memorising a passage of this kind is by keeping in mind the physical progress – escape from the Tower, embarkation for France – and as Clarence is painfully aware of where he is, this would be rather a surprising memorial lapse. Hammond argues that two lines 'seem crucial to the development of the scene' and that the omission must be 'an actor's or copyist's oversight'.[2] However, the audience has just been made aware of Clarence's situation in the preceding dialogue at the end of 1.3 and it is possible that this is an authorial simplification. See Textual Notes 1.4.24n, 26–7n, and 34n.

In F, Rivers, Woodville, and Scales were taken by Shakespeare (misled by his sources) to be three different men; the titles were all those of Rivers. Q corrects (see 2.1.64n) and that change, almost certainly nothing to do with reformation for touring, supports the case for F's underlying manuscript representing an earlier, unrevised, state of the play than the manuscript underlying Q.

Perhaps the most intriguing revisions, surely indicative of artistic insight, and too carefully patterned to be accidental (especially as the pattern occurs twice with different pairs of actors), are the shifts between 'thee', 'thy', 'thou' and 'you', 'your', 'ye' in the exchanges between Anne and Richard in Q from 1.2.135, and those touched on earlier from 1.4.225 between Clarence and the Second Executioner. At a telling moment Anne shifts back to 'you' at the moment we know she has capitulated: 'Well, well, put up your sword' (184). Richard, as he shifts from defence to wooing, tends towards the use of the second person singular in Q. Clarence, when he pleads for his life in Q, 1.4, addresses only the Second Executioner, instead of both Executioners as in F, evidently suspecting that he is the less vicious of the two men: 'Hast thou that holy feeling in thy soul' (225), instead of F's, 'Haue you that holy feeling in your

---

[1] Arden, note to 3.5.49–50.
[2] Arden, note to 1.4.9–10.

soules.' In the second and third lines thereafter, Clarence in Q continues the singular, 'thou . . . thy . . . soule . . . thou', for F's plural, and only at 229 falls back on an appeal to both men in Q and F. These instances of careful dramatic re-ordering betoken artistic change rather than mistaken recall. If, as Foster believes, Shakespeare played Clarence (see p. 16 above), that would support the case for authorial revision.

The Textual Notes point to places where revision is suspected, for example, 1.1.13 ('love' for the more obvious 'lute') and, more certainly, 1.1.26, 'spy' for the bland 'see' (and Q is accepted by Arden), but the warning must be reiterated that it is not possible to be certain that what is suspected as revision may not be the product of an actor's memory; conversely, what has been listed above as memorial substitution may be revision. Further, not all revisions may be authorial; some may have been made at the instigation of the company with or without the author's approval. In the matter of revision, one must walk with extreme delicacy (and I am aware of King Agag's fate). A question-mark indicates more than this general uncertainty.

Summary of possible revisions (not necessarily for touring)

1.1.13, 26, 115, 132, 138?;

1.2.18, 74?, 135, 137, 154–5?, 194, 199, 222?, 234?, 238;

1.3.7, 30, 58, 67, 77, 114–15?, 118, 165–6, 227?, 300, 301?, 317, 329, 337, 350;

1.4.9, 24, 26–7, 34, 65–6, 66, 77, 78, 86, 136, 146–7, 177, 191, 222–3, 224, 225, 231–2, 237–8;

2.1.6, 7, 24–5, 39, 64, 79, 90;

2.4.1–2, 9, 37, 51;

3.1.150 SD, 169–72, 182?, 185, 191, 196;

3.2.5ff., 78, 85?, 87–9, 92 SD, 106–8;

3.3.1, 5, 6, 21;

3.4.0 SD, 91–2, 98–9, 103–4;

3.5.11 SD, 15, 16, 25, 48–9, 54?, 102;

3.7.5–8, 32, 46, 92–3, 131, 200;

4.1.1–2, 5, 9, 64?, 91;

4.2.1 SH, 49–50, 78?, 80?, 84, 94, 98–117, 118;

4.3.35 SD, 46;

4.4.29–31, 48–9, 141, 153, 170, 171–2, 210–11, 260–1, 287, 292–5, 312, 345–6, 348, 370, 404–5;

4.5.2?, 16–18;

5.1.15?;

5.3.9, 38–41.

Thus, a fresh examination of the quarto of *Richard III* indicates to this editor, despite many uncertainties, that it was based on a memorial reconstruction by the actors of a touring version of the play. What was toured would have been revised for touring by a smaller company but the original, London, version would also have undergone revision. The play may have been toured before 1597 (and Professor Foster gives 1596 as a year when *Richard III* was performed), but I suggest that it was for the

1597 tour that it proved necessary to reconstruct the play memorially. Foster does not list its performance in 1597 (and it will be recalled he stressed that his assignments of dates 'must be used with caution'). Under 1596 he states that the play was 'possibly . . . recopied and slightly revised'. Of course, listing a play as performed does not mean it was toured. Thus, he lists three plays as being performed in 1596, *3H6*, *H5*, and *Richard III*; we know of only one place the company visited outside London in 1596 (as Lord Hunsdon's Men): Faversham. We have no way of knowing which of these plays, if any, were performed there, nor how many.

The nature and authorisation of the lost manuscript of the reformed, touring version

It may be objected that a reformed playbook would need to carry the authorisation of the Master of the Revels. Although I do not see this as an insoluble problem, did the text as adapted for touring *Richard III* look significantly different from that used in London? Were there, indeed, two prompt-books, one for London and one for touring, or only a single, combined prompt-book? Anyone who has done even a very modest amount of orchestral playing, especially for musicals, must have come across 're-formed scores' that give the full work but also show cuts, substitutions, cadenzas, rescoring, etc. The different states may be found simultaneously in the full score and the parts and one of the first matters to be sorted out on starting to rehearse is which cuts, substitutions, and rescoring are to be followed.[1]

An excellent example both of a touring version and the loss of a 'text', or part of one, is provided by Mozart's *La finta giardiniera* (1775). Mozart produced a version with spoken dialogue instead of recitatives, *Die Verstellte Gärtnerin*, and it was played as a *singspiel* from 1779 to 1782. Amanda Holden, translator of the 1994 Welsh National Opera production, remarked of the *singspiel*, 'it's good to think that Mozart wanted to cater for a German-speaking audience . . . and a travelling company'. When the music of Act I of *La finta giardiniera* was lost soon afterwards, the *singspiel* provided the only version available for that act until the original was found in Moravia in 1978.[2]

Samuel Foote's *The Diversions of a Morning* (1747; revised 1758), could be played in a variety of different ways in addition to the major changes introduced during revision. Thus, Tate Wilkinson sometimes played Puzzle and sometimes Puzzle was played by Foote. Not only did they act in different ways (Wilkinson imitated Foote imitating

---

[1] Theatre music offers many examples of alternative versions present in the same parts. The Gilbert and Sullivan operettas are notorious for having their parts marked up with cuts, alternatives, and repeats, and an orchestra's first task is to find its way through this minefield of possibilities. Often a player taking over a part in mid-run of a musical show will sit in initially, without playing, simply so that he or she will know what alternatives have been selected. Welsh National Opera's orchestral parts for *La Bohème* give versions in C and D♭ for a tenor aria and the orchestra plays whichever is appropriate for the singer engaged for the performance. Strauss's *Elektra* is arranged for full (indeed, very full) orchestra and for a smaller orchestra (for example, three trumpets instead of six), and many more examples could be given. Information about Welsh National Opera kindly provided by the company's music librarian, Tony Burke, and my son, Simon, who has played (and toured) with WNO for nearly twenty years.

[2] Amanda Holden, 'Mozart's first Munich opera', programme for WNO's *La finta giardiniera* (Cardiff, 1994), p. 14.

Macklin) but, when Foote played Puzzle an additional character, Bounce, was introduced and he was played by Wilkinson. Such alternative versions do not necessarily
require wholly separate versions of the play-text. I have a copy of the stage-manager's
vocal score of the Farjeons' musical play, *The Two Bouquets*, 1936. This came to me on
the death of my mother a year or two ago and had been used by her (she was what
would, in the Elizabethan theatre, be called the bookkeeper), when the show was
played at the Ambassadors and Garrick Theatres in London and on tour. This shows
all the cuts, substitutions of words, and cues to align music with words; it also shows
where vocal and instrumental cadenzas might be performed. There would have been
no problem in presenting this musical play from this copy in its first form, or in all or
part of its revised forms. As it was the only copy, had it, like *Richard III*, Q1, been lost,
it would have had to be reconstituted from memory.

If one turns to what *may* have happened to the manuscript underlying *Richard III*,
we know that there must have been a manuscript underlying Q1 and another (partly
collated with a reprint of Q for 3.1.1–165 and 5.3.44 to the end) underlying F. There
is general agreement that there is no sign of a prompt-book and that the part of the
manuscript underlying F that is different from Q stems from foul papers. From the foul
papers a prompt-book would have been prepared; that would have incorporated
revisions (for example, the elimination of the 'ghost' characters, Woodville and Scales,
whom Shakespeare had mistakenly introduced into his pre-production text – see
2.1.64n – and perhaps the cuts to 4.3. and the Rougemont addition); that would have
been the version first played in London. *Superimposed on that* would have been the
touring alternatives. Thus, when the Keeper spoke in 1.4, a note would indicate that
Brakenbury should enter and speak; Lovell and Vaughan, and their few lines, could be
bracketed for omission as need be, as could the lines of Rivers and Dorset in 2.2, and
the order of the ghosts could be marked for transposition, etc. There would be no need
for a separate text any more than for *The Two Bouquets* and there would be no reason
for such alternatives to require separate authorisation by the Master of the Revels.
Either version could be performed from the same text. I imagine that this combined
prompt-book was lost during the course of a tour in 1596 or 1597, losing, in effect, the
full 'London' version of *Richard III*, and the touring version, at one fell swoop. The
actors then recalled their parts to produce a version to play on tour. There would then
be no prompt-book from which to print the Folio text, hence the resort to foul papers
to print F, and the need for the manuscript underlying Q1 to be specially licensed for
printing (see above p. 11).

Such a theory as I have advanced to account for the nature of Q1 should not be seen
in isolation: it must be related to the exigencies of touring. What happens if a leading
actor is ill, even though leading actors and actresses, unlike their counterparts in opera,
seem remarkable for their ability to perform under the most adverse of circumstances,
as their understudies will attest? Nevertheless, as Tate Wilkinson, the touring impre-
sario *par excellence* of the eighteenth century, confessed, 'illness, like death, will come,
and will not go away when bid'.[1] A brief account of the trials and disasters of touring,

---

[1] *Wandering Patentee*, III, 61.

concentrating on those aspects relevant to what I am proposing for QI, might be useful.

Touring

Touring is still common, but in the sixteenth and later centuries it carried the burden of dramatic representation. Even for Shakespeare's day there is much evidence about touring and in the eighteenth century there is a great mass. I grew up in a theatrical family that toured from the 1870s and whose records in eight bulky volumes are in my possession; my mother managed touring companies in the 1930s; one of my sons has toured for the past twenty years with Welsh National Opera. The continuity of their touring experience with what Tate Wilkinson records is striking. I can think of no more 'dramatic' way of showing this than by comparing the response of companies in the eighteenth and twentieth centuries to sudden disaster. Thus, if a leading actor were unable to appear at short notice, Wilkinson would either have someone read the part from the book, standing in the wings or at the front of the stage; or he would change the play to one that could be presented without that actor. He maintained that, provided he knew by 2.00 pm, he could 'paper the town' advising his prospective audience of such a change. Welsh National Opera does precisely these things. Thus, when a principal in *Così fan tutte* was taken ill at the last moment, one of the chorus, Timothy German, sang the part 'from the book', at first in the wings and then in full view of the audience. When another WNO singer was unavoidably absent at the very last moment so that *Pique Dame* could not be performed in Manchester, *La Bohème* was substituted at two or three hours' notice. In a desperate crisis in 1937 when a tenor lost his voice in a production of the Farjeons' musical, *The Two Bouquets*, my mother (then the chorus mistress and a powerful contralto) sang his part from behind a potted palm whilst he mimed. No one seemed to notice. The main difference between Tate Wilkinson's eighteenth-century practice and that of Welsh National Opera is that Wilkinson set 2.00 pm as his deadline for major change, whereas WNO, with the advantages of telephone, fax, and fast transport, requires an extra half an hour.

Obviously one must be cautious in transferring contemporary, or even eighteenth-century, theatre experience to the late sixteenth century, but I see no reason to believe that practice to cope with such disasters was much different when Shakespeare and the Chamberlain's Men toured. We know, for example, that the Admiral's Men were able to cope with the illness of their leading actor, Edward Alleyn, on tour in Bath in 1593. His father-in-law, Philip Henslowe, wrote to him on 14 August, 'We hard that you weare very sycke at Bathe & that one of youre felowes weare fayne to playe youre parte for you.'[1]

The fortunes of Shakespeare's company may not have sunk to the depths experienced by Munden in the 1780s, but what touring *could* be like is worth bearing in mind. His memoir gives a vivid picture of a small, impoverished company's life on

---

[1] E. K. Chambers, *William Shakespeare: A Study of Facts and Problems* (2 vols., Oxford, 1930), II, 314; as 'Chambers' hereafter.

tour, the kind of company that had first to sweep away the cobwebs and 'the refuse of Ceres's golden grain' in a village barn when preparing for a performance:

The rehearsal over, and the barn-yard cleared, planks were laid and saw-dust strewed for expected company; but in vain was the night appointed; in vain the rehearsal; in vain the barn-yard cleared and the saw-dust strewed to preserve the tender feet of red-cloaked damsels, and rustic swains. No swain, no damsels came; all was solitary, and manager and mate went comfortless to bed [. . .] The two following nights were equally unsuccessful.[1]

Wilkinson records actors going mad, suffering delirium tremens, fighting with the audience, and so forth, but even the most seemingly crippling disasters were usually overcome, although sometimes not without serious damage to the production. Tate Wilkinson records that when he presented Charles Coffey's *The Devil to Pay* at York in 1784, the actor playing Sir John Loverule strained his ankle 'to so violent a degree' that he was unable to move without assistance and did not arrive at the theatre. The company, unaware of his absence when the play began, had 'no resource . . . but getting through as well as they could' without a principal player. As Wilkinson remarks, with wry humour, 'a wretched maimed performance it was'.[2]

Henry Irving's sudden illness when playing Lear at the Lyceum in 1892 illustrates how quickly an actor can learn a major rôle. Irving was taken ill at lunch-time. W. J. Holloway, who played Kent, was appointed to read the part from the stage. Holloway realised that if he were to read the part he would have to wear spectacles and that Lear in pince-nez was an impossibility. In the few hours available to him, he learned the part of Lear and performed it that same night to tumultuous applause. Henry Howe, then the oldest actor on the English stage, called on him to say that 'never in his 60 years upon the stage had he seen anything so marvellous as to study such a part and play it so well without rehearsal at three hours' notice'. By a remarkable coincidence, his son, John, took over as Prospero from John Drinkwater at the Open Air Theatre in Regent's Park in 1933, learning the part overnight and appearing in the matinée the following afternoon.[3]

The Chamberlain's Men's tour of 1597

That the Chamberlain's Men did tour in 1596 and 1597 is recorded. On 28 July 1597 all London theatres were closed following the scandal arising from a production of *The*

---

[1] *Authentic Memoirs of the Green-Room* (2 vols., London, 1806), II, 56–7. Munden was born in 1758. His first name is not given.

[2] *Wandering Patentee*, II, 169–70. Contemporary actors are not as resourceful. When David Williams took an afternoon off instead of turning up for a matinée of the aptly named *Leave Taking* at the National Theatre's Cottesloe in January 1995, it was reported in the press that an announcement had been made by the company that he was 'indisposed' and the performance was cancelled. Geoffrey Wheatcroft, listing 'stage catastrophes' in the *Daily Telegraph* following a disaster-struck performance of *Manon* at Covent Garden in July 1994, recounted the story of the Figaro who disappeared after the first act of *The Marriage of Figaro* at Sadlers Wells. The rest of the cast continued without a Figaro as best they could until they broke down in laughter and the curtain descended.

[3] David Holloway, *Playing the Empire* (London, 1979), pp. 60–2, 190–1. The author was, at the time the book was published, literary editor of the *Daily Telegraph*; he was the grandson and son of W. J. and John Holloway respectively.

Isle of Dogs. The Privy Council evidently intended to suppress stage plays and raze the public theatres to the ground. Options open to companies were to sell their costumes, to allow their plays to be printed, and to tour. We know that the Chamberlain's Men took the second and third options. The Stationers' Register shows that *Richard II* was entered for publication by Andrew Wise on 29 August 1597 and that he entered *Richard III* on 20 October; in August and September the company toured, visiting, as surviving records show, Faversham, Rye, Dover, Bristol, Bath, and Marlborough. The original records have been remarkably inaccurately reproduced in print by Murray, Chambers, Patrick, Dawson, and Hammond.[1] Giles Dawson is rightly hesitant about reconstituting tour itineraries although he makes an exception for Kent. He gives the route he believes to have been 'commonly followed' with an alternative extension round the coast of Thanet.[2] Personal examination of the town chamberlains' account books for Marlborough, Bath, and Bristol,[3] and an analysis of the practical problems, suggest to me that only very exceptionally did London companies make extensive tours and that the Chamberlain's Men may not have played many, if any, more towns than the six for which details have survived, and that any such towns were probably not in Kent; records for Maidstone, Canterbury, Folkestone, Lydd, and New Romney make no mention of their visiting any of these towns in 1597. Apart from 1597 (when they toured because the theatres had been closed down following the *Isle of Dogs* scandal) the only other year the Chamberlain's (or King's) Men are known to have visited as many as six provincial towns (excepting Court appearances) was the terrible plague year of 1603.[4]

What the facts as recorded in town chamberlains' accounts amount to is that the Lord Chamberlain's Men visited Rye not later than 27 August 1597; they visited Dover some time thereafter and not later than 20 September but, in the light of the early position of the record of payment (second of twenty-six), probably on or soon

---

[1] The visits to Faversham in 1596 and 1597 are conflated (so attributing the 1596 date to 1597 – which is undated – and making their reward 16s od instead of 13s 4d) in J. T. Murray, *English Dramatic Companies, 1558–1642* (2 vols., London, 1910), II, 274; Chambers, II, 321; and D. L. Patrick (who does not record the reward and gets the dating wrong), p. 32. Dawson does not include a visit to Dover in the Malone Society's *Collections VII* (Oxford, 1965), but the records of Dover Corporation show that the company received a payment (Folger Shakespeare Library Microfilm, Acc 276.3, f.345). Chambers gives the reward at Marlborough as 6s 8d instead of 6s 4d and records the accounting year at Bath as ending at Midsummer instead of Michaelmas (both of which affect interpretation of the tour). Hammond only lists the six places visited but locates Rye in Kent (Arden, p. 9).

[2] Dawson, pp. xxvii–xxviii.

[3] Records of Wiltshire are held at Trowbridge. The manuscript of the General Accounts for Marlborough, 1572–1757, is call number G22/1/205/2. Wilton records are G25/1/91. Records for Salisbury, Calne, Chippenham, and Malmesbury were checked but, except for Salisbury's Ledger C, 1571–1640, were defective for 1597. Bath records for 1562–1602, ed. F. B. Wardle, were published by Somerset Record Society, vol. xxxviii, 1923; there is also a typescript, prepared by Revd C. W. Shickle, for 1568–1656 (presented to the city in 1904). All relevant entries were checked against the original manuscript. Original manuscript records for Bristol for 1594, 1596, 1597, and 1598 were examined. Records for 1595 and 1602 are missing. For years other than these, Murray was used, II, 216–19. However, Murray is rather inaccurate and (understandably) often confuses 'v' (for five) and 'x' (for ten). A full understanding of provincial touring will not be possible until the *Records of Early English Drama* are published, and also such family records as have as yet not been examined.

[4] Chambers, II, 322–32.

after 3 September, or even a day or two earlier; and that they were in Bristol between 11 and 17 September. There is no information as to when they visited Faversham or Bath; they probably visited Marlborough (from the position of the record of payment) in September, just before, or at the same time, as Lord Chief Justice Popham took the Michaelmas Sessions.[1] There is no record of their receiving payments for playing anywhere else in 1597, although chamberlains' accounts survive for the Kentish towns listed above and for Salisbury, Winchester, and Southampton, all of which could have been on one route to the West that they might have taken. This may mean no more than that the 'local authority' made no payment; it does not mean the players were not allowed to perform.

It is assumed that they left London soon after the sudden closure of the theatres after the *Isle of Dogs* scandal on Thursday, 28 July 1597, having sold Andrew Wise the manuscript of *Richard II* which he entered on 29 August. One might guess that, when the Rose reopened on 11 October with *Jeronimo*,[2] they hastened back to London; certainly, on 20 October, Wise entered *Richard III* – the manuscript that was to be Q1. Both plays were printed in 1597. It may not be coincidental that Pembroke's Men, who, according to Henslowe, with the Admiral's, began playing at his house, the Rose, on 11 October, had preceded the Chamberlain's Men at Bristol by a week or two. They were paid £2, recorded in weeks 10 and 11 (28 August to 10 September), and played twice before the Mayor.[3] Pembroke's and the Chamberlain's both also visited Bath. What, in practical terms, needs to be considered is how the Chamberlain's Men travelled from London to Dover and Bristol and back; how long it would take; the number of performances they would need to give to sustain themselves; whether they might have given other performances *en route*, details of which have not survived; and whether any light might be thrown on the size of the touring company. In other words, what were the economics of the 1597 tour?

There were five modes of transport available to Elizabethans: foot, horseback, boat (by river or sea), cart, and, in the latter part of the sixteenth century, coach. The coach was then (as the *OED* defines it) 'usually a state carriage' and although it had begun to be used by the wealthy towards the end of Elizabeth's reign, it was hardly the kind of conveyance available to itinerant actors, and roads were often bad, especially between provincial towns.[4] Even by 1836, stage coaches only claimed to make the journey from

---

[1] Sir John Popham (1531?–1607) presided over the trials of Essex, Raleigh, and the Gunpowder Plot conspirators. The entry for his being entertained at Marlborough for the Sessions is immediately after that for the Lord Chamberlain's Company: £6 7s 9d was allowed for his 'diet'. Two entries later is a payment of 10s 7d for a gibbet. Popham had acquired Littlecote, about 10 miles to the east of Marlborough, some twenty years earlier, it was said (by Sir John Aubrey) because he allowed its owner, Sir John Dayrell, to escape a charge of murdering his bastard baby. The Chamberlain's Men had also visited Marlborough in 1594, so one must wonder whether Shakespeare came across Popham and whether the Lord Chief Justice in *1H4* and *2H4* is not a flattering portrait of this 'heavie, ugly man', as Aubrey described him.

[2] Henslowe, p. 60.

[3] Murray records twice as 'twist', explaining it as meaning twice; but the spelling, 'twise' is perfectly clear.

[4] Kemp had to make a 6½-mile detour because the road between Long Melford and Bury St Edmunds was so bad; see Arthur Freeman, *Elizabeth's Misfits* (New York, 1978), p. 180, and *Kemps Nine Daies Wonder* (1600), B4ᵛ; see also p. 39, n. 1.

London to Canterbury, 55 miles, in from seven to nine hours – 6 to 8 mph.[1] It is likely that a touring company would require at least one cart in order to carry even a minimum of costumes and props and that would travel at not much above walking pace. In his deposition at the Banbury trial of Richard Bradshaw's company in 1633, Drewe Turner claimed he had done no more on tour than 'drive the horse and beat the drum'.[2] Of course, in such circumstances he may have underplayed his part on tour, but it is certain there was a horse to be *driven* and that suggests drawing a wagon. *Tarltons Iests* records that when the Queen's Players 'were accepted into a Gentlemans house: the Waggon unloading of apparrell, the Waggoner comes to *Tarlton*, & both desire him to speake to the Steward for his horses'.[3] Some of the company might have been able to afford to ride on horseback but, on grounds of cost, that looks impracticable for every member of the company. The Marlborough chamberlain's accounts for 1606 show the expenditure of 18d on two horses to Littlecote, 10 miles away; the Bath records for 1619 enter the hire of a horse for two days at 2s od. Inflation might have affected these charges, but it would be reasonable to estimate the hire of a horse for a week at not less than 6s od. Henslowe's *Diary* shows that on 17 July 1597 he agreed to pay Thomas Hearne 5s od a week for his first year and 6s 8d for the second of a two-year contract. On 8 December 1597, William Kendall was hired for two years at 10s od a week in London but at 5s od a week in the country 'euerie week of his playing', suggesting money was paid only for the weeks he acted.[4] Whether the Chamberlain's Men paid the same amounts, and whether they paid a half-rate in the country is not known. The half-rate on tour may not have been true half-pay but because, when touring, the actors were provided with food and lodging. The Royal Proclamation of 23 July 1589 decreed that wages for joiners (without food) were 7s od a week but only 4s 6d a week with food; similar, usually lower, differential rates were paid for other craftsmen, for example plumbers 6s od and 3s 4d; watermen 3s od and 1s od.[5] Roughly, therefore, hiring a horse cost about as much as hiring an actor, but whereas an actor paid for his sustenance, a horse had also to be fed. That entertainment for men and horses was provided on tour on occasion is clear from the Bath records for 1602 which show that the Queen's Men were paid 3s 2d 'for their horse meate', that is, food for their horse or horses, and 8s od for 'kytchinge' bread, beer, and wine for the players.[6] To equip all the actors and the supporting entourage with horses would at least double the wage bill. Possibly more than one cart was hired so that the the actors did not need to walk, but the pace would be very slow. Even if the better-off actors

---

[1] Alan Bates, *Directory of Stage Coach Services, 1836* (Newton Abbot, 1969), p. 15.

[2] Murray, II, 163–7; Bradley spells Turner's first name 'Drew' (p. 62), but he is quoting Murray.

[3] *Tarltons Iests* (London, 1613), D1ʳ. The jests are possibly apocryphal but their settings (like those for realistic films, however far-fetched their storylines) may give a true picture of theatrical conditions. As 'Tarlton' hereafter.

[4] Henslowe, pp. 238 and 268.

[5] *Tudor Royal Proclamations* (3 vols., New Haven, Conn.), ed. Paul L. Hughes and James F. Larkin, III, 39–41; quoted by Ann Jennalie Cook, *The Privileged Playgoers of Shakespeare's London, 1576–1642* (Princeton, N. J., 1981), Appendix A, pp. 277–9; as 'Cook' hereafter.

[6] I am indebted to Professor John Barnard for pointing out to me what horse meat meant in the sixteenth century.

could afford to ride, progress must have been at walking- or wagon-pace and that, on the roads as they then were, could scarcely mean covering more than 25 miles in a day at most in a ten- or twelve-hour day – about the distance from Tamworth to Leicester (see 5.2.12–13); Tamworth to Bosworth Field is only half as far.

If the Chamberlain's Men left London, say, two days after the theatres were closed down and returned – and here the conjecture is even less sure – three days after Henslowe opened up the Rose, they would be away eleven weeks – seventy-seven days. In that time they would have to journey something like 450 miles. Eighteen days travelling at 25 miles a day would allow a maximum of fifty-nine days for performances – rather less because the towns visited were not spaced in multiples of 25 miles apart and, although actors did sometimes play on a Sunday, that was illegal;[1] twenty-three days walking (an average of about 20 miles a day) would allow fifty-four days for performance, less Sundays. There were eleven Sundays in this period, on some of which the company might have travelled, but, assuming they did not play on Sundays or after anything but a very short journey, they might manage between forty and fifty performances at most. Obviously these figures are guesses; they are designed solely to illustrate the nature of the problem faced by the Chamberlain's Men in getting from place to place in 1597. The company could have saved time and effort by sailing from Dover to Southampton,[2] and they could have travelled between Bristol and Bath by river. The tour has been seen as a single journey, but it is possible the company first visited the south east, returned to London, and then journeyed west.

Earnings and attendances at a London theatre in 1597

Examination of the figures in *Henslowe's Diary* is illuminating.[3] From 24 January to 14 March 1597 inclusive Henslowe records half the gallery receipts and all the door receipts for twenty-five plays in these seven weeks. The half-gallery receipts average out at £4 14s a week. These can usefully be compared with receipts for a later period. For the thirteen weeks 29 July–21 October 1598, Henslowe recorded whole-gallery receipts. These amounted to £117 10s of which half, £4 10s 4½d per week, would go to the players, a sum not too dissimilar from the early 1597 figure. Henslowe's and the players' total receipts (door and gallery) for those seven weeks of 1597 were £155 0s 11d – £6 4s per play; £22 3s per week. Of this, the company would receive (after Henslowe had deducted his half-gallery receipts) £122 2s 11d, about £17 9s per week (£4 17s 8d per play). The acting company, the Admiral's Men, was what Bradley

---

[1] Henslowe, p. xxvii. William Prynne repeats a story of a floor collapsing as retribution for a performance on a Sabbath at Riseley, Bedfordshire, in 1607, killing and hurting spectators (*Histrio-Mastix*, f. 557ʳ, quoting Thomas Beard, *Theater of Gods Iudgements*, 1631 edn, according to Prynne at p. 697). It was not unambiguously argued that performance on Sunday was worse than on weekdays. Sir Geoffrey Fenton, in *A Form of Christian Policy*, 1574, was ambivalent: 'Players . . . ought not to be suffred to prophane that Sabboth day . . . and much lesse to lose time on the dayes of trauayle' (s3ʳ). Editions used are facsimiles in the series, *Theatrum Redivivum*, ed. P. Davison (New York, 1972).
[2] Tarlton and his wife sailed from Southampton 'towards London', Tarlton, D3ʳ. During the journey 'a mightie storme arose'.
[3] Henslowe, pp. xxxiv–xxxv, 56–7, and 94–5.

categorises as a sixteen-cast company.[1] This sixteen represents the number of male, adult actors; it excludes boys (and Bradley posits six for *An Humorous Day's Mirth* under 1597), and back-stage and front-of-house staff – the bookkeeper, wardrobe-master, musicians, stagehands, gatherers, etc. E. K. Chambers, noting that the King's Men had twenty-one hirelings in 1624, of whom at least six were actors (over and above the sharers), concluded, 'we have no reason to suppose that they were very differently staffed in Shakespeare's time'. However, Chambers suggests that when the Blackfriars Theatre had been taken over in 1608 or 1609, there had been 'some elaboration of the provision of music' so that the number of hirelings in 1597 might have been somewhat fewer.[2] On this basis, Bradley's sixteen-cast company would comprise sixteen adult actors plus as many hired men, and also a number of boys: say thirty-two adults and half-a-dozen boys. The Proclamation of 23 July 1589 setting wages for 'the best and most skilful workmen, and hired servants' of many companies in London, and their workmen, journeymen, and hired servants, does not include actors but the wages already mentioned above indicate that to pay a sixteen-actor London company, with its stagehands and bookkeeper, it would need to earn at least £1 a week *per actor* to support itself. Companies permanently sited in the provinces would need much less because wages in the country were considerably lower than in London. By 1655, after over sixty years of inflation and a Civil War, countrymen received (by regulation) roughly what Londoners had been allowed in 1589.[3]

The Chamberlain's Men on tour would receive all they took, plus the amounts received from places they visited: Faversham 13s 4d; Rye, 20s 0d; Dover 13s 4d; Marlborough 6s 4d; Bath 20s 0d; and Bristol (where they performed at the Guildhall) 30s 0d (a total of £5 3s). The company would keep all its receipts, having no 'Henslowe' to pay because it was an independent sharing company, but it had expenses the actors in Henslowe's company in London did not have – the maintenance or hire of a theatre, fees to the Master of the Revels, the cost of touring, etc. This £1 per actor per week (stressing that it does *not* mean each actor received £1 but had to recompense sharers and, roughly, an equivalent number of hirelings), and about £5 in receipts per play given, are useful figures to keep in mind in what follows, rough approximations though they must be.

Another useful figure can be extrapolated from the door receipts. At one penny entrance, the number of people paying at the door at the beginning of 1597 varied from

---

[1] Bradley, pp. 17–20, 71, and 229; and, for the Admiral's Company in 1597, p. 234.

[2] Chambers, II, 80–1. A glance at the 'supporting staff' for the Royal Shakespeare Company will show that the numbers of such 'hirelings' has increased enormously since Shakespeare's day. *King Lear* at the Barbican in 1994 listed 23 actors. Their immediate support numbered 28 of whom 12 were musicians; but stagehands and the like were not listed. In addition, a further 42 staff – directors, heads of departments, and London and Barbican management; 4 resident directors and producers; and 7 administrative staff, 53 in all, were named; these did not include typists and the like.

[3] Wages in Wiltshire were much lower. In 1655, the Justices of the Peace set wages for master carpenters and plumbers at no more than 1s 0d to 1s 3d a day (depending on the time of the year), without meat or drink. With meat and drink they were to be paid no more than 6d and 8d a day – which suggests an expenditure of sixpence a day on meat and drink per man. Journeymen were to be paid no more than 10d and 1s 0d a day on the same terms, and apprentices 7d (whatever the time of year). (B. Howard Cunnington, *Records of the County of Wilts* (Devizes, 1932), pp. 292–3.)

40 to 2,316; the capacity of the theatre was about 3,000;[1] the average attendance was 870. (Admission to the higher-priced seats was dependent upon first paying this penny entrance.) It looks as if, based on these figures, the Admiral's Men, a sixteen-cast company, needed to perform twenty-five plays in a seven-week period and attract an average audience of 870 to keep afloat. The Chamberlain's Men might have received more or less in London, of course, but these figures provide a handy yardstick by which an assessment might be made of what was required to keep a company solvent in London. What about touring?

Implications for the 1597 tour

After Henslowe had taken half the gallery receipts, twenty-five performances by a sixteen-cast company over seven weeks before audiences averaging 870 realised £122 2s 11d (£17 9s per week). Translated into a period of eleven weeks (the time the Chamberlain's Men probably toured), that would require thirty-nine performances with audiences of that size to raise a pro rata amount of £192. What number of performances would be required to raise £192 to sustain a sixteen-cast company over eleven weeks with audiences of different sizes?

Average London audience of 870:   39 performances
75 per cent of average audience (652): 59 performances
50 per cent of average audience (435): 78 performances

The implications will be obvious. An eleven-week tour would include eleven Sundays so there would be a maximum of sixty-six performance days. Henslowe never mentions two performances in a day (but see below) and, on that basis, it would be impossible to fit in seventy-eight performances, and there would be only the eleven Sundays available for travelling (an average of forty-three miles a day, but as some places were close and some far apart, averages underestimate the problems of travel). Thus, an average audience of 50 per cent would be impracticable. On the basis of 75 per cent London attendances, fifty-nine performances would allow eighteen days (including Sundays) for travelling. This assumes that the actors did not perform on the days they travelled and also that they were always allowed to perform, something the records frequently show could not be taken for granted. There can be no doubt that fifty-nine performances and 450 miles of travelling would be an extremely taxing, virtually impossible schedule. The actors would, of course, be giving over twice as many performances in eleven weeks as they had given in those seven weeks in London: fifty-nine to twenty-five.

    Now, if the receipts to be achieved were based on a ten-cast company, the size I have proposed for *Richard III*, ten men and two boys (with an equivalent number of supporting gatherers, stagehands and the bookkeeper), the tour becomes just about

---

[1] Gurr claims the Rose had a capacity of 2,000 in 1587 and 2,400 after the enlargement in 1592. The Theatre, like the Globe for which it provided the frame, had a capacity of 3,000. The private playhouses accommodated 500 to 700, or, at the extreme, 900; see p. 2, n. 5.

financially practicable. If, instead of the men employed as gatherers in London, a couple of actors were taken along – Bradley refers to the well-established actor, Richard Errington, acting as a gatherer on tour in 1627[1] – one or two actors would become available as reserves, but calculations could still be based on plays being performable by a ten-cast company. If a sixteen-cast company needed £17 19s a week, a ten-cast company would, pro rata, need £10 18s a week – £120 instead of £192 for eleven weeks. (Because the company received £5 3s from the six towns visited, they would need slightly less: £114 17s) Whereas 50 per cent of London attendances (435) required seventy-eight performances for a sixteen-cast company, only forty-nine would be needed to support a ten-cast company. That would allow twenty-eight days for travel, an average of 17 miles a day. It would need 75 per cent average attendances – 652 people – to reduce the number of performances to thirty-seven to maintain a ten-cast company: and that would be more or less the intensity of performance Henslowe records for London earlier in 1597 for a sixteen-cast company.

According to the surviving records, the Chamberlain's Men only visited three or more places in the provinces in 1597 (six), 1603 (six, plus the Court performance at Wilton), 1605 (three), 1606 (five), 1607 (three), 1610 (five), and 1613 (four). In the four years 1598, 1599, 1600, and 1604 they seem only to have visited Oxford in 1599–1600. The tour of 1597 was therefore special and six places we know they visited were as many as they visited in any single year. I suggest it almost certainly represents the total number of places visited. For Shakespeare's company we should think not of many-visit tours but of tours targeted on a few places, even at times of theatrical disaster occasioned by plague and theatre-closure. The circumstances of more-or-less permanently touring provincial companies is quite a different matter (just as it would be today).

If the company only visited six places, but stayed a short while at each one, they might, perhaps, have performed on upwards of thirty days – many fewer than the three to four dozen performing days crammed into a many-visit tour, necessary to sustain even a ten-cast company. How might such a targeted tour have been financed? The clue might be provided by examining the curious popularity of Marlborough as a touring venue. Its popularity had nothing to do with the reward the town gave – a mere 6s 4d in 1597 – and little to do with its being on the main London to Bristol road. If Marlborough was simply a stop *en route*, it should not have received more touring companies than either Bath or Bristol; between 1594 and 1622, thirty-seven companies visited Marlborough (none after 1622); twenty-nine visited Bath (and none after 1611), and thirty-one visited Bristol (but at least two account books are missing). Even more curious is that, in a fifty-year period, only two companies visited all three towns: the Chamberlain's Men in 1597 (so, again, this was an unusual tour) and the Queen's Players in 1598. In addition to these visits, another company, the Earl of Hertford's, visited Marlborough and Bath in 1592; and two visits to Marlborough and Bristol were made by Lady Elizabeth's Men in 1613 and 1621. (Only seven companies visited both Bath and Bristol even though they are a mere 13 miles apart and could easily be

[1] Bradley, p. 69.

reached by river.) The Chamberlain's/King's Men visited Marlborough seven times between 1590 and 1622: 1594, 1597, 1606, 1608 (a plague year in Marlborough as well as in London), 1613 (though they might not have performed in the town itself: they were given no 'reward' but wine costing 6s 8d), and twice in 1618 in June and November. Marlborough's popularity with touring companies, despite the small rewards the town could afford, and its tiny population, is strikingly apparent. In a couple of decades after the 1597 tour, James Waylen gives the 'entire number of burgesses' as 'about one hundred'; he names forty-two of those living in Marlborough and fifteen more with freehold property but living outside the town. These facts, with comparative figures for town expenditure for Bath, Bristol, and Marlborough in 1597 suggest that Marlborough's population must have been somewhere between 500 and 1,000, and perhaps at the lower end of that range.[1] Why, then, did so many companies visit Marlborough? What economic explanation can there be for its popularity with touring companies?

Performances in private houses

A clue to the answer may be the year when visits to Marlborough stopped completely. In 1622 three companies visited Marlborough, the Late Queen's, the Prince's, and Lady Elizabeth's. Thereafter, and until the Civil War, nothing. Why? Marlborough formerly had a castle, one of the estates of Edward Seymour, Earl of Hertford (who was a patron of a company of actors). It was this Hertford who had been responsible for the Elvetham Entertainment for Queen Elizabeth in 1591. Hertford was an important figure in Wiltshire. The chamberlain's accounts for 1597 record that in 1597 sums of 16s 0d and £1 16s 5d were paid for sugar loaves for 'my lord of Hertford' (the larger sum being also for a gift of sugar for others), so Hertford was evidently in residence in that year. He died in 1621. Also in 1621, the Countess of Pembroke, who lived at Wilton 30 miles away, died. The estate at Marlborough passed to Hertford's grandson, William, and he conveyed it to his brother, Sir Francis Seymour. Sir Francis devoted himself to erecting a house, 'a great rambling building',[2] and it looks as if that spelt the end of the Hertford interest in visiting companies of actors. The town was to side with the Commonwealth twenty years later, being twice burnt and sacked by the King's

---

[1] The population of London in 1603 is calculated as being 200,000 and Bristol, 12,000. Bath does not appear in the forty-two largest towns after London in 1662 in Chris Cook and John Wroughton, *English Historical Facts 1603–1688* (Totowa, N. J., 1980), pp. 226–8; for the 1603 figures they draw on Peter Clark and Paul Slack, *English Towns in Transition 1500–1700* (Oxford, 1976). In 1597, according to the chamberlain's accounts, Bristol made 1,145 payments amounting to £514 0s 7d; Bath 250 amounting to £153 12s; and Marlborough 37 payments totalling £59 3s 11d. Of Marlborough's expenditure, the three most significant sums, almost 40 per cent of the total, were £13 6s 8d for the schoolteacher, £6 7s 9d and 3s 4d devoted to entertaining the Lord Chief Justice, and £3 4s 7d on 'setting forth of soldiers', leaving £36 1s 7d to run the town for the year. This indicates a very small population. Those named by James Waylen contributed to a gift for Lady Elizabeth on her marriage to Frederick of Bohemia in 1613 (*A History Military and Municipal of . . . Marlborough* (London, 1854), p. 131; as 'Waylen' hereafter). Lady Elizabeth's Players visited Marlborough in that year and on five later occasions to 1622.

[2] Janet H. Stevenson, *Marlborough and Preshute* (reprinted from *The Victoria History of Wiltshire*, vol. XII, Trowbridge, 1990), p. 169. The site is now occupied by Marlborough College.

supporters.¹ It might well have been antipathetic to touring companies, putting up with them only whilst Hertford was alive.

We know that the Pembrokes of Wilton patronised the arts, and, like the Earl of Hertford, had a company of actors, and that the Lord Chamberlain's Men (now renamed The King's Servants) played at Wilton (even smaller in size than Marlborough) in 1603 (for a 'Court' performance). The Wilton records also show that an extraordinarily large sum of £6 5s was given to the King's Men on that occasion by the Master and Burgesses.² Is it too much to suggest that this combination of Pembrokes, Hertfords, and Marlborough are one reason for the popularity of Marlborough as a touring venue? Companies of players visiting Marlborough could well have visited Wilton, 30 miles away, in much the manner that David George shows that Derby's and Dudley's players visited Gawthorpe Hall in Lancashire, also about 30 miles from the seats of their patrons; or, as the Pembrokes had estates at Marlborough, did they travel there to see private performances?³ However speculative this must be, surely it was the patronage of the Hertfords that made it financially practicable for so many companies to visit Marlborough? Prynne complained of stage-players being invited to private houses.⁴ Bradshaw's little run-about company played for Sir Thomas Lucy at Stratford-upon-Avon and for Sir William Spencer at Wormleighton (near Banbury) in 1633.⁵ Robert Armin (who played Lear's Fool for Shakespeare's company) describes a comic incident that took place when a company of players performed at 'a Gentlemans house where Jacke Miller resorted' (probably in Evesham or Pershore, Worcestershire), the actors dressing in the kitchen and making their entries thence into the Hall where the performance took place.⁶ There were also private theatricals, as a manuscript combining the two parts of *Henry IV*, prepared in the winter of 1622–3⁷ for Sir Edward Dering at Surrenden Hall, Kent, bears witness. Much earlier, on 1 January 1596, *Titus Andronicus* was given, presumably by the Lord Chamberlain's Men, for Sir John Harington, the Queen's godson, at Burley-on-the-Hill, Rutland.⁸ It is not, therefore, only towns that were visited, but also private

¹ Waylen, pp. 157–65.
² Leeds Barroll gives details of the visit to Wilton, *Politics, Plague, and Shakespeare's Theater: The Stuart Years* (Ithaca, 1991), pp. 106–14. He does not mention the reward from the town (to be found in chamberlains' records for Wilton, County Record Office, Trowbridge).
³ David George, 'Jacobean actors and the Great Hall at Gawthorpe, Lancashire', *Theatre Notebook*, 37 (1983), 109–21, especially pp. 113–14. The Earls of Pembroke owned Manton estate and mill, which abut onto what was then Hertford's estate (and now part of Marlborough) from 1553–1632. The Earl had been influential in the Borough during Hertford's minority, and he was probably patron of one of Marlborough's MPs in 1558 and 1559, William Daniell (who died in 1604). (Stevenson, pp. 178 and 219.)
⁴ Prynne, p. 47.
⁵ Murray, II, 110.
⁶ *A Shakespeare Jestbook: Robert Armin's 'Foole upon Foole' (1600): A Critical, Old-Spelling Edition*, ed. H. F. Lippincott (Salzburg, 1973), pp. 15–16 and 108.
⁷ The manuscript 'can be confidently dated no later than February, 1623 and probably not much earlier than the beginning of the year', Laetitia Yeandle, 'The dating of Sir Edward Dering's copy of "The History of King Henry the Fourth"', *Shakespeare Quarterly*, 37 (1986), 226.
⁸ *Titus Andronicus*, ed. Jonathan Bate (London, 1995), p. 43. Bate also refers to the play's inclusion in *Englische Comedien und Tragedien* (Leipzig (?), 1620). This is heavily cut and with 'a reduction of the cast to twelve parts (with some doubling possible) and a couple of all-purpose silent extras (who serve as soldiers, carriers on of the table for the bloody banquet, and so on)', p. 44. He quotes W. Braeckman that

estates, and the latter provide clues as to why certain places were visited and how touring was financed. The year 1596 was not, incidentally, one in which Donald Foster believes *Titus Andronicus* was performed: he gives 1591, 1593, and 1594.

The amounts paid by private houses for which records survive were not large. Possibly the Hertfords and Pembrokes were more munificent. The Clifford manuscripts show sums of £1–2 per play, but the members of the companies would be fed and housed and the records show that they sometimes received additional gifts of money. The earnings per visit were often more worthwhile than these sums suggest because they might stay for several days and play twice a day, once after dinner and again after supper.[1] The amounts paid by the Shuttleworths in Lancashire to the ten seemingly local companies who came to Smithills between 1586 and 1596 were very small, averaging 3s 0d a visit. Between 1609 and 1618, better-known companies – Derby's, Dudley's, Monteagle's, Stafford's, and the Queen's Players – visited the Shuttleworths' new house, Gawthorpe Manor. The smallest payment was a single shilling to three (unattached?) players; the largest, £2 10s to Monteagle's on 11 August 1612 (though in the preceding month they had received only 6s 8d). The average payment, depressed a little by that shilling, was 15s 0d. David George, on the basis of these figures, has calculated that companies of '10 actors were the norm for these itinerant companies'.[2]

'The "reporter" responsible for the text was one Frederick Menius' ('The relationship of Shakespeare's *Titus Andronicus* to the German play of 1620 and to Jan Vos's *Aran en Titus*'. *Studia Germanica Gandensia*, 9 (1967), 22–5.

[1] See Lawrence Stone, 'Companies of players entertained by the Earl of Cumberland and Lord Clifford, 1607–39', Malone Society, *Collections V*, 1959 (Oxford, 1960), pp. 17–28. The King's Players stayed at Londesborough from a Tuesday to a Friday in February 1620 and gave five plays. The company numbered fourteen, presumably including boys and, perhaps, the bookkeeper, and possibly even a stagehand. They were paid £5.

[2] The visits of players (and waits and minstrels) are summarised in *The House and Farm Accounts of the Shuttleworths of Gawthorpe Hall in the County of Lancaster at Smithills and Gawthorpe, September 1582–1621*, ed. John Harland (4 vols., Chetham Society, 1856–8), vol. IV (as vol. XLVI), 893–4. See also David George (p. 47, n. 3), who illustrates the Hall and its screen and gives useful measurements (see also the Lancashire volume in the REED series, Toronto, 1993). No payments are given by G. W. Boddy in his excellent account of strolling players in Yorkshire in the early seventeenth century, but as they often visited the homes of yeomen, their payments may not have been much above their keep. His account of Hudson and Lester's little company (these two men and five children and youths of seven to sixteen years) shows that they played in thirty houses in the fifty-two days from 29 December 1615 to 18 February 1616 (and the tour was certainly longer). They walked some 150 miles over the North Yorkshire moors in winter but do not seem to have journeyed more than 10 miles in any one day. This puts into perspective Shakespeare's colleagues' travels in 1597 and shows that to travel 475 miles in seventy-seven days they must have been hard pressed. See G. W. Boddy, 'Players of interludes in North Yorkshire in the early seventeenth century', *North Yorkshire County Record Office Journal*, 3 (1976), 95–130, especially pp. 111–13. I am deeply grateful to Martin Butler of Leeds University for drawing my attention to this article and providing me with a copy, and also for his helpful comments. There seem to be no surviving documents in the possession of the Earl of Hertford's descendants and I am grateful to the Dukes of Northumberland and Somerset, and the Marquess of Hertford, for answering my inquiries so promptly. A search through the as yet uncatalogued accounts of the Duke of Somerset at Exeter and Trowbridge Record Office might yet reveal something pertinent to 1597.

Conclusion

The case for Q1 being based on a memorial reconstruction of a lost prompt-book designed for use in London with a full company and on tour with a reduced-size company – what Bradley would categorise as a ten-cast company – has been based on an analysis of variants in the context of touring practice over the past four hundred years. Inevitably the strength of the argument (to reiterate Kane) 'must vary with the character of the evidence available; it cannot be uniform any more than it can be exactly determinable. In the last analysis all decisions about originality are provisional only.'[1] This cannot be too strongly stressed, yet I believe that despite this, and despite flying in the face of current opinions about sizes of touring companies and the rôles boy-actors played, the grounds for asserting that this is how Q1 came to be as it is are surer than the alternatives others have put forward. One final crux, which has been mentioned in passing, might suitably conclude this study. It cannot prove the case made here but it might illustrate to advantage the nature of the problem, the conflicting answers recently adduced, and the solution proposed here.

In Q1, the ghosts of the two young princes enter before that of Hastings (5.3.142 SD and 5.3.150 SD respectively). The order in Q1 is repeated in Q2 but Q3, which at this point provides copy for F, prints Hastings before the young princes, the order in which their deaths occurred. There is no authority for Q3's change. Hammond regards this as 'a positively inspired correction' by the Q3 compositor: 'no doubt the error in Q1 arose through some confusion in the reporting process'.[2] The *Textual Companion* to the Oxford Shakespeare states:

We can see no way of attributing Q1's arrangement to casting difficulties, nor does it seem to have any obvious dramatic advantages; however, the slight deviation from chronological order is in itself well within the range of Shakespeare's practice, which characteristically disregards such pedantic niceties. The Q1 order *could* result from simple memorial error; but such an error, involving the entrances of three actors who were apparently involved in the reconstruction, is most unlikely. It thus seems to us (*a*) that there is nothing intrinsically unShakespearian about the Q1 order (*b*) that Q1's order cannot be convincingly explained as the result of mechanical constraints or collective memorial error, and (*c*) that Q3's arrangement, however tidy, is without discernible authority. There are at least four explanations of how the variant could have arisen in Q3: (1) a miscorrected eyeskip, (2) deliberate but unauthorized editorial sophistication, (3) the use, as copy for Q3, of a copy of Q2 used as the prompt-book for a production of the play, (4) access to an authoritative manuscript which was completely ignored throughout the rest of the text. Any of the first three options seems considerably more plausible than the fourth.[3]

The Oxford *Original-Spelling Edition* retains Q1's order; Arden maintains that Q3/F's order must be adopted.

Were Q1 arranged for a tightly doubled cast (as I have suggested), the order of the ghosts could well present casting difficulties; Shakespeare's concern might be expected to be artistic niceties rather than the rhetorically suspect 'pedantic niceties';

---

[1] Kane, p. 149; and quoted at p. 6, n. 1 above.
[2] Arden, note to 5.3.147–51.
[3] *A Textual Companion*, note to 5.5.99.2–107 / 3190.2–3198, p. 248.

certainly a memorial reconstruction involving three people should not have got the order wrong and so, for the purposes of touring, there was no error. Ironically, both orders can be correct, depending upon which text is being edited. For a full-cast edition, Arden is correct; a touring version, planned for a cast of ten men and two boys, would require Q1's order. This explanation does not *prove* my thesis is correct, but it might suggest a very simple answer to what is patently a crux that elicits from contemporary scholars diametrically opposed answers.

The re-ordering of the ghosts in 5.3, and, among many variants, the omission of Lovell from 3.4, 3.5, and 4.2, the neat excision of the niece from 4.1 (see 1–2n), the Priest becoming a mute in 3.2 (see 106–8n), and Vaughan's remarkable silence at his execution (see 3.3.6n), are but the more obvious elements in a mass of information pointing to a very tight recasting of *Richard III* for a small number of players.

The Tragedy of King Richard III

CHARACTERS IN ORDER OF APPEARANCE

(Numbers in parentheses are those of the actors listed in figure 3, 'Conjectural disposition of rôles')

Richard, Duke of GLOUCESTER; later KING RICHARD III (1)
The Duke of CLARENCE, his brother (10)
Sir Robert BRAKENBURY (4)
Lord William HASTINGS (3)
Lady ANNE; later Duchess of Gloucester (Boy 2)
TRESSEL (Mute) (Boy 1)
BERKELEY (Mute) (7)
Two HALBERDIERS (1 mute) (5 and 6)
Four ATTENDANTS (3 mute) (2, 4, 8, and 10)
Queen ELIZABETH, wife of King Edward IV (8)
Lord RIVERS, her brother (4)
Lord GREY, her son (Boy 2 or perhaps actor 2)
Marquess of DORSET, her son (Boy 1)
Duke of BUCKINGHAM (9)
Stanley, Earl of DERBY (10)
Queen MARGARET, widow of King Henry VI (7)
Sir William CATESBY (6)
Two EXECUTIONERS (5 and 6)
King EDWARD IV (7)
DUCHESS OF YORK, mother of King Edward IV, Gloucester, and Clarence (2)
BOY (son to Clarence) (Boy 1)
GIRL (Daughter to Clarence) (Boy 2)
Sir Richard RATCLIFFE (5)
Three CITIZENS (2, 5, and 7)
CARDINAL Bourchier, Archbishop of Canterbury (4)
Young Duke of YORK, younger son of King Edward IV (Boy 2)

Edward, PRINCE of Wales, elder son of King Edward IV (Boy 1)
Lord MAYOR of London (7)
MESSENGER to Hastings (2)
Hastings, a PUSUIVANT (8)
A PRIEST (Mute) (7)
Sir Thomas VAUGHAN (Mute) (Boy 1)
A HALBERDIER (Mute) (2)
Bishop of ELY (8)
A SCRIVENER (8)
Two BISHOPS (Mutes) (3 and 4)
A CITIZEN (off) (Boy 2)
LIEUTENANT of the Tower (4)
A PAGE (Boy 1)
Sir James TYRREL (5)
Four MESSENGERS to Richard (3, 4, Boys 2 and 1)
Sir Christopher URSWICK, a Priest (4)
Earl of RICHMOND, later King Henry VII (3)
Three LORDS attendant on Richmond (4, 8, and 10)
Sir James BLUNT (4)
Duke of NORFOLK (2)
GHOSTS of PRINCE EDWARD, son of Henry VI (8); HENRY VI (7); CLARENCE (10); RIVERS (4), GREY (5), and VAUGHAN (6); Young Duke of YORK and Edward, PRINCE of Wales (Boys 1 and 2); HASTINGS (2); LADY ANNE (Boy 2); BUCKINGHAM (9)
Another MESSENGER to Richard (9)
GUARDS, ATTENDANTS, LORDS, SOLDIERS (all Mutes)

THE TRAGEDY OF KING RICHARD III

[1.1] *Enter* RICHARD, DUKE OF GLOUCESTER, *alone*

[GLOUCESTER] Now is the winter of our discontent
    Made glorious summer by this son of York;
    And all the clouds that loured upon our House
    In the deep bosom of the ocean buried.
    Now are our brows bound with victorious wreaths,   5
    Our bruised arms hung up for monuments,
    Our stern alarms changed to merry meetings,
    Our dreadful marches to delightful measures.
    Grim-visaged war hath smoothed his wrinkled front,
    And now instead of mounting barbed steeds   10
    To fright the souls of fearful adversaries,
    He capers nimbly in a lady's chamber
    To the lascivious pleasing of a love.
    But I that am not shaped for sportive tricks,
    Nor made to court an amorous looking-glass,   15
    I that am rudely stamped and want love's majesty
    To strut before a wanton ambling nymph;
    I that am curtailed of this fair proportion,
    Cheated of feature by dissembling Nature,
    Deformed, unfinished, sent before my time   20
    Into this breathing world scarce half made up,
    And that so lamely and unfashionable
    That dogs bark at me as I halt by them:
    Why I in this weak piping time of peace
    Have no delight to pass away the time,   25
    Unless to spy my shadow in the sun
    And descant on mine own deformity.
    And therefore since I cannot prove a lover
    To entertain these fair well-spoken days,
    I am determined to prove a villain,   30
    And hate the idle pleasures of these days.
    Plots have I laid, inductions dangerous,
    By drunken prophecies, libels and dreams,

[1.1]] *There are no act and scene divisions in* Q; *the play is divided into Acts and Scenes throughout in* F   0   SD *Enter* RICHARD, DUKE OF GLOUCESTER, *alone] Enter Richard Duke of Glocester solus.* Q (*Glocester*), F (*Gloster*)   13   love] Q; Lute F   *19   Nature] F; nature Q   26   spy] Q; see F   *32   inductions] Q3, F; inductious Q1 -2

To set my brother Clarence and the King
In deadly hate the one against the other.   35
And if King Edward be as true and just
As I am subtle, false, and treacherous,
This day should Clarence closely be mewed up
About a prophecy which says that 'G'
Of Edward's heirs the murderers shall be.   40
Dive thoughts, down to my soul, here Clarence comes:

     Enter CLARENCE [*and* BRAKENBURY] *with a guard of men*

Brother, good days! What means this armed guard
That waits upon your grace?
CLARENCE   His Majesty,
Tendering my person's safety, hath appointed
This conduct to convey me to the Tower.   45
GLOUCESTER Upon what cause?
CLARENCE   Because my name is George.
GLOUCESTER Alack, my lord, that fault is none of yours.
He should for that commit your godfathers.
O, belike his Majesty hath some intent
That you shall be new christened in the Tower.   50
But what's the matter, Clarence, may I know?
CLARENCE Yea, Richard, when I know; for I protest
As yet I do not, but as I can learn,
He hearkens after prophecies and dreams,
And from the cross-row plucks the letter 'G'   55
And says a wizard told him that by 'G'
His issue disinherited should be.
And for my name of George begins with 'G',
It follows in his thought that I am he.
These, as I learn, and such like toys as these,   60
Have moved his Highness to commit me now.
GLOUCESTER Why, this it is when men are ruled by women:
'Tis not the King that sends you to the Tower:
My Lady Grey, his wife, Clarence – 'tis she
That tempers him to this extremity.   65
Was it not she and that good man of worship,
Anthony Woodville, her brother there,
That made him send Lord Hastings to the Tower,

*39 'G'] *Arden (and elsewhere)*; G. Q, F   40 murderers] Q1–2 (murtherers); murtherer Q3–6, F   41 SD] Q (*offset to right against 41's two lines*); *Enter Clarence, and Brakenbury, guarded.* F   42 days] Q; day F   *43–5 That waits . . . the Tower] *lineation as Pope*; That waits . . . grace? / His Maiesty . . . ap- / po"nted / . . . the tower Q; That waits . . . Grace? / His Maiesty . . . safety, / Hath appointed . . . th'Tower F   50 shall be] Q; should be F   52 for] Q; but F   61 Have] Q; Hath F   *64 Grey] F (*in italic*); Gray Q   65 tempers] Q1; tempts Q2, 4–6, F; temps Q3 extremity] Q; harsh Extremity F

From whence this present day he is delivered?
We are not safe, Clarence, we are not safe!   70
CLARENCE By heaven, I think there is no man is secured
    But the Queen's kindred and night-walking heralds
    That trudge betwixt the King and Mistress Shore.
    Heard ye not what an humble suppliant
    Lord Hastings was to her for his delivery?   75
GLOUCESTER Humbly complaining to her deity
    Got my Lord Chamberlain his liberty.
    I'll tell you what: I think it is our way,
    If we will keep in favour with the King,
    To be her men and wear her livery.   80
    The jealous o'er-worn widow and herself,
    Since that our brother dubbed them gentlewomen,
    Are mighty gossips in this monarchy.
BRAKENBURY I beseech your Graces both to pardon me:
    His Majesty hath straitly given in charge   85
    That no man shall have private conference
    Of what degree soever with his brother.
GLOUCESTER Even so; and please your worship, Brakenbury,
    You may partake of anything we say.
    We speak no treason, man; we say the King   90
    Is wise and virtuous, and his noble Queen
    Well struck in years, fair, and not jealous.
    We say that Shore's wife hath a pretty foot,
    A cherry lip, a bonny eye, a passing pleasing tongue;
    And that the Queen's kindred are made gentlefolks.   95
    How say you, sir? Can you deny all this?
BRAKENBURY With this, my lord, myself have naught to do.
GLOUCESTER Naught to do with Mistress Shore! I tell thee, fellow,
    He that doth naught with her, excepting one,
    Were best he do it secretly, alone.   100
BRAKENBURY What one, my lord?
GLOUCESTER Her husband, knave! Wouldst thou betray me?
BRAKENBURY I beseech your Grace to pardon me, and withal
    Forbear your conference with the noble Duke.
CLARENCE We know thy charge, Brakenbury, and will obey.   105
GLOUCESTER We are the Queen's abjects and must obey.
    Brother, farewell; I will unto the King,
    And, whatsoever you will employ me in –
    Were it to call King Edward's widow 'Sister' –

---

71 is secured] Q; secure F   74 ye] Q; you F   75 was to her for his] Q; was, for her F   83 this] Q; our F   *84 SH
BRAKENBURY] *Bro.* Q; *Bra.* F   87 SH his] Q; your F   100 he] Q; to F   *101–2 What one . . . betray me?] Q2–8, F; *om.*
Q1   103 beseech] Q1–6; do beseech F

I will perform it to enfranchise you.   110
Meantime, this deep disgrace in brotherhood
Touches me deeper than you can imagine.
CLARENCE I know it pleaseth neither of us well.
GLOUCESTER Well, your imprisonment shall not be long;
I will deliver you – or lie for you.   115
Meantime, have patience.
CLARENCE   I must perforce. Farewell.
                        Exeunt Clar[ence, Brakenbury and guard]
GLOUCESTER Go tread the path that thou shalt ne'er return.
Simple, plain Clarence, I do love thee so
That I will shortly send thy soul to heaven –
If heaven will take the present at our hands.   120
But who comes here? The new-delivered Hastings?

                    Enter LORD HASTINGS

HASTINGS Good time of day unto my gracious lord.
GLOUCESTER As much unto my good Lord Chamberlain:
Well are you welcome to the open air.
How hath your lordship brooked imprisonment?   125
HASTINGS With patience, noble lord, as prisoners must.
But I shall live, my lord, to give them thanks
That were the cause of my imprisonment.
GLOUCESTER No doubt, no doubt – and so shall Clarence too,
For they that were your enemies are his   130
And have prevailed as much on him as you.
HASTINGS More pity that the eagle should be mewed
While kites and buzzards prey at liberty.
GLOUCESTER What news abroad?
HASTINGS No news so bad abroad as this at home: 135
The King is sickly, weak, and melancholy,
And his physicians fear him mightily.
GLOUCESTER Now by Saint Paul, this news is bad indeed.
Oh, he hath kept an evil diet long
And overmuch consumed his royal person.   140
'Tis very grievous to be thought upon.
What? Is he in his bed?
HASTINGS   He is.
GLOUCESTER Go you before and I will follow you.
                                            Exit Hast[ings]
He cannot live, I hope, and must not die
Till George be packed with post-horse up to heaven.   145

---

115 or lie] Q; or else lye F   124 the] Q1–2; this Q3–6, F   132 eagle] Q; Eagles F   133 While] Q; Whiles F   prey] Q1–6; play F   138 Saint Paul] Q; S. Iohn F   this] Q; that F   142 What] Q; Where F

I'll in to urge his hatred more to Clarence
With lies well-steeled with weighty arguments,
And, if I fail not in my deep intent,
Clarence hath not another day to live;
Which done, God take King Edward to his mercy   150
And leave the world for me to bustle in.
For then I'll marry Warwick's youngest daughter:
What though I killed her husband and her father?
The readiest way to make the wench amends
Is to become her husband and her father –   155
The which will I, not all so much for love
As for another secret close intent,
By marrying her, which I must reach unto.
But yet I run before my horse to market;
Clarence still breathes, Edward still lives and reigns.   160
When they are gone, then must I count my gains.

                                                        Exit

[1.2] *Enter* LADY ANNE *with the hearse of* HENRY VI [*with Halberdiers to guard it,* TRESSEL, BERKELEY, *and* ATTENDANTS]

ANNE Set down, set down your honourable load –
          If honour may be shrouded in a hearse –
          Whilst I awhile obsequiously lament
          The untimely fall of virtuous Lancaster.
          Poor key-cold figure of a holy king,   5
          Pale ashes of the House of Lancaster,
          Thou bloodless remnant of that royal blood:
          Be it lawful that I invocate thy ghost
          To hear the lamentations of poor Anne,
          Wife to thy Edward, to thy slaughtered son,   10
          Stabbed by the selfsame hands that made these holes.
          Lo! In those windows that let forth thy life
          I pour the helpless balm of my poor eyes.
          Cursed be the hand that made these fatal holes;
          Cursed be the heart that had the heart to do it.   15
          More direful hap betide that hated wretch
          That makes us wretched by the death of thee
          Than I can wish to adders, spiders, toads,
          Or any creeping venomed thing that lives.

0 SD *Enter . . . Attendants*] *Enter Lady Anne with the hearse of Harry the 6.*] Q; *Enter the Coarse of Henrie the sixt with Halberds to guard it, / Lady Anne being the Mourner.* F   *1 load] F; lo Q1; lord Q2; Lord Q3–8   11 hands] Q; hand F   holes] Q; wounds F   12 those] Q; these F   14 Cursed] Q; O cursed F   fatal holes] Q; holes F   15 Cursed be] Q (Curst be); Cursed F   15–16 do it. / More direful] Q; do it: / Cnrsed the Blood, that let this blood from hence: / More direfull F ('Cnrsed' *sic*)   18 adders] Q; Wolues, to F

If ever he hath child, abortive be it,   20
Prodigious and untimely brought to light,
Whose ugly and unnatural aspect
May fright the hopeful mother at the view.
If ever he have wife, let her be made
As miserable by the death of him   25
As I am made by my poor lord and thee.
Come now towards Chertsey with your holy load,
Taken from Paul's to be interred there;
And still, as you are weary of the weight,
Rest you whiles I lament King Henry's corse.   30

Enter GLOUCESTER

GLOUCESTER Stay, you that bear the corse, and set it down.
ANNE What black magician conjures up this fiend
    To stop devoted charitable deeds?
GLOUCESTER Villain, set down the corse, or by Saint Paul
    I'll make a corse of him that disobeys.   35
HALBERDIER My lord, stand back and let the coffin pass.
GLOUCESTER Unmannered dog! Stand thou when I command.
    Advance thy halberd higher than my breast,
    Or by Saint Paul I'll strike thee to my foot
    And spurn upon thee, beggar, for thy boldness.   40
ANNE What! Do you tremble? Are you all afraid?
    Alas, I blame you not, for you are mortal,
    And mortal eyes cannot endure the devil.
    Avaunt, thou dreadful minister of hell!
    Thou hadst but power over his mortal body;   45
    His soul thou canst not have: therefore, begone!
GLOUCESTER Sweet saint, for charity, be not so curst.
ANNE Foul devil, for God's sake hence and trouble us not,
    For thou hast made the happy earth thy hell,
    Filled it with cursing cries and deep exclaims.   50
    If thou delight to view thy heinous deeds,
    Behold this pattern of thy butcheries.
    Oh gentlemen! See, see dead Henry's wounds
    Open their congealed mouths and bleed afresh!
    Blush! Blush! Thou lump of foul deformity;   55
    For 'tis thy presence that exhales this blood
    From cold and empty veins where no blood dwells.
    Thy deed inhuman and unnatural

23-4 view. / If ever] Q; view, / And that be Heyre to his vnhappinesse. / If euer F   25-6 As . . . As] Q; More . . . Then
F   25 death] Q, F; life *Cibber*   26 poor] Q; young F   29 the] Q; this F   34 Villain] Q; Villaines F   37 Stand] Q
(stand); Stand'st F   58 deed] Q; Deeds F

Provokes this deluge most unnatural.
Oh God, which this blood madest, revenge his death!   60
Oh earth, which this blood drinkst, revenge his death!
Either heaven with lightning strike the murderer dead
Or earth gape open wide and eat him quick,
As thou dost swallow up this good King's blood
Which his hell-governed arm hath butchered.   65

GLOUCESTER Lady, you know no rules of charity,
    Which renders good for bad, blessings for curses.

ANNE Villain, thou knowest no law of God nor man:
    No beast so fierce but knows some touch of pity.

GLOUCESTER But I know none, and therefore am no beast.   70

ANNE Oh wonderful, when devils tell the truth!

GLOUCESTER More wonderful when angels are so angry.
    Vouchsafe, divine perfection of a woman,
    Of these supposed evils to give me leave,
    By circumstance, but to acquit myself.   75

ANNE Vouchsafe, diffused infection of a man,
    For these known evils but to give me leave,
    By circumstance, to curse thy cursed self.

GLOUCESTER Fairer than tongue can name thee, let me have
    Some patient leisure to excuse myself.   80

ANNE· Fouler than heart can think thee, thou canst make
    No excuse current but to hang thyself.

GLOUCESTER By such despair I should accuse myself.

ANNE And by despairing shouldst thou stand excused
    For doing worthy vengeance on thyself,   85
    Which didst unworthy slaughter upon others.

GLOUCESTER Say that I slew them not!

ANNE   Why then, they are not dead –
    But dead they are and, devilish slave, by thee.

GLOUCESTER I did not kill your husband.

ANNE Why then, he is alive.   90

GLOUCESTER Nay, he is dead, and slain by Edward's hand.

ANNE In thy foul throat thou liest. Queen Margaret saw
    Thy bloody falchion smoking in his blood,
    The which thou once didst bend against her breast
    But that thy brothers beat aside the point.   95

GLOUCESTER I was provoked by her slanderous tongue,
    Which laid their guilt upon my guiltless shoulders.

ANNE Thou wast provoked by thy bloody mind,

---

68 no] Q; nor F   74   evils] Q; Crimes F   76   a man] Q; man F   77   For] Q; Of F   78   to curse] Q, F; t'accuse *Arden*,
after Spedding   84   shouldst] Q; shalt F   86   Which didst] Q; That did'st F   87   Why then . . . dead] Q; Then say they
were not slaine F   91   hand] Q; hands F   93   bloody] Q; murd'rous F   97   Which] Q; That F

Which never dreamt on aught but butcheries.
Didst thou not kill this King?

GLOUCESTER   I grant ye –   100

ANNE Dost grant me, hedgehog? Then God grant me too
Thou mayest be damned for that wicked deed.
Oh, he was gentle, mild, and virtuous –

GLOUCESTER The fitter for the King of Heaven that hath him.

ANNE He is in heaven, where thou shalt never come.   105

GLOUCESTER Let him thank me that holp to send him thither,
For he was fitter for that place than earth.

ANNE And thou unfit for any place but hell.

GLOUCESTER Yes, one place else, if you will hear me name it.

ANNE Some dungeon?

GLOUCESTER   Your bed-chamber!   110

ANNE Ill rest betide the chamber where thou liest.

GLOUCESTER So will it, madam, till I lie with you.

ANNE I hope so.

GLOUCESTER I know so. But, gentle Lady Anne,
To leave this keen encounter of our wits,   115
And fall somewhat into a slower method.
Is not the causer of the timeless deaths
Of these Plantagenets, Henry and Edward,
As blameful as the executioner?

ANNE Thou art the cause and most accursed effect.   120

GLOUCESTER Your beauty was the cause of that effect,
Your beauty, which did haunt me in my sleep,
To undertake the death of all the world
So I might rest one hour in your sweet bosom.

ANNE If I thought that, I tell thee, homicide,   125
These nails should rend that beauty from my cheeks.

GLOUCESTER These eyes could never endure sweet beauty's wrack;
You should not blemish them if I stood by:
As all the world is cheered by the sun,
So I by that: it is my day, my life.   130

ANNE Black night overshade thy day, and death thy life.

GLOUCESTER Curse not thyself, fair creature, thou art both.

ANNE I would I were, to be revenged on thee.

GLOUCESTER It is a quarrel most unnatural
To be revenged on him that loveth you.   135

ANNE It is a quarrel just and reasonable

---

99 Which never dreamt] Q; That neuer dream'st F **•100** ye] F; yea Q1–2; yee Q3–6 **104** fitter] Q; better F
116 somewhat] Q; something F **120** art] Q; was't F **122** which] Q; that F **124** rest] Q; liue F **126** rend] Q; rent
F **127** never . . . sweet] Q; not . . . that F **128** them] Q; it F **•129** sun] F; sonne Q **135** you] Q; thee F

To be revenged on him that slew my husband.

GLOUCESTER He that bereft thee, lady, of thy husband,
Did it to help thee to a better husband.

ANNE His better doth not breathe upon the earth.   140

GLOUCESTER Go to, he lives that loves you better than he could.

ANNE Name him!

GLOUCESTER   Plantagenet.

ANNE   Why, that was he!

GLOUCESTER The selfsame name, but one of better nature.

ANNE Where is he?

GLOUCESTER   Here.

She spits at him
Why dost thou spit at me?

ANNE Would it were mortal poison for thy sake.   145

GLOUCESTER Never came poison from so sweet a place.

ANNE Never hung poison on a fouler toad.
Out of my sight! Thou dost infect my eyes.

GLOUCESTER Thine eyes, sweet lady, have infected mine.

ANNE Would they were basilisks to strike thee dead.   150

GLOUCESTER I would they were that I might die at once,
For now they kill me with a living death.
Those eyes of thine from mine have drawn salt tears,
Shamed their aspect with store of childish drops.
I never sued to friend nor enemy,   155
My tongue could never learn sweet soothing words,
But now thy beauty is proposed my fee;
My proud heart sues and prompts my tongue to speak.
[She looks scornfully at him]
Teach not thy lips such scorn, for they were made
For kissing, lady, not for such contempt.   160
If thy revengeful heart cannot forgive,
Lo, here I lend thee this sharp-pointed sword,
Which, if thou please to hide in this true bosom,
And let the soul forth that adoreth thee,
I lay it naked to the deadly stroke,   165
And humbly beg the death upon my knee.
[He lays his breast open, she offers at [it] with his sword]
Nay, do not pause, 'twas I that killed your husband,

---

137 slew] Q; kill'd F 138 thee] Q; the F 141 Go to, he] Q; He F you] Q; thee F 144 SD *She spits at him*] Q (*spitteth*)
placed against Where is he ? ; *Spits at him.* (*placed as here*) F 148 my] Q; mine F 154 aspect] Q; Aspects F 154–
5 drops. / I never] Q; drops. / These eyes, which neuer shed remorsefull teare, / [*ten lines*] / Thy Beauty hath, and made
them blinde with weeping. / I neuer F 156 soothing words] Q; smoothing word F *158 SD *She . . . him*] F; *om.* Q
159 lips . . . they were] Q; lip . . . it was F 163 bosom] Q; brest F *166 SD *He lays . . . sword*] F; *om.* Q 167 'twas
I . . . husband] Q; For I did kill King *Henrie* F

But 'twas thy beauty that provoked me.
Nay now, dispatch, 'twas I that killed King Henry,
But 'twas thy heavenly face that set me on.   170
                Here she lets fall the sword
Take up the sword again or take up me.

ANNE Arise, dissembler, though I wish thy death
    I will not be the executioner.

GLOUCESTER Then bid me kill myself, and I will do it.

ANNE I have already.

GLOUCESTER   Tush! That was in thy rage.   175
    Speak it again, and even with the word,
    That hand, which for thy love did kill thy love,
    Shall for thy love, kill a far truer love:
    To both their deaths shall thou be accessary.

ANNE I would I knew thy heart.   180

GLOUCESTER 'Tis figured in my tongue.

ANNE I fear me both are false.

GLOUCESTER Then never was man true.

ANNE Well, well, put up your sword.

GLOUCESTER Say then my peace is made.   185

ANNE That shall you know hereafter.

GLOUCESTER But shall I live in hope?

ANNE All men, I hope, live so.

GLOUCESTER Vouchsafe to wear this ring.

ANNE To take is not to give.   190

GLOUCESTER Look how this ring encompasseth thy finger!
    Even so thy breast encloseth my poor heart.
    Wear both of them, for both of them are thine,
    And if thy poor devoted suppliant may
    But beg one favour at thy gracious hand,   195
    Thou dost confirm his happiness for ever.

ANNE What is it?

GLOUCESTER That it would please thee leave these sad designs
    To him that hath more cause to be a mourner
    And presently repair to Crosby Place,   200
    Where, after I have solemnly interred
    At Chertsey Monastery this noble King,
    And wet his grave with my repentant tears,
    I will, with all expedient duty, see you.
    For divers unknown reasons, I beseech you   205

169 killed King Henry] Q; stabb'd yong *Edward* F   **170** SD] *right margin of 170–1* Q; *She fals the Sword.* F (*against 170*)   **173** the] Q; thy F   **175** Tush! That] Q; That F   **177** That] Q; This F   **183** was man] Q; Man was F   **186** shall you] Q; shalt thou F   **190** To take is not to give.] Q; *om.* F   **191** this] Q; my F   **194** suppliant] Q; Seruant F   **198** would] Q; may F   thee] Q; you F   **199** more] Q; most F   **200** Place] Q (place); House F

Grant me this boon.

ANNE With all my heart, and much it joys me too,
      To see you are become so penitent.
      Tressel and Berkeley, go along with me.

GLOUCESTER Bid me farewell.

ANNE   'Tis more than you deserve: 210
      But since you teach me how to flatter you
      Imagine I have said farewell already.

                              Exit [with Tressel and Berkeley]

GLOUCESTER Sirs, take up the corse.

ATTENDANT Towards Chertsey, noble lord?

GLOUCESTER No, to Whitefriars. There attend my coming.   215

                              Exeunt [all but] Gloucester

      Was ever woman in this humour wooed?
      Was ever woman in this humour won?
      I'll have her, but I will not keep her long.
      What? I that killed her husband and his father,
      To take her in her heart's extremest hate,   220
      With curses in her mouth, tears in her eyes,
      The bleeding witness of her hatred by,
      Having God, her conscience, and these bars against me?
      And I, nothing to back my suit at all
      But the plain devil and dissembling looks!   225
      And yet, to win her, all the world to nothing! Ha!
      Hath she forgot already that brave prince,
      Edward, her lord, whom I, some three months since,
      Stabbed in my angry mood at Tewkesbury?
      A sweeter and a lovelier gentleman,   230
      Framed in the prodigality of nature,
      Young, valiant, wise, and no doubt right royal,
      The spacious world cannot again afford.
      And will she yet debase her eyes on me,
      That cropped the golden prime of this sweet prince,   235
      And made her widow to a woeful bed?
      On me, whose all not equals Edward's moiety?
      On me, that halt, and am unshapen thus?
      My dukedom to a beggarly denier,
      I do mistake my person all this while!   240
      Upon my life she finds, although I cannot,
      Myself to be a marvellous proper man!
      I'll be at charges for a looking glass,

---

*212 SD *Exit . . . Berkeley*] *Exit* Q; *Exit two with Anne* F *214 SH ATTENDANT] *Ser.* Q; *Gent.* F *215 SD
Exeunt . . . Gloucester] *Exeunt. manet Gl.* Q; *Exit Coarse* F 222 her] Q; my F 224 nothing] Q; no Friends F at all] Q1–
2; withall Q3–6, F 234 debase] Q; abase F 238 halt] Q; halts F unshapen] Q; mishapen F

And entertain some score or two of tailors
To study fashions to adorn my body.   245
Since I am crept in favour with myself,
I will maintain it with some little cost.
But first, I'll turn yon fellow in his grave,
And then return, lamenting, to my love.
Shine out, fair sun, till I have bought a glass,   250
That I may see my shadow as I pass.

Exit

[**1.3**] *Enter* QUEEN [ELIZABETH], LORD RIVERS, [LORD] GREY[, *and the* MARQUESS *of* DORSET]

RIVERS Have patience, madam, there's no doubt his Majesty
    Will soon recover his accustomed health.
GREY In that you brook it ill, it makes him worse;
    Therefore, for God's sake entertain good comfort
    And cheer his Grace with quick and merry words.   5
ELIZABETH If he were dead, what would betide of me?
RIVERS No other harm but loss of such a lord.
ELIZABETH The loss of such a lord includes all harm.
GREY The heavens have blessed you with a goodly son
    To be your comforter when he is gone.   10
ELIZABETH Oh he is young, and his minority
    Is put unto the trust of Richard Gloucester,
    A man that loves not me nor none of you.
RIVERS Is it concluded he shall be Protector?
ELIZABETH It is determined, not concluded yet,   15
    But so it must be if the King miscarry.

Enter BUCK[INGHAM *and*] DERBY

GREY Here come the Lords of Buckingham and Derby.
BUCKINGHAM Good time of day unto your royal Grace.
DERBY God make your Majesty joyful, as you have been.
ELIZABETH The Countess Richmond, good my lord of Derby,   20
    To your good prayers will scarcely say, 'Amen'.
    Yet, Derby, notwithstanding she's your wife,
    And loves not me, be you, good lord, assured
    I hate not you for her proud arrogance.
DERBY I do beseech you, either not believe   25
    The envious slanders of her false accusers,

244 some] Q; a F   **3** it ill, it] Q2–6, F; it, ill it Q1   **5** with quick] Q2–6, F; quick Q1   words] Q; eyes F   **6** *line repeated, second with* Ifhe *unspaced, in* F   of] Q; on F (*in both settings*)   **7** SH RIVERS] Q (*Ry.*); *Gray.* F   **8** harm] Q; harmes F   **12** Richard] F; Rich. Q   **17** come] Q; comes F   Lords] Q; Lord F   **21** prayers] Q; prayer F

Or if she be accused in true report,
Bear with her weakness, which I think proceeds
From wayward sickness and no grounded malice.
RIVERS Saw you the King today, my lord of Derby?   30
DERBY But now the Duke of Buckingham and I
Came from visiting his Majesty.
ELIZABETH With likelihood of his amendment, lords?
BUCKINGHAM Madam, good hope; his Grace speaks cheerfully.
ELIZABETH God grant him health. Did you confer with him?   35
BUCKINGHAM Madam, we did. He desires to make atonement
Betwixt the Duke of Gloucester and your brothers,
And betwixt them and my Lord Chamberlain,
And sent to warn them to his royal presence.
ELIZABETH Would all were well, but that will never be.   40
I fear our happiness is at the highest.

Enter GLOUCESTER [*and* HASTINGS]

GLOUCESTER They do me wrong and I will not endure it!
Who are they that complains unto the King
That I forsooth am stern and love them not?
By holy Paul, they love his Grace but lightly   45
That fill his ears with such dissentious rumours.
Because I cannot flatter and speak fair,
Smile in men's faces, smooth, deceive, and cog,
Duck with French nods and apish courtesy,
I must be held a rancorous enemy.   50
Cannot a plain man live and think no harm
But thus his simple truth must be abused
By silken, sly, insinuating Jacks?
RIVERS To whom in all this presence speaks your Grace?
GLOUCESTER To thee that hast nor honesty nor grace.   55
When have I injured thee? When done thee wrong?
Or thee? Or thee? Or any of your faction?
A plague upon you all! His royal person
(Whom God preserve better than you would wish)
Cannot be quiet scarce a breathing while   60
But you must trouble him with lewd complaints.
ELIZABETH Brother of Gloucester, you mistake the matter.
The King, of his own royal disposition,
And not provoked by any suitor else,
Aiming belike at your interior hatred,   65

27 in] Q; on F   30 SH RIVERS] Q (*Ry.*); *Qu.* F   32 Came] Q; Are come F   33 With] Q; What F   36 Madam, we did] Q; I Madam F   37–8 Betwixt . . . betwixt] Q; Betweene . . betweene F   41 highest] Q; height F   43 are they that complains] Q1–7; is it that complaines F; are they that complaine Q8   47 speak] Q; looke F   •48 deceive] F; dcceiue Q   53 By] Q; With F   54 SH RIVERS] Q (*Ry.*); *Grey.* F   whom] Q; who F   58 person] Q; Grace F   63 of] Q; on F

                    Which in your outward actions shows itself,
                    Against my kindred, brother, and myself,
                    Makes him to send that thereby he may gather
                    The ground of your ill will and to remove it.
GLOUCESTER   I cannot tell; the world is grown so bad   70
                    That wrens make prey where eagles dare not perch.
                    Since every Jack became a gentleman,
                    There's many a gentle person made a jack.
ELIZABETH   Come, come, we know your meaning brother Gloucester.
                    You envy my advancement and my friends'.   75
                    God grant we never may have need of you.
GLOUCESTER   Meantime, God grants that we have need of you.
                    Our brother is imprisoned by your means,
                    Myself disgraced, and the nobility
                    Held in contempt, whilst many fair promotions   80
                    Are daily given to ennoble those
                    That scarce some two days since were worth a noble.
ELIZABETH   By Him that raised me to this careful height
                    From that contented hap which I enjoyed,
                    I never did incense his Majesty   85
                    Against the Duke of Clarence but have been
                    An earnest advocate to plead for him.
                    My lord, you do me shameful injury
                    Falsely to draw me in these vile suspects.
GLOUCESTER   You may deny that you were not the cause   90
                    Of my Lord Hastings' late imprisonment.
RIVERS   She may, my lord –
GLOUCESTER   She may, Lord Rivers. Why? Who knows not so?
                    She may do more, sir, than denying that;
                    She may help you to many fair preferments,   95
                    And then deny her aiding hand therein,
                    And lay those honours on your high deserts.
                    What may she not? She may, yea, marry may she!
RIVERS   What, marry may she?
GLOUCESTER   What marry may she? Marry with a king,   100
                    A bachelor, a handsome stripling too.
                    Iwis, your grandam had a worser match.
ELIZABETH   My lord of Gloucester, I have too long borne
                    Your blunt upbraidings and your bitter scoffs.
                    By heaven, I will acquaint his Majesty   105

66   Which] Q; That F   actions] Q; action F   67   kindred, brother] Q; Children, Brothers F   68–9   Makes … gather /
The ground … remove it.] Q; Makes him to send, that he may learne the ground. F   73   jack] Iacke Q; Iaeke F   77   we]
Q; I F   80   whilst many fair] Q; while great F   90   cause] Q; meane F   *92   lord -] Lord. Q; Lord, for——F
97   deserts] Q; desert F   98   yea] Q; I F   101   a] Q; and a F

With those gross taunts I often have endured.
I had rather be a country servant maid
Than a great queen with this condition
To be thus taunted, scorned, and baited at.

Enter QU[EEN] MARGARET

Small joy have I in being England's queen.   110
MARGARET And lessened be that small, God I beseech thee,
 Thy honour, state, and seat is due to me.
GLOUCESTER What! Threat you me with telling of the King?
 Tell him and spare not. Look, what I have said
 I will avouch't in presence of the King.   115
 'Tis time to speak; my pains are quite forgot.
MARGARET Out, devil! I remember them too well.
 Thou slewest my husband Henry in the Tower
 And Edward, my poor son, at Tewkesbury.
GLOUCESTER Ere you were Queen, yea, or your husband King,   120
 I was a packhorse in his great affairs,
 A weeder-out of his proud adversaries,
 A liberal rewarder of his friends.
 To royalise his blood I spilt mine own.
MARGARET Yea, and much better blood than his or thine.   125
GLOUCESTER In all which time, you and your husband, Grey,
 Were factious for the House of Lancaster;
 And Rivers, so were you. Was not your husband
 In Margaret's battle at Saint Albans slain?
 Let me put in your minds, if yours forget,   130
 What you have been ere now, and what you are;
 Withall, what I have been, and what I am.
MARGARET A murderous villain, and so still thou art.
GLOUCESTER Poor Clarence did forsake his father, Warwick,
 Yea, and forswore himself (which Jesu pardon).   135
MARGARET Which God revenge.
GLOUCESTER To fight on Edward's party for the crown.
 And for his meed, poor lord, he is mewed up.
 I would to God my heart were flint like Edward's,
 Or Edward's soft and pitiful like mine.   140
 I am too childish-foolish for this world.
MARGARET Hie thee to hell for shame and leave the world,

---

106 With] Q; Of F I often] Q; that oft I F 109 thus . . . baited] Q; so baited, scorn'd, and stormed F 109 SD
Enter . . . MARGARET] Q (*Qu. rt. margin of 109, 110*); *Enter old Queene Margaret* F (*after* 110) 111 thee] Q; him F
114 Tell him . . . said] Q; *om.* F *115 avouch't] F; auouch Q 115–16 King. / 'Tis] Q; King: / I dare aduenture to be
sent to th'Towre. / 'Tis F 117 I] Q; I do F 118 slewest] Q; killd'st F 124 spilt] Q; spent F 130 yours] Q; you
F 131 now] Q; this F *141 childish-foolish] *Theobald*; childish, foolish Q1–2; childish foolish Q3–6 F 142 the] Q;
this F

      Thou cacodemon: there thy kingdom is!

RIVERS My lord of Gloucester, in those busy days,
      Which here you urge to prove us enemies,   145
      We followed then our lord, our lawful king.
      So should we you, if you should be our king.

GLOUCESTER If I should be? I had rather be a pedlar.
      Far be it from my heart the thought of it.

ELIZABETH As little joy, my lord, as you suppose   150
      You should enjoy, were you this country's king;
      As little joy may you suppose in me
      That I enjoy, being the Queen thereof.

MARGARET A little joy enjoys the Queen thereof,
      For I am she and altogether joyless.   155
      I can no longer hold me patient.
      Hear me, you wrangling pirates, that fall out
      In sharing that which you have pilled from me.
      Which of you trembles not that looks on me?
      If not, that I being Queen you bow like subjects,   160
      Yet that by you deposed you quake like rebels.
      O gentle villain, do not turn away.

GLOUCESTER Foul wrinkled witch, what makest thou in my sight?

MARGARET But repetition of what thou hast marred:
      That will I make before I let thee go.   165
      A husband and a son thou owest to me;
      And thou a kingdom; all of you, allegiance.
      The sorrow that I have by right is yours,
      And all the pleasures you usurp are mine.

GLOUCESTER The curse my noble father laid on thee,   170
      When thou didst crown his warlike brows with paper,
      And with thy scorn drewst rivers from his eyes,
      And then to dry them gavest the Duke a clout
      Steeped in the faultless blood of pretty Rutland –
      His curses then, from bitterness of soul   175
      Denounced against thee, are all fallen upon thee,
      And God, not we, hath plagued thy bloody deed.

ELIZABETH So just is God to right the innocent.

HASTINGS O, 'twas the foulest deed to slay that babe,
      And the most merciless that ever was heard of.   180

RIVERS Tyrants themselves wept when it was reported.

146 lawful] Q; Soueraigne F 149 of it] Q; thereof F 150 SH ELIZABETH] *Qu.* Q1, F; *Q.M(ar)*. Q3–4, Q6–7; *Qu. Nar.* Q5 152 may you] Q; you may F 159 of] Q; off F 160 being] Q; am F 165–6 go. / A husband] Q; goe. / *Rich.* Wert thou not banished, on paine of death? / *Q.M.* I was: but I doe find more paine in banishment, / Then death can yeeld me here, by my abode. / A Husband F 168 The] Q; This F 172 scorn] Q; scornes F drewst] Q; drew'st F 180 ever] Q; ere F

DORSET No man but prophesied revenge for it.

BUCKINGHAM Northumberland, then present, wept to see it.

MARGARET What? Were you snarling all before I came,
   Ready to catch each other by the throat   185
   And turn you all your hatred now on me?
   Did York's dread curse prevail so much with heaven
   That Henry's death, my lovely Edward's death,
   Their kingdom's loss, my woeful banishment,
   Could all but answer for that peevish brat?   190
   Can curses pierce the clouds and enter heaven?
   Why then, give way, dull clouds, to my quick curses!
   If not by war, by surfeit die your King,
   As ours by murder, to make him a king.
   Edward thy son, which now is Prince of Wales,   195
   For Edward my son, which was Prince of Wales,
   Die in his youth by like untimely violence;
   Thyself a queen, for me that was a queen,
   Outlive thy glory like my wretched self.
   Long mayest thou live to wail thy children's loss,   200
   And see another, as I see thee now,
   Decked in thy rights, as thou art stalled in mine.
   Long die thy happy days before thy death,
   And after many lengthened hours of grief,
   Die neither mother, wife, nor England's Queen.   205
   Rivers and Dorset, you were standers-by,
   And so wast thou, Lord Hastings, when my son
   Was stabbed with bloody daggers. God, I pray him,
   That none of you may live your natural age,
   But by some unlooked accident cut off.   210

GLOUCESTER Have done thy charm, thou hateful withered hag.

MARGARET And leave out thee? Stay, dog, for thou shalt hear me.
   If heaven have any grievous plague in store
   Exceeding those that I can wish upon thee,
   O, let them keep it till thy sins be ripe,   215
   And then hurl down their indignation
   On thee, the troubler of the poor world's peace.
   The worm of conscience still begnaw thy soul,
   Thy friends suspect for traitors while thou livest
   And take deep traitors for thy dearest friends;   220
   No sleep close up that deadly eye of thine,
   Unless it be whilst some tormenting dream

---

190 Could] Q; Should F 193 If] Q; Though F 195 which] Q; that F 196 my] Q; our F which] Q; that F
200 loss] Q; death F 202 rights] Q; Rights F; glorie Q2–6 209 your] Q; his F *212 thee ? Stay] F (stay); the stay
Q 222 whilst] Q; while F

Affrights thee with a hell of ugly devils.
Thou elvish-marked, abortive, rooting hog,
Thou that was sealed in thy nativity   225
The slave of nature, and the son of hell,
Thou slander of thy mother's heavy womb,
Thou loathed issue of thy father's loins,
Thou rag of honour, thou detested, &c.

GLOUCESTER Margaret!
MARGARET   Richard!
GLOUCESTER   Ha?
MARGARET   I call thee not.   230
GLOUCESTER Then I cry thee mercy, for I had thought
          That thou hadst called me all these bitter names.
MARGARET Why, so I did, but looked for no reply.
          O, let me make the period to my curse.
GLOUCESTER 'Tis done by me, and ends in 'Margaret'!   235
ELIZABETH Thus have you breathed your curse against yourself.
MARGARET Poor painted queen, vain flourish of my fortune:
          Why strewest thou sugar on that bottled spider,
          Whose deadly web ensnareth thee about?
          Fool! Fool! Thou whetst a knife to kill thyself.   240
          The time will come that thou shalt wish for me
          To help thee curse that poisonous bunch-backed toad.
HASTINGS False-boding woman, end thy frantic curse,
          Lest to thy harm thou move our patience.
MARGARET Foul shame upon you, you have all moved mine.   245
RIVERS Were you well served you would be taught your duty.
MARGARET To serve me well you all should do me duty.
          Teach me to be your queen and you my subjects:
          O, serve me well, and teach yourselves that duty.
DORSET Dispute not with her, she is lunatic.   250
MARGARET Peace, Master Marquess: you are malapert.
          Your fire-new stamp of honour is scarce current:
          O, that your young nobility could judge
          What 'twere to lose it and be miserable.
          They that stand high have many blasts to shake them,   255
          And if they fall they dash themselves to pieces.
GLOUCESTER Good counsel, marry! Learn it, learn it, Marquess!
DORSET It toucheth you, my lord, as much as me.
GLOUCESTER Yea, and much more; but I was born so high.
          Our aery buildeth in the cedar's top,   260

---

227 mother's heavy] Q; heauie Mothers F   229 detested, &c.] Q; detested——F   231 Then . . . thought] Q; I cry thee
mercie then: for I did thinke F   241 time] Q; day F   242 that] Q; this F   *255 blasts] F; blast Q   258 toucheth] Q;
touches F

And dallies with the wind, and scorns the sun.
MARGARET And turns the sun to shade, alas, alas!
   Witness my son, now in the shade of death,
   Whose bright outshining beams thy cloudy wrath
   Hath in eternal darkness folded up.   265
   Your aery buildeth in our aery's nest,
   O God that seest it, do not suffer it!
   As it was won with blood, lost be it so.
BUCKINGHAM Have done, for shame, if not for charity.
MARGARET Urge neither charity nor shame to me;   270
   Uncharitably with me have you dealt,
   And shamefully by you my hopes are butchered.
   My charity is outrage, life my shame,
   And in my shame still live my sorrow's rage.
BUCKINGHAM Have done!   275
MARGARET O princely Buckingham, I will kiss thy hand
   In sign of league and amity with thee.
   Now fair befall thee and thy princely house;
   Thy garments are not spotted with our blood,
   Nor thou within the compass of my curse.   280
BUCKINGHAM Nor no one here, for curses never pass
   The lips of those that breathe them in the air.
MARGARET I'll not believe but they ascend the sky,
   And there awake God's gentle sleeping peace.
   O Buckingham, beware of yonder dog!   285
   Look when he fawns, he bites, and when he bites,
   His venom tooth will rankle thee to death.
   Have not to do with him, beware of him:
   Sin, death, and hell have set their marks on him,
   And all their ministers attend on him.   290
GLOUCESTER What doth she say, my lord of Buckingham?
BUCKINGHAM Nothing that I respect, my gracious lord.
MARGARET What? Dost thou scorn me for my gentle counsel,
   And soothe the devil that I warn thee from?
   O, but remember this another day   295
   When he shall split thy very heart with sorrow,
   And say, poor Margaret was a prophetess.
   Live each of you the subjects of his hate,
   And he to yours, and all of you to God's.

                                             Exit

---

268 was] Q; is F   269 Have done] Q; Peace, peace F   272 by you my hopes] Q; my hopes (by you) F   274 my] Q;
that F   275 Have done] Q; Haue done, haue done F   276 I will] Q; Ile F   278 princely] Q; Noble F   283 I'll not
believe] Q; I will not thinke F   285 beware] Q; take heede F   *287 rankle] F; rackle Q   thee to] Q; to the F   298 of |
Q; to F   *299 yours] F; your Q1–2; you Q3–6

HASTINGS My hair doth stand on end to hear her curses. 300
RIVERS And so doth mine; I wonder she's at liberty.
GLOUCESTER I cannot blame her, by God's holy mother.
    She hath had too much wrong, and I repent
    My part thereof that I have done.
ELIZABETH I never did her any to my knowledge. 305
GLOUCESTER But you have all the vantage of this wrong.
    I was too hot to do somebody good
    That is too cold in thinking of it now.
    Marry, as for Clarence, he is well repaid;
    He is franked up to fatting for his pains. 310
    God pardon them that are the cause of it.
RIVERS A virtuous and a Christianlike conclusion
    To pray for them that have done scathe to us.
GLOUCESTER So do I ever, being well advised.
    [*To himself*] For had I cursed, now I had cursed myself. 315

[Enter CATESBY]

CATESBY Madam, his Majesty doth call for you,
    And for your Grace, and you my noble lords.
ELIZABETH Catesby, we come. Lords, will you go with us?
RIVERS Madam, we will attend your Grace.
                            Exeunt all but Gloucester
GLOUCESTER I do the wrong, and first began to brawl. 320
    The secret mischiefs that I set abroach
    I lay unto the grievous charge of others.
    Clarence, whom I indeed have laid in darkness,
    I do beweep to many simple gulls,
    Namely to Hastings, Derby, Buckingham, 325
    And say it is the Queen and her allies
    That stir the King against the Duke, my brother.
    Now they believe me, and withal, whet me
    To be revenged on Rivers, Vaughan, Grey.
    But then I sigh, and with a piece of scripture, 330
    Tell them that God bids us do good for evil,
    And thus I clothe my naked villainy
    With old odd ends stolen out of Holy Writ,

300 SH HASTINGS] Q; *Buc.* F on] Q; an F 301 wonder] Q; muse why F 304 done] Q; done to her F 306 But] Q; Yet F this] Q; her F 311 of it] Q; thereof F *315 SD *To himself*] *Speakes to himselfe.* F (*after* 314); *not in* Q 315 cursed, now I] Q; curst now, I F *315 SD *Enter* CATESBY] F; *om.* Q *317 and you my noble lords] Q (Lo: Q1– 2; Lord Q3–6); yours my gracious Lord F 318 we] Q; I F us] Q; mee F 319 Madam, we will attend] Q; We wait vpon F 319 SD *Exeunt . . . Gloucester*] *Exeunt man. Ri.* Q; *Exeunt all but Gloster.* F 320 began] Q; begin F 323 whom] Q; who F laid] Q; cast F 325 Hastings, Derby] Q; *Derby, Hastings* F 326 say it is] Q; tell them 'tis F 328 believe me] Q; beleeue it F 329 Vaughan] Q; *Dorset* F 333 old odd] Q; odde old F out] Q; forth F

And seem a saint when most I play the devil.
But soft, here come my executioners.   335

Enter EXECUTIONERS

How now, my hardy, stout, resolved mates!
Are you now going to despatch this deed?
EXECUTIONER We are, my lord, and come to have the warrant
        That we may be admitted where he is.
GLOUCESTER It was well thought upon. I have it here about me.   340
        When you have done, repair to Crosby Place.
        But sirs, be sudden in the execution,
        Withal obdurate, do not hear him plead,
        For Clarence is well spoken, and perhaps
        May move your hearts to pity, if you mark him.   345
EXECUTIONER Tush, fear not my lord, we will not stand to prate.
        Talkers are no good doers; be assured
        We come to use our hands and not our tongues.
GLOUCESTER Your eyes drop millstones when fools' eyes drop tears.
        I like you lads: about your business!   350

                                                    Exeunt

[1.4.] *Enter* CLARENCE [*and*] BRAKENBURY

BRAKENBURY Why looks your Grace so heavily today?
CLARENCE O, I have passed a miserable night,
        So full of ugly sights, of ghastly dreams,
        That as I am a Christian, faithful man,
        I would not spend another such a night   5
        Though 'twere to buy a world of happy days,
        So full of dismal terror was the time.
BRAKENBURY What was your dream? I long to hear you tell it.
CLARENCE Methoughts I was embarked for Burgundy,
        And in my company my brother Gloucester,   10
        Who from my cabin tempted me to walk
        Upon the hatches; thence we looked toward England,
        And cited up a thousand fearful times

---

335 SD *Enter* EXECUTIONERS] Q; *Enter two murtherers* F (*after* 334) 337 deed] Q; thing F 338, 346 SH EXECU-
TIONER] Q (*Execu., Exec.*); *Vil.* F 340 It was well] Q; Well F 346 Tush, fear not my lord] Q; Tut, tut, my Lord F
348 come] Q; go F 349 drop] Q; fall F 350 business !] Q; businesse straight. / Go, go, dispatch. / *Vil.* We will my
Noble Lord. F 0 SD BRAKENBURY] *Brokenbury* Q; *Keeper* F; SHs *Bro(k). for Keeper* 3 ugly sights, of ghastly dreams]
Q; fearefull Dreames, of vgly sights F 8 What . . . tell it] Q; What was your dream my Lord, I pray you tel me
F 9 Methoughts . . . Burgundy] Q (Me thoughts); Me thoughts that I had broken from the Tower, / And was embark'd
to crosse to Burgundy F 12 thence] Q1–5, F; There Q6, F toward] Q1–5, F; towards Q6 13 fearful] Q; heauy F

During the wars of York and Lancaster
That had befallen us. As we paced along   15
Upon the giddy footing of the hatches,
Methought that Gloucester stumbled, and in stumbling,
Struck me – that thought to stay him – overboard
Into the tumbling billows of the main.
Lord, Lord, methought what pain it was to drown;   20
What dreadful noise of waters in my ears,
What ugly sights of death within my eyes.
Methought I saw a thousand fearful wrecks;
Ten thousand men that fishes gnawed upon,
Wedges of gold, great anchors, heaps of pearl,   25
Inestimable stones, unvalued jewels.
Some lay in dead men's skulls, and in those holes
Where eyes did once inhabit, there were crept
(As 'twere in scorn of eyes) reflecting gems,
Which wooed the slimy bottom of the deep   30
And mocked the dead bones that lay scattered by.
BRAKENBURY Had you such leisure in the time of death
To gaze upon the secrets of the deep?
CLARENCE Methought I had, for still the envious flood
Kept in my soul and would not let it forth   35
To seek the empty, vast, and wandering air,
But smothered it within my panting bulk,
Which almost burst to belch it in the sea.
BRAKENBURY Awaked you not with this sore agony?
CLARENCE O no, my dream was lengthened after life.   40
O, then began the tempest to my soul,
Who passed methought the melancholy flood,
With that grim ferryman which poets write of,
Unto the kingdom of perpetual night.
The first that there did greet my stranger soul   45
Was my great father-in-law, renowned Warwick,
Who cried aloud, 'What scourge for perjury
Can this dark monarchy afford false Clarence?'
And so he vanished. Then came wandering by
A shadow like an angel in bright hair   50
Dabbled in blood; and he squeaked out aloud,

17 stumbling] Q; falling F   20 Lord, Lord] Q; O Lord F   21 waters] Q1–5; water Q6, F   my] Q1; mine Q2–6, F
22 ugly sights of] Q; sights of ugly F   my] Q1; mine Q2–6, F   23 Methought] Q (Me thought); Me thoughts F
24 Ten] Q; A F   26–7 jewels. / Some] Q; Iewels, / All scattred in the bottome of the Sea. / Some F   27 those] Q; the
F   30 Which] Q; That F   *32 such] F; such Q   33 the secrets] Q; these secrets F   34 I had … flood] Q; I had, and
often did I striue / To yeeld the Ghost: but still the enuious Flood F   35 Kept] Q; Stop'd F   36 seek] Q1–2; keepe Q3–
6; find F   38 Which] Q; Who F   39 with] Q; in F   40 O no] Q; No, no F   42 Who] Q; I F   43 grim] Q; sowre F
47 cried] Q; spake F   50 in] Q; with F   *51 squeaked] Q2–3, 5–6 (squeakt); squakt Q1; sqaueakt Q4; shriek'd F

'Clarence is come! False, fleeting, perjured Clarence,
That stabbed me in the field by Tewkesbury!
Seize on him Furies! Take him to your torments!'
With that methoughts a legion of foul fiends   55
Environed me about, and howled in mine ears
Such hideous cries, that with the very noise
I trembling, waked, and for a season after
Could not believe but that I was in hell,
Such terrible impression made the dream.   60
BRAKENBURY No marvel, my lord, though it affrighted you –
I promise you, I am afraid to hear you tell it.
CLARENCE O Brakenbury, I have done those things,
Which now bear evidence against my soul,
For Edward's sake, and see how he requites me.   65
I pray thee, gentle Keeper, stay by me.
My soul is heavy and I fain would sleep.
BRAKENBURY I will, my lord. God give your Grace good rest.
                        [*Clarence sleeps*]
Sorrow breaks seasons and reposing hours
Makes the night morning and the noontide night,   70
Princes have but their titles for their glories,
An outward honour for an inward toil;
And for unfelt imagination
They often feel a world of restless cares,
So that betwixt their titles and low names   75
There's nothing differs but the outward fame.

                        The Murderers enter

In God's name, what are you and how came you hither?
1 EXECUTIONER I would speak with Clarence – and I came hither on my legs.
BRAKENBURY Yea, are you so brief?
2 EXECUTIONER O sir, it is better to be brief than tedious.   80
Show him our commission. Talk no more.
BRAKENBURY (*He reads it*) I am in this commanded to deliver
The noble Duke of Clarence to your hands.

54 to your torments] Q; vnto Torment F   55   methoughts] Q (me thoughts); (me thought) F   56   me about] Q; me F
60 the] Q; my F   61   my lord,] Q (my Lo:); Lord, F   62   promise you, I am afraid] Q; am affraid (me thinkes) F   63   O
Brakenbury] Q (Brokenbury); Ah Keeper, Keeper F those] Q; these F   64   Which now bear] Q; That now giue
F   65–6 me. / I pray] Q; mee. / O God! if my deep prayres cannot appease thee, / [*two lines*] / O spare my guiltlesse
Wife, and my poore children. F   66   I pray . . . by me] Q; Keeper, I prythee sit by me a-while F   68   SD *not required in*
Q; *Enter Brakenbury the Lieutenant.* F   •69 breaks] F; breake Q   73   imagination] Q; Imaginations F   75   betwixt] Q;
betweene F names] Q; Name F   76   SD *The Murderers enter*] Q (murtherers); *Enter two Murtherers /* 1. *Mur.* Ho, who's
heere? F   77   In God's . . . hither?] Q; *Bra.* What would'st thou Fellow? And how camm'st / thou hither F   78   SH 1
EXECUTIONER] *Execu.* Q; 2 *Mur.* F   79   Yea, are you] Q; What F   80   SH 2 EXECUTIONER] Q (2 *Exe.*); 1. F; *from here
F, and from 90, Q indicate Executioners only by numbers,* 1 *and* 2 O sir . . . tedious] Q; 'Tis better (Sir) then to be tedious F
81   Show . . . Talk] Q; Let him see our Commission, and talke F   82   SD *He reads it*] Q (*He readeth it.*); *Reads* F; *both
follow* 81

I will not reason what is meant hereby,
Because I will be guiltless of the meaning.   85
Here are the keys; there sits the Duke asleep.
I'll to his Majesty and certify his Grace
That thus I have resigned my charge to you.   [*Exit*]

1 EXECUTIONER   Do so, it is a point of wisdom.
2 EXECUTIONER   What, shall I stab him as he sleeps?   90
1 EXECUTIONER   No, then he will say 'twas done cowardly – when he wakes.
2 EXECUTIONER   When he wakes? Why fool, he shall never wake till the
                Judgement Day.
1 EXECUTIONER   Why, then he will say we stabbed him sleeping.
2 EXECUTIONER   The urging of that word 'Judgement' hath bred a kind of 95
                remorse in me.
1 EXECUTIONER   What? Art thou afraid?
2 EXECUTIONER   Not to kill him, having a warrant for it; but to be
                damned for killing him, from which no warrant can defend us.
1 EXECUTIONER   Back to the Duke of Gloucester! Tell him so.   100
2 EXECUTIONER   I pray thee, stay a while. I hope my holy humour
                will change. 'Twas wont to hold me but while one would
                tell twenty.
                            [*A silence*]
1 EXECUTIONER   How dost thou feel thyself now?
2 EXECUTIONER   Faith, some certain dregs of conscience are yet within me. 105
1 EXECUTIONER   Remember our reward when the deed is done.
2 EXECUTIONER   Zounds, he dies! I had forgot the reward.
1 EXECUTIONER   Where is thy conscience now?
2 EXECUTIONER   In the Duke of Gloucester's purse.
1 EXECUTIONER   So, when he opens his purse to give us our reward,   110
                thy conscience flies out?
2 EXECUTIONER   Let it go – there's few or none will entertain it.
1 EXECUTIONER   How if it come to thee again?
2 EXECUTIONER   I'll not meddle with it; it is a dangerous thing. It
                makes a man a coward. A man cannot steal but it accuses him. 115
                He cannot swear but it checks him. He cannot lie with his
                neighbour's wife but it detects him. It is a blushing, shamefaced
                spirit that mutinies in a man's bosom. It fills one full of

85 of] Q; from F   86 Here ... asleep] Q; There lies the Duke asleepe, and there the Keyes F   87 I'll ... Grace] Q; Ile
to the King, and signifie to him F   88 my charge to you] Q1–2; my place to you Q3–6; to you my charge F   •88   SD *Exit*]
F; *om.* Q   89 Do ... wisdom] Q; You may sir, 'Tis a point of wisedome: / Far you well. F   90 I] Q1–2; we Q3–6, F
91 then he will] Q; hee'l F   92 When ... fool] Q; Why F   till] Q; vntill F   the] Q; the great F   98 warrant for it] Q;
Warrant F   99 which] Q; the which F   us] Q; me F   99–100 us. / Back] Q; I I thought thou had'st bin resolute. / 2 So
I am, to let him liue. / Ile backe F   100 Tell] Q; and tell F   101–3 I pray ... twenty] Q; Nay, I prythee stay a little:
/ I hope this passionate humor of mine, will change, / It was wont to hold me but while one tels twenty F   105 Faith,
some] Q; Some F   107 Zounds] Q; Come F   109 In] Q; O, in F   110 So, when] Q; When F   112 Let] Q; 'Tis no
matter, let F   113 How] Q; What F   114 it; it is a dangerous thing. It] Q; it, it F   116 He ... He] Q; A man ... A man
F   •117 shamefaced] shamefast Q; shamefac'd F   118 one] Q; a man F

obstacles; it made me once restore a purse of gold that I
found. It beggars any man that keeps it. It is turned out   120
of all towns and cities for a dangerous thing; and every
man that means to live well, endeavours to trust to himself
and to live without it.

1 EXECUTIONER Zounds, it is even now at my elbow, persuading me
  not to kill the Duke.   125

2 EXECUTIONER Take the devil in thy mind and believe him not; he
  would insinuate with thee to make thee sigh.

1 EXECUTIONER Tut, I am strong in fraud, he cannot prevail with
  me, I warrant thee.

2 EXECUTIONER Spoke like a tall fellow that respects his   130
  reputation. Come, shall we to this gear?

1 EXECUTIONER Take him over the costard with the hilts of thy
  sword, and then we will chop him in the malmsey butt in the
  next room.

2 EXECUTIONER Oh excellent device: make a sop of him.   135

1 EXECUTIONER Hark! He stirs. Shall I strike?

2 EXECUTIONER No, first let's reason with him.

CLARENCE Where art thou Keeper? Give me a cup of wine.

1 EXECUTIONER You shall have wine enough, my lord, anon.

CLARENCE In God's name, what art thou?   140

2 EXECUTIONER A man, as you are.

CLARENCE But not as I am, royal.

2 EXECUTIONER Nor you as we are, loyal.

CLARENCE Thy voice is thunder, but thy looks are humble.

2 EXECUTIONER My voice is now the King's, my looks mine own.   145

CLARENCE How darkly and how deadly dost thou speak.
    Tell me who are you? Wherefore come you hither?

BOTH To, to, to –

CLARENCE To murder me?

BOTH Ay.   150

CLARENCE You scarcely have the hearts to tell me so,
    And therefore cannot have the hearts to do it.
    Wherein, my friends, have I offended you?

1 EXECUTIONER Offended us you have not, but the King.

CLARENCE I shall be reconciled to him again.   155

119 that I] Q; that (by chance) I F   121 all towns] Q; Townes F   *122 to himself] F; to / To himselfe Q   123 to live]
Q; liue F   124 Zounds, it is] Q; 'Tis F   125 Duke] Q; Dkue F   127 to] Q; but to F   128-9 Tut . . . thee] Q; I am
strong fram'd, he cannot preuaile with me F   130 fellow] Q; man F   his] Q; thy F   131 to this gear] Q; fall to worke F
132 over] Q; on F   133 we will chop him in] Q; throw him into F   135 make] Q; and make F   136-7 1 EXECU-
TIONER Hark . . . with him] Q; 1 Soft, he wakes. / 2 Strike. / 1 No, wee'l reason with him F   139 SH 1 EXECUTIONER]
Q (1); 2 F   141, 143, 145 SHS 2 EXECUTIONER] Q (2); 1 F   *142 But] F; Bnt Q   146-7 speak . . . hither?] Q; speake? /
Your eyes do menace me: why looke you pale? / Who sent you hither? Wherefore do you come? F   148 SH BOTH] Q
(Am.); 2 F   150 SH BOTH] Q (Am.); Both. F   Ay] Q (I); I, I F

2 EXECUTIONER Never, my lord. Therefore, prepare to die.
CLARENCE Are you called forth from out a world of men
    To slay the innocent? What is my offence?
    Where are the evidence that do accuse me?
    What lawful quest have given their verdict up   160
    Unto the frowning judge? Or who pronounced
    The bitter sentence of poor Clarence' death
    Before I be convict by course of law?
    To threaten me with death is most unlawful.
    I charge you, as you hope to have redemption,   165
    By Christ's dear blood, shed for our grievous sins,
    That you depart and lay no hands on me.
    The deed you undertake is damnable.
1 EXECUTIONER What we will do, we do upon command.
2 EXECUTIONER And he that hath commanded is the King.   170
CLARENCE Erroneous vassal! The great King of Kings
    Hath in the tables of His law commanded
    That thou shalt do no murder, and wilt thou then
    Spurn at His edict and fulfil a man's?
    Take heed! For He holds vengeance in His hands   175
    To hurl upon their heads that break His law.
2 EXECUTIONER And that same vengeance doth He throw on thee,
    For false forswearing – and for murder too.
    Thou didst receive the holy sacrament
    To fight in quarrel of the House of Lancaster.   180
1 EXECUTIONER And like a traitor to the name of God
    Didst break that vow, and with thy treacherous blade
    Unripst the bowels of thy sovereign's son.
2 EXECUTIONER Whom thou wert sworn to cherish and defend.
1 EXECUTIONER How canst thou urge God's dreadful law to us   185
    When thou hast broke it in so dear degree?
CLARENCE Alas! For whose sake did I that ill deed?
    For Edward, for my brother, for his sake.
    Why sirs! He sends ye not to murder me for this,
    For in this sin he is as deep as I.   190
    If God will be revenged for this deed,
    Take not the quarrel from His powerful arm.
    He needs no indirect nor lawless course
    To cut off those that have offended Him.

157 called forth from out] Q; drawne forth among F 159 are] Q; is F 165–7 to have . . . That] Q; for any goodnesse, / That F 170 the] Q; our F 171 vassal] Q (Vassaile); Vassals F 172 tables] Q; Table F 173 and wilt thou] Q; Will you F 175 hands] Q; hand F 177 throw] Q; hurle F 179–80 holy sacrament / To fight in quarrel] Q; Sacrament, to fight / In quarrell F 184 wert] Q; was't F 186 so] Q; such F 189 Why sirs ! He sends ye] Q; He sends you F 190 this] Q; that F 191 revenged for this] Q; auenged for the F 191–2 deed, / Take] Q; deed, / O know you yet, he doth it publiquely, / Take F 193 nor] Q; or F

1 EXECUTIONER Who made thee then a bloody minister   195
    When gallant-springing, brave Plantagenet,
    That princely novice, was struck dead by thee?
CLARENCE My brother's love, the devil, and my rage.
1 EXECUTIONER Thy brother's love, the devil, and thy fault
    Have brought us hither now to murder thee.   200
CLARENCE O, if you love my brother, hate not me.
    I am his brother and I love him well.
    If you be hired for meed, go back again,
    And I will send you to my brother Gloucester,
    Who will reward you better for my life   205
    Than Edward will for tidings of my death.
2 EXECUTIONER You are deceived: your brother Gloucester hates you.
CLARENCE O no, he loves me, and he holds me dear.
    Go you to him from me.
BOTH   Ay, so we will.
CLARENCE Tell him, when that our princely father, York,   210
    Blessed his three sons with his victorious arm,
    And charged us from his soul to love each other,
    He little thought of this divided friendship.
    Bid Gloucester think of this, and he will weep.
BOTH Ay, millstones, as he lessoned us to weep.   215
CLARENCE O, do not slander him, for he is kind.
1 EXECUTIONER Right as snow in harvest; thou deceiv'st thyself,
    'Tis he hath sent us hither now to slaughter thee.
CLARENCE It cannot be, for when I parted with him,
    He hugged me in his arms, and swore with sobs   220
    That he would labour my delivery.
2 EXECUTIONER Why, so he doth; now he delivers thee
    From this world's thraldom to the joys of heaven.
1 EXECUTIONER Make peace with God, for you must die, my lord.
CLARENCE Hast thou that holy feeling in thy soul   225
    To counsel me to make my peace with God?
    And art thou yet to thy own soul so blind
    That thou wilt war with God by murdering me?
    Ah sirs, consider: he that set you on
    To do this deed will hate you for this deed.   230

*197 struck] F (strucke); stroke Q1; strooke Q2–6 199 the devil] Q; our Duty F   fault] Q; Faults F 200 Have brought] Q; Prouoke F   murder] Q; slaughter F 201 O, if you] Q; If you do F 203 be] Q; are F   meed] Q (meede); neede Q2; need Q3–6; meed F 205 will] Q; shall F 209, 215 SHS BOTH] *Am.* Q; 1 F 212 And charged . . . other,] Q; *om.* F 214 of] Q1–5; on Q6, F 217 thou deceiv'st thyself] Q; Come, you deceiue your selfe F 218 hath . . . thee] Q; that sends vs to destroy you heere F 219 when . . . him] Q; he bewept my Fortune F 222 SH 2 EXECUTIONER] Q (2); 1 F   now] Q; when F 223 world's] Q; earths F 224 SH 1 EXECUTIONER] Q (1); 2 F *Make] F; Makes Q 225 Hast thou] Q; Haue you F   thy soul] Q; your soules F 227 thou] Q; you F   thy] Q; your F   soul] Q; soules F 228 thou wilt] Q; you will F 229 he] Q; they F 230 this] Q; the F

2 EXECUTIONER What shall we do?

CLARENCE   Relent, and save your souls.

1 EXECUTIONER Relent? 'Tis cowardly and womanish.

CLARENCE Not to relent is beastly, savage, devilish.

   [*To 2 Executioner*] My friend, I spy some pity in thy looks:

   O, if thy eye be not a flatterer,   235

   Come thou on my side and entreat for me.

   A begging prince, what beggar pities not?

1 EXECUTIONER Ay, thus, and thus! (*He stabs him*) If this will not serve,

   I'll chop thee in the malmsey butt in the next room.   [*Exit*]

2 EXECUTIONER A bloody deed and desperately performed.   240

   How fain like Pilate would I wash my hand

   Of this most grievous guilty murder done.

      [*Enter* 1 EXECUTIONER]

1 EXECUTIONER Why dost thou not help me?

   By heavens, the Duke shall know how slack thou art.

2 EXECUTIONER I would he knew that I had saved his brother.   245

   Take thou the fee, and tell him what I say,

   For I repent me that the Duke is slain.   *Exit*

1 EXECUTIONER So do not I. Go, coward, as thou art!

   Now I must hide his body in some hole

   Until the Duke take order for his burial.   250

   And when I have my meed I must away:

   For this will out, and here I must not stay.   *Exeunt*

[2.1] [*Flourish*]. *Enter* KING [EDWARD *sick*], QUEEN [ELIZABETH], HASTINGS,
RIVERS, DORSET, [BUCKINGHAM, *and* GREY]

EDWARD So, now I have done a good day's work.

   You peers, continue this united league.

   I every day expect an embassage

   From my Redeemer to redeem me hence,

   And now in peace my soul shall part to heaven,   5

231–2 souls. / Relent] Q; soules: / Which of you, if you were a Princes Sonne, / [*three lines*] / Were you in my distresse.
/ Relent F 232 'Tis] Q (tis); no: 'Tis F •234 SD *To 2 Executioner*] *after Arden; not in* Q, F 235 thy] Q; thine
F 237–8 pities not ? / Ay, thus] Q; pitties not. / 2 Looke behinde you, my Lord. / 1 Take that F 238 Ay, thus . . . not
serve] Q (SD *at end of line*); Take that, and that, if all this will not do, *Stabs him.* F 239 chop thee] Q; drowne you F in
the next room] Q; within F •SD *Exit.*] F; *om.* Q 240 performed] Q; dispatcht F 241 hand] Q; hands
F 242 grievous guilty murder done] Q; greeuous murther F •242 SD *Enter* 1 EXECUTIONER] F (*Murtherer*); *om.*
Q 243 Why . . . me?] Q; How now? what mean'st thou that thou help'st me not? F 244 heavens] Q; Heauen F thou
art] Q; you have beene F 249 Now . . . his] Q; Well, Ile go hide the F 250 Until] Q; Till F take] Q; giue
F 251 must] Q; will F 252 here] Q; then F 0 SD *Flourish . . .* GREY] *Enter King, Queene, Hastings, Ryuers, Dorcet,
&c.* Q; F *adds* Catesby *and* Woodville (*for* Rivers) *and omits* Grey 1 So] Q; Why so F I have] Q; haue I F 5 now in]
Q; more to F to] Q1 (*three copies*), Q3–6, F; *from* Q1 (*two copies*), Q2

   Since I have set my friends at peace on earth
   Rivers and Hastings, take each other's hand:
   Dissemble not your hatred; swear your love.
RIVERS By heaven, my heart is purged from grudging hate,
   And with my hand I seal my true heart's love.   10
HASTINGS So thrive I, as I truly swear the like.
EDWARD Take heed you dally not before your King
   Lest he that is the supreme King of Kings
   Confound your hidden falsehood and award
   Either of you to be the other's end.   15
HASTINGS So prosper I, as I swear perfect love.
RIVERS And I, as I love Hastings with my heart.
EDWARD Madam, your self are not exempt in this,
   Nor your son, Dorset; Buckingham, nor you.
   You have been factious one against the other.   20
   Wife, love Lord Hastings, let him kiss your hand,
   And what you do, do it unfeignedly.
ELIZABETH Here, Hastings, I will never more remember
   Our former hatred, so thrive I and mine.
DORSET This interchange of love, I here protest,   25
   Upon my part shall be inviolable.
HASTINGS And so swear I, my lord.
        [They embrace]
EDWARD Now, princely Buckingham, seal thou this league
   With thy embracements to my wife's allies,
   And make me happy in your unity.   30
BUCKINGHAM Whenever Buckingham doth turn his hate
   On you or yours, but with all duteous love
   Doth cherish you and yours, God punish me
   With hate, in those where I expect most love.
   When I have most need to employ a friend,   35
   And most assured that he is a friend,
   Deep, hollow, treacherous, and full of guile
   Be he unto me: this do I beg of God,
   When I am cold in zeal to you or yours.
EDWARD A pleasing cordial, princely Buckingham,   40
   Is this thy vow unto my sickly heart.
   There wanteth now our brother Gloucester here
   To make the perfect period of this peace.

---

6 set] Q; made F 7 Rivers and Hastings] Q; *Dorset and Riuers* F 9 heart] Q; soule F 18 are] Q; is F in] Q; from
F 19 your] Q; you F 23 Here] Q; There F 24–5 mine. / DORSET This] Q; mine. / *King. Dorset,* imbrace him: /
Hastings, loue Lord Marquesse. / *Dor.* This F *26 inviolable] F; vnuiolable Q 27 I, my lord] Q; I F *27 SD *They
embrace*] Capell; *not in* Q, F 32 On you or yours] Q; Vpon your Grace F 38 God] Q; heauen F 39 zeal] Q; loue F
yours.] Q; yours. *Embrace* F 43 perfect] Q; blessed F

BUCKINGHAM And in good time: here comes the noble Duke.

Enter GLOUCEST[ER]

GLOUCESTER Good morrow to my sovereign King and Queen,   45
    And princely peers: a happy time of day!
EDWARD Happy indeed, as we have spent the day.
    Brother, we have done deeds of charity,
    Made peace of enmity, fair love of hate,
    Between these swelling, wrong-incensed peers.   50
GLOUCESTER A blessed labour, my most sovereign liege.
    Amongst this princely heap, if any here
    By false intelligence or wrong surmise,
    Hold me a foe, if I unwittingly or in my rage
    Have aught committed that is hardly borne   55
    By any in this presence, I desire
    To reconcile me to his friendly peace.
    'Tis death to me to be at enmity.
    I hate it, and desire all good men's love.
    First, madam, I entreat true peace of you,   60
    Which I will purchase with my duteous service;
    Of you, my noble cousin Buckingham
    If ever any grudge were lodged between us;
    Of you, Lord Rivers, and Lord Grey, of you,
    That all without desert have frowned on me: 65
    Dukes, earls, lords, gentlemen, indeed of all.
    I do not know that Englishman alive,
    With whom my soul is any jot at odds,
    More than the infant that is born tonight.
    I thank my God for my humility.   70
ELIZABETH A holy day shall this be kept hereafter;
    I would to God all strifes were well compounded.
    My sovereign liege, I do beseech your majesty,
    To take our brother Clarence to your grace.
GLOUCESTER Why, madam, have I offered love for this –   75
    To be thus scorned in this royal presence?
    Who knows not that the noble Duke is dead?
             [*They all start*]
    You do him injury to scorn his corse.
RIVERS Who knows not he is dead! Who knows he is?

44 the noble Duke] Q; Sir *Richard Ratcliffe*, and the Duke F   44 SD *Enter* GLOUCESTER | Q (*Glocest.*); *Enter Ratcliffe, and Gloster.* F   48 Brother] Q; Gloster F   51 liege] Q; Lord F   52 Amongst] Q; Among F   54 unwittingly] Q; vnwillingly F   56 By] Q; To F   64 Of . . . of you] Q; Of you and you, Lord *Riuers* and of *Dorset* F   65–6 me: / Dukes] Q; me: / Of you Lord *Wooduill*, and Lord *Scales* of you, / Dukes F   73 liege] Q; Lord F   majesty] Q; Highnesse F   76 thus scorned] Q; so flowted F   77 noble] Q; gentle F   •77 SD *They all start*] F; *not in* Q   79 SH RIVERS] Q (*Ryu.*); King. F

ELIZABETH All-seeing heaven, what a world is this?   80
BUCKINGHAM Look I so pale, Lord Dorset, as the rest?
DORSET Ay, my good lord, and no one in this presence
 But his red colour hath forsook his cheeks.
EDWARD Is Clarence dead? The order was reversed.
GLOUCESTER But he, poor soul, by your first order died,   85
 And that a winged Mercury did bear;
 Some tardy cripple bore the countermand
 That came too lag to see him buried.
 God grant that some, less noble and less loyal,
 Nearer in bloody thoughts, but not in blood,   90
 Deserve not worse than wretched Clarence did,
 And yet go current from suspicion.

Enter DERBY

DERBY A boon, my sovereign, for my service done!
EDWARD I pray thee peace, my soul is full of sorrow.
DERBY I will not rise unless your Highness grant –   95
EDWARD Then speak at once: what is it thou demand'st?
DERBY The forfeit, Sovereign, of my servant's life,
 Who slew today a riotous gentleman
 Lately attendant on the Duke of Norfolk.
EDWARD Have I a tongue to doom my brother's death,   100
 And shall the same give pardon to a slave?
 My brother slew no man; his fault was thought,
 And yet his punishment was cruel death.
 Who sued to me for him? Who, in my rage,
 Kneeled at my feet and bad me be advised?   105
 Who spake of brotherhood? Who of love?
 Who told me how the poor soul did forsake
 The mighty Warwick, and did fight for me?
 Who told me, in the field by Tewkesbury,
 When Oxford had me down, he rescued me,   110
 And said, 'Dear brother, live, and be a king'?
 Who told me, when we both lay in the field,
 Frozen almost to death, how he did lap me
 Even in his own garments, and gave himself
 All thin and naked to the numb-cold night?   115
 All this from my remembrance brutish wrath

82 Ay...no one in this] Q (I); I...no man in the F 85 soul] Q; man F *86 winged] Q2 6, F; wingled
Q1 87 bore] Q; bare F *89 some, less noble] *ed;* some less noble, Q, F 90 but] Q; and F *blood] Q4–6, F; blond Q1;
bloud Q2–3 94 pray thee] Q; prethee F 95 grant] Q; heare me F 96 speak] Q; say F demand'st] Q; requests
F 101 the same] Q; that tongue F 102 slew] Q; kill'd F 103 cruel] Q; bitter F 104 rage] Q; wrath F 105 at] Q;
and F bad] Q; bid F 106 spake] Q; spoke F Who] Q; who spoke F 109 by] Q; at F 114 own garments] Q;
Garments F gave] Q; did giue F

> Sinfully plucked and not a man of you
> Had so much grace to put it in my mind.
> But when your carters, or your waiting vassals,
> Have done a drunken slaughter, and defaced　　　　　120
> The precious image of our dear Redeemer,
> You straight are on your knees for 'Pardon! Pardon!'
> And I, unjustly too, must grant it you.
> But for my brother, not a man would speak,
> Nor I, ungracious, speak unto myself　　　　　125
> For him, poor soul. The proudest of you all
> Have been beholding to him in his life:
> Yet none of you would once plead for his life.
> O God! I fear Thy justice will take hold
> On me, and you, and mine, and yours for this.　　　　　130
> Come, Hastings, help me to my closet.
> O poor Clarence!

　　　　　　　　　　[*Exeunt, except Gloucester and Buckingham*]

GLOUCESTER This is the fruit of rashness. Marked you not
> How that the guilty kindred of the Queen
> Looked pale when they did hear of Clarence' death?　　　　　135
> O, they did urge it still unto the King!
> God will revenge it. But come, let's in
> To comfort Edward with our company.

　　　　　　　　　　　　　　　　　　　　Exeunt

[2.2] *Enter* [*the old*] DUCHESS OF YORK, *with* [*the two*] CHILDREN *of* CLARENCE

BOY Tell me, good Granam, is our father dead?
DUCHESS No, boy.
BOY Why do you wring your hands, and beat your breast,
> And cry, 'O Clarence, my unhappy son'?
GIRL Why do you look on us and shake your head,　　　　　5
> And call us wretches, orphans, castaways,
> If that our noble father be alive?
DUCHESS My pretty cousins, you mistake me much.
> I do lament the sickness of the King,
> As loath to lose him – not your father's death:　　　　　10

•117 plucked] Q2–6, F (pluckt); puckt Q1　128 plead] Q; begge F　132 SD *Exeunt . . . Buckingham*] *Exit.* Q (*after* 130);
Exeunt some with K. & Queen. F (*after* 132)　133 fruit] Q; fruits F　137 But come, lets in] Q; Come Lords will you go,
F　138 company.] Q; company. / *Buc.* We wait vpon your Grace. F　•0 SD *Enter . . .* CLARENCE] F; *Enter Dutches of
Yorke, with Clarence Children.* Q　1 SH BOY] Q; *Edw.* F　Tell . . . Granam] Q; Good Grandam tell vs F　3 SH BOY] Q;
Daugh. F　you wring your hands] Q; do weepe so oft F　5 SH GIRL] Q; *Boy* F　6 wretches, orphans] Q; Orphans,
Wretches F　7 be] Q; were F　8 much] Q; both F　•10 lose] F; loose Q

It were lost labour to weep for one that's lost.

BOY Then, Granam, you conclude that he is dead:
The King, my uncle, is to blame for this.
God will revenge it, whom I will importune
With daily prayers, all to that effect.   15

DUCHESS Peace, children, peace. The King doth love you well.
Incapable and shallow innocents,
You cannot guess who caused your father's death.

BOY Granam, we can: for my good uncle Gloucester
Told me the King, provoked by the Queen,   20
Devised impeachments to imprison him;
And when he told me so, he wept,
And hugged me in his arm, and kindly kissed my cheek,
And bad me rely on him as in my father,
And he would love me dearly as his child.   25

DUCHESS O, that deceit should steal such gentle shapes,
And with a virtuous visard hide foul guile!
He is my son, yea, and therein my shame,
Yet from my dugs he drew not this deceit.

BOY Think you my uncle did dissemble, Granam?   30

DUCHESS Ay, boy.

BOY I cannot think it. Hark, what noise is this?

Enter the QUEE[N *with her hair about her ears*]

ELIZABETH O! Who shall hinder me to wail and weep?
To chide my fortune, and torment myself?
I'll join with black despair against my soul,   35
And to myself become an enemy.

DUCHESS What means this scene of rude impatience?

ELIZABETH To make an act of tragic violence:
Edward, my lord, your son, our King, is dead.
Why grow the branches now the root is withered?   40
Why wither not the leaves, the sap being gone?
If you will live, lament; if die, be brief,
That our swift-winged souls may catch the King's,
Or, like obedient subjects, follow him
To his new kingdom of perpetual rest.   45

---

11 labour to weep for] Q; sorrow to waile F   12 Granam . . . that] Q; you conclude, (my Grandam) F   13 my] Q; mine
F *to] F; too Q   this] Q; it F   15 daily] Q; earnest F   15–16 effect. / Peace] Q; effect. / *Daugh.* And so will I. / *Dut.*
Peace F   19 Granam] Q; Grandam F   20 by] Q; to it by F   22 he] Q; my Vnckle F   23 hugged me in his arm] Q;
pittied me F *cheek] Q2–5, F; checke Q1; cheekes Q6   24 And bad] Q; Bad F   as in] Q; as on F   25 his] Q; a F
26 shapes] Q; shape F   27 visard] Q; Vizor F   foul guile] Q; deepe vice F   30 Granam] Q; Grandam F   32 SD
Enter . . . ears] *Enter the* / *Quee.* Q (*end of* 32–3); *Enter the Queene with her haire about her ears,* / *Riuers & Dorset after her.*
F   39 your] Q; thy F   40 now] Q; when F   withered] Q; gone F   41 the sap being gone] Q; that want their sap F
45 perpetual rest] Q; nere-changing night F

DUCHESS Ah, so much interest have I in thy sorrow
    As I had title in thy noble husband.
    I have bewept a worthy husband's death,
    And lived by looking on his images;
    But now two mirrors of his princely semblance   50
    Are cracked in pieces by malignant death;
    And I for comfort have but one false glass,
    Which grieves me when I see my shame in him.
    Thou art a widow, yet thou art a mother,
    And hast the comfort of thy children left thee;   55
    But death hath snatched my husband from mine arms
    And plucked two crutches from my feeble limbs:
    Edward and Clarence. O, What cause have I,
    Thine being but a moiety of my grief,
    To overgo thy plaints and drown thy cries?   60
BOY Good aunt, you wept not for our father's death,
    How can we aid you with our kindred's tears?
GIRL Our fatherless distress was left unmoaned;
    Your widow's dolours likewise be unwept.
ELIZABETH Give me no help in lamentation;   65
    I am not barren to bring forth laments.
    All springs reduce their currents to mine eyes,
    That I being governed by the watery moon,
    May send forth plenteous tears to drown the world.
    O for my husband! For my heir, Lord Edward!   70
CHILDREN O for our father, for our dear Lord Clarence!
DUCHESS Alas for both, both mine Edward and Clarence.
ELIZABETH What stay had I but Edward, and he is gone.
CHILDREN What stay had we but Clarence, and he is gone.
DUCHESS What stays had I but they, and they are gone.   75
ELIZABETH Was never widow had so dear a loss.
CHILDREN Was never orphans had a dearer loss.
DUCHESS Was never mother had a dearer loss.
    Alas, I am the mother of these moans.
    Their woes are parcelled, mine are general.   80
    She for Edward weeps, and so do I;
    I for a Clarence weep, so doth not she;
    These babes for Clarence weep, and so do I;

46 I in] Q; in F 49 by] Q; with F *50 But] F; Bnt Q 53 Which] Q; That F 55 left thee] Q; left F
*56 husband F; children Q 57 limbs] Q; hands F 58 Edward and Clarence] Q; *Clarence*, and *Edward* F
*59 Thine] F; Then Q *a moiety] F; moity Q grief] Q; moane F 60 plaints] Q; woes F 61 Good] Q; Ah F
62 kindred's] Q (kindreds); Kindred F 64 widow's dolours] Q (widdowes); widdow-dolour F 66 laments] Q; complaints F *68 moon] F; moane Q 70 heir] Q (eire); dear F 71, 74, 77 SHS CHILDREN] *Ambo, Am., Ambo.* Q; Chil.
F 77 and 78 a dearer] Q; so deere a F 79 moans] Q; Greefes F 80 are] Q; is F 81 for] Q; for an F 82 weep] Q;
weepes F 83–4 and so do I; / I for an Edward weep,] Q; *om.* F

I for an Edward weep, so do not they.
Alas, you three, on me threefold distressed,   85
Pour all your tears; I am your sorrow's nurse,
And I will pamper it with lamentations.

Enter GLOUCEST[ER, BUCKINGHAM, DERBY, HASTINGS, *and* RATCLIFFE]

GLOUCESTER Madam, have comfort, all of us have cause
        To wail the dimming of our shining star,
        But none can cure their harms by wailing them.   90
        Madam my mother, I do cry you mercy;
        I did not see your Grace. Humbly on my knee
        I crave your blessing.
DUCHESS God bless thee, and put meekness in thy mind,
        Love, charity, obedience, and true duty.   95
GLOUCESTER Amen; [*Aside*] and make me die a good old man:
        That's the butt-end of a mother's blessing.
        I marvel why her Grace did leave it out.
BUCKINGHAM You cloudy princes and heart-sorrowing peers
        That bear this mutual heavy load of moan,   100
        Now cheer each other in each other's love.
        Though we have spent our harvest of this king,
        We are to reap the harvest of his son.
        The broken rancour of your high-swollen hearts,
        But lately splintered, knit, and joined together,   105
        Must gently be preserved, cherished, and kept.
        Me seemeth good that with some little train,
        Forthwith from Ludlow the young Prince be fetched
        Hither to London, to be crowned our King.
GLOUCESTER Then be it so, and go we to determine   110
        Who they shall be that straight shall post to Ludlow.
        Madam, and you my mother, will you go
        To give your censures in this weighty business?
ELIZABETH, DUCHESS With all our hearts.
                        Exeunt all except Gloucester and Buckingham
BUCKINGHAM My lord, whoever journeys to the Prince,   115
        For God's sake let not us two stay behind,
        For by the way I'll sort occasion,

---

86 Pour] Q; Proue Q2; Powre Q3–6; Power F   87   lamentations.] Q; Lamentation. F [*then follow seven lines for Dorset and
five for Rivers*]   *87 SD *Enter . . . *RATCLIFFE] F; *Enter Glocest. with others.* Q   88 Madam] Q; Sister F   90 cure their]
Q; helpe our F   94 mind] Q; breast F   98 why] Q; that F   100 mutual heavy] Q; heauie mutuall F   104 hearts] Q;
hates F   105 splintered] Q1 (splinterd); splinted Q2–6; splinter'd F   * together] Q2–6, F; etogether Q1   109–10 King.
/ Then be it so] Q; King. / [*then follow nineteen lines divided between Rivers, Buckingham, Richard, Hastings*] / Then be it
so F   111 Ludlow] Q; London F   112 mother] Q; Sister F   113 weighty business] Q; businesse F   114 SH
ELIZABETH, DUCHESS With all our hearts] Q (*Ans.*); *not in* F   114 SD *Exeunt . . . Buckingham*] Exeunt man. Glo. Buck.
Q; *Exeunt. / Manet Buckingham, and Richard.* F   116 behind] Q; at home F

As index to the story we late talked of,
To part the Queen's proud kindred from the King.
GLOUCESTER My other self, my counsel's consistory,   120
My oracle, my prophet, my dear cousin:
I, like a child, will go by thy direction.
Towards Ludlow then, for we will not stay behind.

                                                                    [*Exeunt*]

[**2.3**] *Enter two* CITIZENS

1 CITIZEN Neighbour, well met! Whither away so fast?
2 CITIZEN I promise you, I scarcely know myself.
1 CITIZEN Hear you the news abroad?
2 CITIZEN Ay, that the King is dead.
1 CITIZEN Bad news, by'r Lady; seldom comes the better.   5
I fear, I fear, 'twill prove a troublous world.

                          Enter another CITIZEN

3 CITIZEN Good morrow, neighbours. Doth this news hold of good King
Edward's death?
1 CITIZEN It doth.
3 CITIZEN Then masters, look to see a troublous world.   10
1 CITIZEN No, no; by God's good grace his son shall reign.
3 CITIZEN Woe to that land that's governed by a child!
2 CITIZEN In him there is a hope of government,
That in his nonage counsel under him,
And in his full and ripened years himself,   15
No doubt shall then, and till then govern well.
1 CITIZEN So stood the state when Harry the Sixth
Was crowned at Paris, but at nine months old.
3 CITIZEN Stood the state so? No, good my friend, not so,
For then this land was famously enriched   20
With politic grave counsel. Then the King
Had virtuous uncles to protect his Grace.
2 CITIZEN So hath this, both by the father and mother.
3 CITIZEN Better it were they all came by the father
Or by the father there were none at all;   25

119 King] Q; Prince F   122 like] Q; as F   123 Towards Ludlow] Q; Toward London F   *123 SD *Exeunt*] F; *om.* Q
0 SD *Enter two Citizens*] Q; *Enter one Citizen at one doore, and another at / the other.* F   1 Neighbour, well met] Q; Good
morrow Neighbour F   3, 5, 9, 39 SHS 1 CITIZEN] Q (1); 2. F   4, 23, 32 SHS 2 CITIZEN] Q (2); 1. F   4 Ay] Q (I); Yes F
5 Bad] Q; Ill F   6 troublous] Q; troublesome Q2–6; giddy F   7 Good . . . news] Q; Neighbours, God speed. / 1. Giue
you good morrow sir. / 3. Doth the newes F   9 SH 1 CITIZEN It doth.] Q; 2. I sir, it is too true, God helpe the while. F
14 That] Q; Which F   17 Harry] Q; *Henry* F   18 at] Q; in F   19 No . . . so] Q; No, no, good friends, God wot F
23 So] Q; Why so F   23, 24, 25 the] Q; his F

For emulation now, who shall be nearest
Will touch us all too near, if God prevent not.
O, full of danger is the Duke of Gloucester,
And the Queen's kindred, haughty and proud;
And were they to be ruled, and not to rule,   30
This sickly land might solace as before.
2 CITIZEN Come, come. We fear the worst; all shall be well.
3 CITIZEN When clouds appear, wise men put on their cloaks;
            When great leaves fall, the winter is at hand;
            When the sun sets, who doth not look for night?   35
            Untimely storms make men expect a dearth.
            All may be well, but if God sort it so,
            'Tis more than we deserve or I expect.
1 CITIZEN Truly, the souls of men are full of dread.
            Ye cannot, almost, reason with a man   40
            That looks not heavily and full of fear.
3 CITIZEN Before the times of change, still is it so:
            By a divine instinct, men's minds mistrust
            Ensuing dangers, as by proof we see
            The waters swell before a boisterous storm.   45
            But leave it all to God. Whither away?
2 CITIZEN We are sent for to the Justice.
3 CITIZEN And so was I; I'll bear you company.

                                                            Exeunt

[2.4] *Enter* CARDINAL, DUCHESS OF YORK, QUEE[N ELIZABETH,
and the] *young* [DUKE OF] YORK

CARDINAL Last night, I hear, they lay at Northampton;
            At Stony Stratford will they be tonight;
            Tomorrow, or next day, they will be here.
DUCHESS I long with all my heart to see the Prince;
            I hope he is much grown since last I saw him.   5
ELIZABETH But I hear no; they say my son of York
            Hath almost overta'en him in his growth.
YORK Ay, mother; but I would not have it so.
DUCHESS Why, my young cousin, it is good to grow.

26 now, who shall] Q; who shall now F   29 kindred, haughty] Q; Sons, and Brothers, haught F   32 shall be] Q
(shalbe); will be F   33 appear] Q; are seen F   34 the] Q; then F   36 make] Q; makes F   39 souls] Q; hearts F •dread]
Q3–6; bread Q1–2; fear F   40 Ye] Q (Yee); Ye Q2–6; You F   almost, reason] Q; reason (almost) F   41 fear] Q; dread
F   42 times] Q; dayes F   44 Ensuing] Q (*and* F *catchword*); Pursuing F   dangers] Q; danger F   45 waters] Q; Water
F   47 We are] Q; Marry we were F   Justice] Q; Iustices F   0 SD CARDINAL] Q; *Arch-bishop* [*of York*] F (*see Introduction,
p. 27*)   1 SH CARDINAL] Q (*Car.*); *Arch.* F (*throughout scene*)   1 hear] Q1–2; heard Q3–6, F   Northampton] Q; Stony
Stratford F   2 At . . . be] Q; And at Northampton they do rest F   9 my young] Q; my good F

YORK   Grandam, one night as we did sit at supper,   10
        My uncle Rivers talked how I did grow
        More than my brother. 'Ay', quoth my uncle Gloucester,
        'Small herbs have grace, great weeds grow apace.'
        And since, methinks, I would not grow so fast,
        Because sweet flowers are slow, and weeds make haste.   15
DUCHESS Good faith, good faith, the saying did not hold
        In him that did object the same to thee.
        He was the wretchedest thing when he was young –
        So long a-growing, and so leisurely
        That if this were a true rule, he should be gracious   20
CARDINAL Why, madam, so no doubt he is.
DUCHESS I hope so too, but yet let mothers doubt.
YORK   Now by my troth, if I had been remembered,
        I could have given my uncle's Grace a flout
        That should have nearer touched his growth than he did mine.   25
DUCHESS How, my pretty York? I pray thee, let me hear it.
YORK   Marry, they say my uncle grew so fast
        That he could gnaw a crust at two hours' old;
        'Twas full two years ere I could get a tooth.
        Granam, this would have been a biting jest!   30
DUCHESS I pray thee, pretty York, who told thee so?
YORK   Granam, his nurse.
DUCHESS His nurse? Why, she was dead ere thou wert born.
YORK   If 'twere not she, I cannot tell who told me.
ELIZABETH A perilous boy! Go to, you are too shrewd!   35
CARDINAL Good madam, be not angry with the child.
ELIZABETH Pitchers have ears.

                        Enter DORSET

CARDINAL Here comes your son, Lord Marquess Dorset.
        What news, Lord Marquess?
DORSET Such news, my lord, as grieves me to unfold.   40
ELIZABETH How fares the Prince?
DORSET Well, madam, and in health.
DUCHESS What is thy news then?
DORSET Lord Rivers and Lord Gray are sent to Pomfret;
        With them, Sir Thomas Vaughan, prisoners.   45

*12 uncle] F; Nnckle Q 13 grow] Q; do grow F 20 this were a true rule] Q; his rule were true F 21 SH CARDI-
NAL] Q; *Yor.* F Why . . . is] Q; And so no doubt he is, my gracious Madam F 22 so . . . doubt] Q (yer; yet Q2–8); he is,
but yet let Mothers doubt F 25 That . . . mine] Q; To touch his growth, neerer then he toucht mine F 26 pretty] Q;
yong F 30, 32 Granam] Q; Grandam F *30 been] F; heene Q 31 so] Q; this F 33 wert] Q; wast F 35 perilous]
Q; parlous F 36 SH CARDINAL] Q; *Dut.* F 37 SD DORSET] Q; *a Messenger* F 38–9 your . . . Marquess] Q; *a
Messenger:* What Newes? F (*one line*) 40 unfold] Q; report F 41 fares] Q; doth F 43 news then] Q; Newes F
45 With] Q; and with F

DUCHESS Who hath committed them?
DORSET The mighty dukes, Gloucester and Buckingham.
CARDINAL For what offence?
DORSET The sum of all I can I have disclosed.
          Why, or for what, these nobles were committed   50
          Is all unknown to me, my gracious lady.
ELIZABETH Ay me! I see the downfall of our house!
          The tiger now hath seized the gentle hind;
          Insulting tyranny begins to jet
          Upon the innocent and lawless throne.   55
          Welcome destruction, death, and massacre;
          I see, as in a map, the end of all.
DUCHESS Accursed and unquiet wrangling days,
          How many of you have mine eyes beheld?
          My husband lost his life to get the crown,   60
          And often up and down my sons were tossed
          For me to joy and weep their gain and loss;
          And being seated, and domestic broils
          Clean overblown themselves, the conquerors
          Make war upon themselves, blood against blood,   65
          Self against self. O, preposterous
          And frantic outrage, end thy damned spleen,
          Or let me die, to look on death no more.
ELIZABETH Come, come my boy, we will to sanctuary.
DUCHESS I'll go along with you.   70
ELIZABETH You have no cause.
CARDINAL   My gracious lady, go,
          And thither bear your treasure and your goods.
          For my part, I'll resign unto your Grace
          The seal I keep, and so betide to me
          As well I tender you and all of yours.   75
          Come, I'll conduct you to the sanctuary.

                                              Exeunt

[3.1] *The Trumpets sound. Enter young* PRINCE [EDWARD], *the* DUKES OF
GLOUCESTER *and* BUCKINGHAM, CARDINAL, [CATESBY,] *etc.*

BUCKINGHAM Welcome, sweet Prince, to London, to your chamber.
GLOUCESTER Welcome, dear cousin, my thoughts' sovereign.

50 these] Q; the F   51 lady] Q; Lord F   52 downfall of our] Q; ruine of my F   54 jet] Q; Iutt F   55 lawless] Q;
awelesse F   56 death] Q; Blood F   65 themselves, blood against blood] Q; themselues, Brother to Brother; / Blood to
blood F   68 death] Q; earth F   69 sanctuary.] Q; Sanctuary. / Madam, farwell. F   70 I'll go along] Q; Stay, I will go
F   76 Come] Q; Go F

The weary way hath made you melancholy.

PRINCE No, uncle, but our crosses on the way
    Have made it tedious, wearisome, and heavy. 5
    I want more uncles here to welcome me.

GLOUCESTER Sweet Prince, the untainted virtue of your years
    Hath not yet dived into the world's deceit,
    Nor more can you distinguish of a man
    Than of his outward show, which God he knows, 10
    Seldom or never jumpeth with the heart.
    Those uncles which you want were dangerous;
    Your Grace attended to their sugared words,
    But looked not on the poison of their hearts.
    God keep you from them, and from such false friends! 15

PRINCE God keep me from false friends – but they were none.

GLOUCESTER My Lord, the Mayor of London comes to greet you.

Enter LORD MAYOR

MAYOR God bless your Grace with health and happy days.

PRINCE I thank you, good my lord – and thank you all.
    I thought my mother and my brother York 20
    Would long ere this have met us on the way.
    Fie! What a slug is Hastings that he comes not
    To tell us whether they will come or no.

Enter L[ORD] HAST[INGS]

BUCKINGHAM And in good time: here comes the sweating lord.

PRINCE Welcome my lord. What, will our mother come? 25

HASTINGS On what occasion – God he knows, not I –
    The Queen your mother and your brother York
    Have taken sanctuary. The tender Prince
    Would fain have come with me to meet your Grace,
    But by his mother was perforce withheld. 30

BUCKINGHAM Fie! What an indirect and peevish course
    Is this of hers? Lord Cardinal, will your Grace
    Persuade the Queen to send the Duke of York
    Unto his princely brother presently?
    If she deny, Lord Hastings, go with him 35
    And from her jealous arms pluck him perforce.

CARDINAL My Lord of Buckingham, if my weak oratory
    Can from his mother win the Duke of York,
    Anon expect him here; but if she be obdurate
    To mild entreaties, God in heaven forbid 40

9 Nor] Q1–6; No F   40 in heaven] Q1–2; *om.* Q3–6, F

We should infringe the holy privilege
Of blessed sanctuary. Not for all this land
Would I be guilty of so deep a sin.
BUCKINGHAM You are too senseless-obstinate, my lord,
  Too ceremonious and traditional.   45
  Weigh it but with the grossness of this age!
  You break not sanctuary in seizing him;
  The benefit thereof is always granted
  To those whose dealings have deserved the place,
  And those who have the wit to claim the place.   50
  This Prince hath neither claimed it nor deserved it,
  And therefore, in mine opinion, cannot have it.
  Then taking him from thence that is not there,
  You break no privilege nor charter there.
  Oft have I heard of sanctuary-men,   55
  But sanctuary-children – never till now!
CARDINAL My lord, you shall o'er-rule my mind for once.
  Come on, Lord Hastings, will you go with me?
HASTINGS I go, my lord.
PRINCE Good lords, make all the speedy haste you may.   60
                              [*Exeunt Cardinal and Hastings*]
  Say, uncle Gloucester, if our brother come,
  Where shall we sojourn till our coronation?
GLOUCESTER Where it seems best unto your royal self.
  If I may counsel you, some day or two
  Your Highness shall repose you at the Tower.   65
  Then, where you please, and shall be thought most fit
  For your best health and recreation.
PRINCE I do not like the Tower of any place.
  Did Julius Caesar build that place, my lord?
BUCKINGHAM He did, my gracious lord, begin that place,   70
  Which since, succeeding ages have re-edified.
PRINCE Is it upon record, or else reported
  Successively from age to age, he built it?
BUCKINGHAM Upon record, my gracious lord.
PRINCE But say, my lord, it were not registered,   75
  Methinks the truth should live from age to age,
  As 'twere retailed to all posterity,
  Even to the general all-ending day.
GLOUCESTER [*Aside*] So wise, so young, they say do never live long.
PRINCE What say you, uncle?   80

---

43 deep] Q1–2; great Q3–6, F •60 SD *Exeunt . . . Hastings*] at 59 Q3–6, F; *om.* Q1–2 63 seems] Q1–2; think'st Q3–6,
F 78 all-ending] Q; ending Q2–6, F

GLOUCESTER I say, without characters fame lives long.
   [*Aside*] Thus, like the formal Vice, Iniquity,
   I moralize two meanings in one word.
PRINCE That Julius Caesar was a famous man;
   With what his valour did enrich his wit,   85
   His wit set down to make his valour live.
   Death makes no conquest of this conqueror,
   For now he lives in fame though not in life.
   I'll tell you what, my cousin Buckingham –
BUCKINGHAM What, my gracious lord?   90
PRINCE And if I live until I be a man,
   I'll win our ancient right in France again,
   Or die a soldier as I lived a king.
GLOUCESTER Short summers lightly have a forward spring.

    Enter young YORK, HASTINGS, [*and*] CARDINAL

BUCKINGHAM Now in good time, here comes the Duke of York. 95
PRINCE Richard of York: how fares our loving brother?
YORK Well, my dread lord – so must I call you now.
PRINCE Ay, brother, to our grief, as it is yours;
   Too late he died that might have kept that title,
   Which by his death hath lost much majesty.   100
GLOUCESTER How fares our cousin, noble lord of York?
YORK I thank you, gentle uncle. O my lord,
   You said that idle weeds are fast in growth:
   The Prince my brother hath outgrown me far.
GLOUCESTER He hath, my lord.
YORK   And therefore – is he idle?   105
GLOUCESTER O my fair cousin, I must not say so!
YORK Then he is more beholding to you than I.
GLOUCESTER He may command me as my sovereign,
   But you have power in me as in a kinsman.
YORK I pray you, uncle, give me this dagger.   110
GLOUCESTER My dagger, little cousin? With all my heart.
PRINCE A beggar, brother?
YORK Of my kind uncle that I know will give,
   And being but a toy, which is no grief to give.
GLOUCESTER A greater gift than that I'll give my cousin. 115
YORK A greater gift? O, that's the sword to it!
GLOUCESTER Ay, gentle cousin, were it light enough.
YORK O, then I see you will part but with light gifts;

---

*86 valour] Q3–6, F; valure Q1–2 87 this] Q1; his Q2–6, F 96 loving] Q1–2; noble Q3–6, F (Noble) 97 dread] Q1–2; deare Q3–6, F

In weightier things you'll say a beggar nay.
GLOUCESTER It is too heavy for your Grace to wear.   120
YORK I weigh it lightly were it heavier.
GLOUCESTER What, would you have my weapon, little lord?
YORK I would, that I might thank you as you call me.
GLOUCESTER How?
YORK Little!   125
PRINCE My lord of York will still be cross in talk.
    Uncle, your Grace knows how to bear with him.
YORK You mean to bear me, not to bear with me.
    Uncle, my brother mocks both you and me;
    Because that I am little, like an ape,   130
    He thinks that you should bear me on your shoulders.
BUCKINGHAM With what a sharp-provided wit he reasons!
    To mitigate the scorn he gives his uncle
    He prettily and aptly taunts himself.
    So cunning and so young is wonderful.   135
GLOUCESTER My lord, will't please you pass along?
    Myself and my good cousin, Buckingham,
    Will to your mother to entreat of her
    To meet you at the Tower and welcome you.
YORK What, will you go unto the Tower, my lord?   140
PRINCE My Lord Protector needs will have it so.
YORK I shall not sleep in quiet at the Tower.
GLOUCESTER Why, what should you fear?
YORK Marry, my uncle Clarence' angry ghost!
    My Granam told me he was murdered there.   145
PRINCE I fear no uncles dead.
GLOUCESTER Nor none that live, I hope.
PRINCE And if they live, I hope I need not fear:
    But come, my lord. With a heavy heart,
    Thinking on them, go I unto the Tower.   150

              Exeunt Prin[ce,] Yor[k,] Hast[ings, and all except]
              [Gloucester,] Buck[ingham, and Catesby]

BUCKINGHAM Think you, my lord, this little prating York
    Was not incensed by his subtle mother
    To taunt and scorn you thus opprobriously?
GLOUCESTER No doubt, no doubt. O, 'tis a perilous boy –
    Bold, quick, ingenious, forward, capable –   155
    He is all the mother's, from the top to toe.

---

120 heavy] Q1; waightie Q2, 4; weightie Q3, 5, 6, F   **123** as] Q; as as Q3; as, as, F   **141** needs] Q1; *om.* Q2–6, F
145 Granam] Q1–6; Grandam F   **149** With] Q1–6 (with); and with F   **150** SD *Exeunt . . . Catesby*] *Exeunt Prin. Yor. Hast. Dors. manet, Rich. Buck.* Q; *A Senet. Exeunt Prince, Yorke, Hastings, and Dorset. / Manet Richard, Buckingham, and Catesby.* F

BUCKINGHAM Well, let them rest. Come hither, Catesby.
       Thou art sworn as deeply to effect what we intend
       As closely to conceal what we impart.
       Thou knowest our reasons urged upon the way.   160
       What thinkest thou? Is it not an easy matter
       To make William Lord Hastings of our mind
       For the instalment of this noble Duke
       In the seat royal of this famous isle?
CATESBY He for his father's sake so loves the Prince   165
       That he will not be won to aught against him.
BUCKINGHAM What thinkest thou then of Stanley? What will he?
CATESBY He will do all in all as Hastings doth.
BUCKINGHAM Well then, no more but this:
       Go gentle Catesby, and as it were afar off,   170
       Sound thou Lord Hastings, how he stands affected
       Unto our purpose – if he be willing,
       Encourage him and show him all our reasons.
       If he be leaden, icy, cold, unwilling,
       Be thou so too, and so break off your talk   175
       And give us notice of his inclination:
       For we tomorrow hold divided Councils
       Wherein thyself shalt highly be employed.
GLOUCESTER Commend me to Lord William; tell him, Catesby,
       His ancient knot of dangerous adversaries   180
       Tomorrow are let blood at Pomfret Castle,
       And bid my friend, for joy of this good news,
       Give Mistress Shore one gentle kiss the more.
BUCKINGHAM Good Catesby, effect this business soundly.
CATESBY My good lords both, with all the heed I may.   185
GLOUCESTER Shall we hear from you, Catesby, ere we sleep?
CATESBY You shall, my lord.
GLOUCESTER At Crosby Place, there shall you find us both.

                                          [Exit Catesby]

BUCKINGHAM Now, my lord, what shall we do if we perceive
       William, Lord Hastings, will not yield to our complots?   190
GLOUCESTER Chop off his head, man! Somewhat we will do.
       And look when I am king, claim thou of me
       The earldom of Hereford and the moveables
       Whereof the King my brother stood possessed.

---

167 What will] Q; Will not F   172–3 Unto . . . Encourage] Q; to our purpose, / And summon him to morrow to the
Tower, / To sit about the Coronation. / If thou do'st finde him tractable to vs, / Encourage F   173 show] Q; tell F
175 your] Q; the F   182 friend] Q; Lord F   184 effect] Q; goe effect F   185 lords] Q (Lo:), F Lords   may] Q; can F
188 Place] Q (place); House F   *188 SD *Exit Catesby*] Q3–6, F; *om.* Q1–2   190 William, Lord] Q; Lord F   *191 off]
F; of Q   head, man] Q; Head F   Somewhat we will do] Q; Something wee will determine F (*on line on its own*)   193 and]
Q; and all F   194 stood] Q; was F

BUCKINGHAM I'll claim that promise at your Grace's hands.   195
GLOUCESTER And look to have it yielded with all willingness.
          Come, let us sup betimes, that afterwards
          We may digest our complots in some form.

                                                  Exeunt

[3.2] *Enter a* MESSENGER *to* LORD HASTINGS['*s door*]

MESSENGER   What ho, my lord!
HASTINGS Who knocks at the door?
MESSENGER A messenger from the Lord Stanley.

                    Enter HASTINGS

HASTINGS What's o'clock?
MESSENGER   Upon the stroke of four.
HASTINGS Cannot thy master sleep these tedious nights?   5
MESSENGER So it should seem by that I have to say.
          First he commends him to your noble lordship.
HASTINGS And then?
MESSENGER   And then he sends you word
          He dreamt tonight the boar had raised his helm;
          Besides, he says there are two Councils held,   10
          And that may be determined at the one
          Which may make you and him to rue at the other.
          Therefore he sends to know your lordship's pleasure,
          If presently you will take horse with him
          And with all speed post into the north   15
          To shun the danger that his soul divines.
HASTINGS Go, fellow, go; return unto thy lord,
          Bid him not fear the separated Councils;
          His honour and myself are at the one,
          And at the other is my servant, Catesby,   20
          Where nothing can proceed that toucheth us
          Whereof I shall not have intelligence.
          Tell him his fears are shallow, wanting instance,
          And for his dreams, I wonder he is so fond

195 hands] Q; hand F   196 willingness] Q; kindnesse F   *0 SD Enter ... door] *Enter a Messenger to the Doore of Hastings.* F; *Enter a Messenger to Lo: Hastings.* Q   1 What ho, my lord] Q; My Lord, my Lord F   2 Who ... door] Q; Who knockes F   3 A messenger] Q; One F   3 SD *Enter* HASTINGS] Q (*end of line 3*); *Enter Lord Hastings.* F (*after line 5*)   4 What's] Q; What is't F   5 thy master] Q; my Lord *Stanley* F   6 should seem] Q; appeares F   7 lordship] Q; selfe F   8 And then?] Q; What then? F   8–9 And then he sends ... tonight] Q; Then certifies your Lordship, that this Night / He dreamt, F   *9 boar] F (Bore); beare Q   raised] Q1–4 (raste); caste Q5–6; rased off F   10 held] Q; kept F   14 presently you will] Q; you will presently F   15 into] Q; with him toward F   18 Councils] Q (counsels); Councell F   20 servant] Q; good friend F   23 wanting] Q; without F   24 he is so fond] Q; hee's so simple F

To trust the mockery of unquiet slumbers.   25
To fly the boar before the boar pursues us
Were to incense the boar to follow us
And make pursuit where he did mean no chase.
Go, bid thy master rise and come to me,
And we will both together to the Tower,   30
Where he shall see the boar will use us kindly.
MESSENGER My gracious lord, I'll tell him what you say.   [*Exit*]

Enter CATES[BY]

CATESBY Many good morrows to my noble lord.
HASTINGS Good morrow, Catesby. You are early stirring.
What news, what news in this our tottering state?   35
CATESBY It is a reeling world indeed, my lord,
And I believe it will never stand upright
Till Richard wear the garland of the realm.
HASTINGS How? Wear the garland? Dost thou mean the crown?
CATESBY Ay, my good lord.   40
HASTINGS I'll have this crown of mine cut from my shoulders
Ere I will see the crown so foul misplaced.
But canst thou guess that he doth aim at it?
CATESBY Upon my life, my lord, and hopes to find you forward
Upon his party for the gain thereof,   45
And thereupon he sends you this good news,
That this same very day, your enemies,
The kindred of the Queen, must die at Pomfret.
HASTINGS Indeed, I am no mourner for that news,
Because they have been still mine enemies;   50
But that I'll give my voice on Richard's side
To bar my master's heirs in true descent –
God knows I will not do it – to the death.
CATESBY God keep your lordship in that gracious mind.
HASTINGS But I shall laugh at this a twelvemonth hence,   55
That they who brought me in my master's hate,
I live to look upon their tragedy.
I tell thee, Catesby –
CATESBY   What, my lord?
HASTINGS Ere a fortnight make me elder,
I'll send some packing that yet think not on it.   60
CATESBY 'Tis a vile thing to die, my gracious lord,
When men are unprepared and look not for it.
HASTINGS O monstrous, monstrous! And so falls it out

26 pursues us] Q; pursues F   **32** My . . . I'll] Q; Ile goe, my Lord, and F   **37** it will] Q1 2; twill Q3–8; will F   **42** Ere
I will] Q; Before Ile F   **44** Upon my life, my lord,] Q; I, on my life, F   **50** mine enemies] Q; my aduersaries F   **56** who]
Q; which F   **58** I tell . . . my lord?] Q; Well *Catesby*, F   **59** elder] Q; older F   **60** on it] Q; on't F

With Rivers, Vaughan, Grey; and so 'twill do
With some men else who think themselves as safe   65
As thou and I, who, as thou knowest, are dear
To princely Richard and to Buckingham.
CATESBY The Princes both make high account of you –
[*Aside*] For they account his head upon the bridge.
HASTINGS I know they do, and I have well deserved it.   70

Enter LORD STANLEY [EARL OF DERBY]

What, my lord: where is your boar-spear, man?
Fear you the boar and go so unprovided?
DERBY My lord, good morrow; good morrow, Catesby.
You may jest on, but by the holy rood,
I do not like these several Councils, I.   75
HASTINGS My lord, I hold my life as dear as you do yours,
And never in my life, I do protest,
Was it more precious to me than it is now:
Think you, but that I know our state secure
I would be so triumphant as I am?   80
DERBY The lords at Pomfret, when they rode from London,
Were jocund and supposed their states was sure;
And they indeed had no cause to mistrust;
But yet you see how soon the day overcast.
This sudden scab of rancour I misdoubt;   85
Pray God, I say, I prove a needless coward.
But come, my lord, shall we to the Tower?
HASTINGS I go – but stay: hear you not the news?
This day those men you talked of are beheaded.
DERBY They for their truth might better wear their heads   90
Than some that have accused them wear their hats.
But come my lord, let us away.

Enter HASTIN[GS,] *a Pursu*[*iv*]*ant*

HASTINGS Go you before, I'll follow presently.
                              [*Exit Lord Stanley and Catesby*]
Well met, Hastings; how goes the world with thee?
PURSUIVANT The better that it please your lordship to ask.   95
HASTINGS I tell thee, fellow, 'tis better with me now

---

65 who] Q; that F   *70 SD *Enter . . .* DERBY] *Enter Lord Stanley* Q, F   71 What, my lord] Q; Come on, come on F
76 you do yours] Q; yours F   77 life] Q; dayes F   78 more] Q; so F   than it is] Q (then); as 'tis F   82 was] Q; were
F   85 scab] Q1–6; stab F   87 But . . . Tower?] Q; What, shall we toward the Tower? the day is spent. F   88 I
go . . . news?] Q; Come, come, haue with you: / Wot you what, my Lord, F   89 This . . . talked] Q; To day the Lords you
talke F   92 SD *Enter . . . Pursuivant*] Q (*Pursuant*); *Enter a Pursuiuant* F;   93 you] Q; on F   I'll follow presently] Q; Ile
talke with this good fellow F   *93 SD *Exit . . . Catesby*] F; om. Q   94 Well met, Hastings] Q; How now, Sirrah? F
95 that . . . lordship] Q; that your Lordship please F   96 fellow] Q; man F

Than when I met thee last where now we meet!
Then was I going prisoner to the Tower
By the suggestion of the Queen's allies;
But now I tell thee – keep it to thyself –   100
This day those enemies are put to death,
And I in better state than ever I was.

PURSUIVANT God hold it to your honour's good content.
HASTINGS Gramercy, Hastings! Hold: spend thou that.

He gives him his purse

PURSUIVANT God save your lordship.   [*Exit*]   105

Enter a PRIEST

HASTINGS What, Sir John, you are well met:
I am beholding to you for your last day's exercise.
Come the next sabbath and I will content you.

He whispers in his ear

Enter BUCKINGHAM

BUCKINGHAM How now, Lord Chamberlain! What – talking with a priest?
Your friends at Pomfret, they do need the priest;   110
Your honour hath no shriving work in hand.
HASTINGS Good faith, and when I met this holy man,
Those men you talk of came into my mind.
What, go you to the Tower, my lord?
BUCKINGHAM I do, but long I shall not stay,   115
I shall return before your lordship thence.
HASTINGS 'Tis like enough, for I stay dinner there.
BUCKINGHAM [*Aside*] And supper too, although thou knowest it not.
Come, shall we go along?

Exeunt

[3.3] *Enter* SIR RICHARD RATCLIFFE, *with the* LO[RDS] RIVERS, GREY, *and*
VAUGHAN, *prisoners,* [*guarded by a Halberdier*]

RATCLIFFE Come, bring forth the prisoners.
RIVERS Sir Richard Ratcliffe, let me tell thee this:

97 I met thee] Q; thou met'st me F   104 Hastings . . . that] Q; fellow: there, drinke that for me F   104 SD
He . . . purse] Q; *Throwes him his Purse.* F   105 God . . . lordship] Q; I thanke your Honor F   *105 SD *Exit*] *Exit*
Pursuiuant F; *om.* Q   106–7 . What . . . exercise] Q; *Priest* Well met, my Lord, I am glad to see your Honor. / *Hast.* I thanke
thee, good Sir *Iohn*, with all my heart. / I am in your debt, for your last Exercise F   108 content you. *He whispers in his
ear.*] Q; content you. / *Priest.* Ile wait vpon your Lordship. F   109 How . . . priest?] Q; What, talking with a Priest, Lord
Chamberlaine? F   113 Those] Q; The F   114 to . . . Lord] Q; toward the Tower F   115 do] Q; doe, my Lord F   shall
not stay] Q; cannot stay there F   117 'Tis] Q; Nay F   119 shall we go along?] Q; will you goe? / *Hast.* Ile wait vpon your
Lordship. F   *0 SD *Enter . . . Halberdier*] *Enter Sir Rickard Ratliffe, with the Lo: Riuers, / Gray, and Vaughan, prisoners.*
Q; *Enter Sir Richard Ratcliffe, with Halberds, carrying / the Nobles to death at Pomfret.* F   1 RATCLIFFE . . . prisoners.] Q;
not in F   *2 Ratcliffe] F (*Ratcliffe*); Ratliffe Q

        Today shalt thou behold a subject die,
        For truth, for duty, and for loyalty.
GREY God keep the Prince from all the pack of you: 5
        A knot you are of damned bloodsuckers.
RIVERS O Pomfret, Pomfret! O thou bloody prison,
        Fatal and ominous to noble peers!
        Within the guilty closure of thy walls
        Richard the Second here was hacked to death;   10
        And for more slander to thy dismal soul,
        We give thee up our guiltless bloods to drink.
GREY Now Margaret's curse is fallen upon our heads,
        For standing by when Richard stabbed her son.
RIVERS Then cursed she Hastings, then cursed she Buckingham,   15
        Then cursed she Richard. O, remember God,
        To hear her prayers for them as now for us,
        And for my sister, and her princely son:
        Be satisfied, dear God, with our true bloods,
        Which, as thou knowest, unjustly must be spilt.   20
RATCLIFFE Come, come: dispatch! The limit of your lives is out.
RIVERS Come Grey, come Vaughan, let us all embrace
        And take our leave until we meet in heaven.

                              Exeunt

[3.4] *Enter* [BUCKINGHAM, DERBY, HASTINGS, BISHOP OF ELY, *and* CATESBY
at a table]

HASTINGS My lords, at once! The cause why we are met
        Is to determine of the coronation:
        In God's name, say! When is this royal day?
BUCKINGHAM Are all things fitting for that royal time?
DERBY It is, and wants but nomination.   5
ELY Tomorrow, then, I guess a happy time.
BUCKINGHAM Who knows the Lord Protector's mind herein?
        Who is most inward with the noble Duke?

5 keep] Q; blesse F 6–7 bloodsuckers. / RIVERS O Pomfret] Q; Blood-suckers. / *Vaugh.* You liue, that shall cry woe for this heere- / after. / *Rat.* Dispatch, the limit of your Liues is out. / *Riuers.* O Pomfret F *10 Richard] Richard Q2–6, F; Richatd Q 11 soul] Q; Seat F 12 thee up] Q; to thee F bloods] Q; blood F 13–14 heads, / For] Q; Heads, / When shee exclaim'd on *Hastings*, you, and I, / For F 15 Hastings] Q; *Richard* F 16 Richard] Q; *Hastings* F 17 prayers] Q; prayer F 18 son] Q; Sonnes F 19 bloods] Q; blood F 21 RATCLIFFE . . . out.] Q; *sense of line precedes* 7 *in* F: *see* 6–7 *above.* *lives] Q3–6; linea Q1; lines Q2; Liues F (*in its line* 7) 22 all] Q; here F 23 And take our leave] Q; Farewell, F meet] Q; meet againe F *0 SD *Enter . . . table*] *Enter the Lords to Councell.*] Q; *Enter Buckingham, Darby, Hastings, Bishop of Ely, / Norfolke, Ratcliffe, Louell, with others, / at a Table.* F 1 My lords, at once] Q; Now Noble Peeres F 3 say] Q; speake F this] Q; the F 4 Are] Q; Is F fitting] Q; ready F that] Q; the F *6 SH ELY] F; *Ryu.* Q1; *Riu.* Q2; *Bish.* Q3–6 6 guess] Q; judge F time] Q; day F

ELY   Why, you my lord, methinks you should soonest know his mind.
BUCKINGHAM   Who I, my lord? We know each other's faces,   10
      But for our hearts, he knows no more of mine
      Than I of yours – nor I no more of his than you of mine!
      Lord Hastings, you and he are near in love.
HASTINGS   I thank his Grace. I know he loves me well,
      But for his purpose in the coronation –   15
      I have not sounded him nor he delivered
      His gracious pleasure any way therein.
      But you, my noble lords, may name the time,
      And in the Duke's behalf I'll give my voice,
      Which I presume he will take in gentle part.   20
ELY   Now in good time, here comes the Duke himself.

                    Enter GLO[UCESTER]

GLOUCESTER   My noble lords and cousins all, good morrow.
      I have been long a sleeper, but I hope
      My absence doth neglect no great designs
      Which by my presence might have been concluded.   25
BUCKINGHAM   Had not you come upon your cue, my lord,
      William, Lord Hastings, had now pronounced your part –
      I mean your voice for crowning of the King.
GLOUCESTER   Than my Lord Hastings no man might be bolder;
      His lordship knows me well, and loves me well.   30
HASTINGS   I thank your Grace.
GLOUCESTER   My Lord of Ely –
ELY   My Lord?
GLOUCESTER   When I was last in Holborn
      I saw good strawberries in your garden there: 35
      I do beseech you, send for some of them
ELY   I go my lord.   *Exit*
GLOUCESTER   Cousin Buckingham, a word with you.   [*They step aside*]
      Catesby has sounded Hastings in our business
      And finds the testy gentleman so hot   40
      As he will lose his head ere give consent
      His master's son, as worshipfully he terms it,
      Shall lose the royalty of England's throne.

9   Why . . . should] Q; Your Grace, we thinke, should F   10   Who I, my lord? We] Q; We F   11   But for] Q; for F
12   nor I no more of his] Q; Or I of his, my lord F   *17   gracious] F; Graces Q   18   noble lords] Q (noble Lo:);
Honourable Lords F   21   Now . . . time] Q; In happie time F   *21   SD *Enter* GLOUCESTER] *Ent. Glo.* Q (*end of* 22); *Enter*
Gloucester. F (*after* 20)   23   hope] Q; trust F   24   designs] Q; designe F   26   not you] Q; you not F   27   had now] Q;
now F   30–4   well . . . When] Q; well. / My Lord of Ely, when F   37   I go my lord] Q; Mary and will, my Lord, with
all my heart. F   *37   SD *Exit*] *Exit Bishop.* F; *om.* Q   38   Cousin] Q; Cousin of F   41   As] Q; That F   *ere] Q2 (*four*
copies), Q3–4, Q6, F; care Q1, Q2 (*three copies*); are Q5   42   son] Q; Child F   *worshipfully] F; worshipfull Q

BUCKINGHAM Withdraw you hence my lord; I'll follow you.

                           Ex[eunt] Gl[oucester and Buckingham]

DERBY We have not yet set down this day of triumph;   45
      Tomorrow, in mine opinion, is too sudden,
      For I myself am not so well provided
      As else I would be were the day prolonged.

                Enter B[ISHOP] OF ELY

ELY Where is my Lord Protector? I have sent for these strawberries.
HASTINGS His Grace looks cheerfully and smooth today;   50
      There's some conceit or other likes him well
      When he doth bid good morrow with such a spirit.
      I think there is never a man in Christendom
      That can lesser hide his love or hate than he,
      For by his face straight shall you know his heart.   55
DERBY What of his heart perceive you in his face
      By any livelihood he shewed today?
HASTINGS Marry, that with no man here he is offended,
      For if he were, he would have shown it in his looks.
DERBY I pray God he be not, I say.   60

        Enter GLOUCESTER [and BUCKINGHAM]

GLOUCESTER I pray you all, what do they deserve
      That do conspire my death with devilish plots
      Of damned witchcraft, and that have prevailed
      Upon my body with their hellish charms?
HASTINGS The tender love I bear your Grace, my lord,   65
      Makes me most forward in this noble presence
      To doom the offenders whatsoever they be.
      I say, my lord, they have deserved death.
GLOUCESTER Then be your eyes the witness of this ill.
      See how I am bewitched: behold mine arm   70
      Is like a blasted sapling withered up!
      This is that Edward's wife, that monstrous witch,
      Consorted with that harlot strumpet Shore,
      That by their witchcraft thus have marked me.
HASTINGS If they have done this thing, my gracious lord –   75
GLOUCESTER If! Thou protector of this damned strumpet,

---

44 you . . . follow] Q; your selfe a while, Ile goe with F   *44 SD *Exeunt . . . Buckingham] Ex. Gl.* Q; *Exeunt.* F   46 mine
opinion] Q; my iudgement F   sudden] Q1, F; soone Q2–8   49 Lord Protector] Q (L. protector); Lord, the Duke of Gloster
F   these] Q, F; Q BM *appears to be* those   50 today] Q; this morning F   52 he doth bid] Q; that he bids F   a spirit] Q;
spirit F   *57 livelihood] F; likelihood Q   59 if he were, he would have] Q; were he, he had F   60 DERBY I . . . say.]
Q; *not in* F   60 SD *Enter . . . BUCKINGHAM] Enter Glocester.* Q; *Enter Richard, and Buckingham.* F   61 what do] Q; tell me
what F   66 noble] Q; Princely F   67 whatsoever] Q; whosoe're F   69 this ill] Q; their euill F   70 See] Q; Looke F
72 This is that] Q; And this is F   75 thing] Q; deed F   gracious] Q; Noble F

Tell'st thou me of ifs? Thou art a traitor!
Off with his head! Now by Saint Paul,
I will not dine today I swear
Until I see the same. Some see it done.   80
The rest that love me, come and follow me.

Exeunt except Cat[esby] with Ha[stings]

HASTINGS Woe, woe for England, not a whit for me,
For I, too fond, might have prevented this.
Stanley did dream the boar did raze his helm,
But I disdained it and did scorn to fly.   85
Three times today my footcloth horse did stumble,
And started when he looked upon the Tower,
As loath to bear me to the slaughterhouse.
O, now I want the priest that spake to me;
I now repent I told the pursuivant,   90
As 'twere triumphing at mine enemies,
How they at Pomfret bloodily were butchered,
And I myself secure in grace and favour.
O Margaret, Margaret, now thy heavy curse
Is lighted on poor Hastings' wretched head.   95
CATESBY Dispatch, my lord. The Duke would be at dinner.
Make a short shrift – he longs to see your head.
HASTINGS O momentary state of worldly men,
Which we more hunt for than the grace of heaven.
Who builds his hopes in air of your fair looks,   100
Lives like a drunken sailor on a mast,
Ready with every nod to tumble down
Into the fatal bowels of the deep.
Come, lead me to the block: bear him my head.
They smile at me that shortly shall be dead.   *Exeunt*   105

[3.5] *Enter* DUKE OF GLOUCESTER *and* BUCKINGHAM *in armour*

GLOUCESTER Come cousin, canst thou quake and change thy colour,
Murder thy breath in middle of a word,

77 Tell'st thou me] Q; Talk'st thou to me F   78 Paul,] Q; *Paul* I sweare, F   79–80 today . . . done] Q; vntill I see the same. / *Louell and Ratcliffe*, looke that it be done F   81 come] Q; rise F   81 SD *Exeunt . . . Hastings*] *Exeunt. / manet Cat. with Ha.* Q (*right margin of* 81–2); *Exeunt* F (*right margin of* 80); *Manet Louell and Ratcliffe, with the / Lord Hastings.* F (*following* 81)   84 raze his helm] Q (race); rowse our Helmes F   85 But . . . fly] Q; And I did scorne it, and disdaine to flye F   •87 started] F; startled Q1–6   89 want] Q; need F   91 'twere] Q; too F   at] Q; how F   92 How they] Q; To day F   96 SH CATESBY] Q; *Ra.* F   Dispatch, my lord] Q (Lo:); Come, come, dispatch F   98 state of worldly] Q; grace of mortall F   99 heaven] Q; God F   100 hopes] Q; hope F   fair] Q; good F   103–4 deep. / Come] Q; Deepe. / *Lou.* Come, come, dispatch, 'tis bootlesse to exclaime. / *Hast.* O bloody *Richard*: miserable England, / I prophecie the fearefull'st time to thee, / That euer wretched Age hath look'd vpon. / Come F   105 that] Q; who F   0 SD *Enter . . . armour*] Q (armonr; in] *Huntington copy;* In] *Huth copy);* Enter Richard, and Buckingham, in rotten Armour, maruellous ill-fauoured F

And then begin again and stop again,
As if thou wert distraught and mad with terror?
BUCKINGHAM Tut, fear not me,   5
I can counterfeit the deep tragedian,
Speak, and look back, and pry on every side,
Intending deep suspicion. Ghastly looks
Are at my service like enforced smiles,
And both are ready in their offices   10
To grace my stratagems.

Enter MAYOR

GLOUCESTER   Here comes the Mayor.
BUCKINGHAM [*Aside*] Let me alone to entertain him. – Lord Mayor!
GLOUCESTER Look to the drawbridge there!
BUCKINGHAM [*To the Mayor*] The reason we have sent for you –
GLOUCESTER Buckingham – overlook the walls!   15
BUCKINGHAM Hark! I hear a drum.
GLOUCESTER Look back! Defend thee, here are enemies.
BUCKINGHAM God and our innocence defend us!

Enter CATESBY *with* HAST[INGS'S] *head*

GLOUCESTER O, O be quiet! It is Catesby.
CATESBY Here is the head of that ignoble traitor,   20
The dangerous and unsuspected Hastings.
GLOUCESTER So dear I loved the man that I must weep.
I took him for the plainest harmless man
That breathed upon this earth, a Christian –
Look ye, my Lord Mayor! –   25
Made him my book, wherein my soul recorded
The history of all her secret thoughts.
So smooth he daubed his vice with show of virtue
That, his apparent open guilt omitted –
I mean his conversation with Shore's wife –   30
He lived from all attainder of suspect.
BUCKINGHAM Well, well, he was the covertest sheltered traitor
That ever lived. Would you have imagined,

---

3   begin again] Q; againe begin F   4   wert] Q; were F   5   Tut, fear not me] Q; Tut F   7–8   side, / Intending] Q; side,
/ Tremble and start at wagging of a Straw: / Intending F   11   To] Q; At any time to F   11–12   stratagems . . . Mayor]
Q; Stratagemes. / But what, is *Catesby* gone? / *Rich.* He is, and see he brings the Maior along. / *Enter the Maior, and
Catesby. / Buck.* Lord Maior F   14   The reason . . . you –] Q; Lord Maior, the reason we haue sent. (*following* 15, o're-
looke the Walls.) F   *15   Buckingham] *this edn*; Catesby Q, F   16   Hark . . . drum] Q; Hearke, a Drumme F (*precedes* 15)
18   innocence . . . us] Q; Innocencie defend, and guard vs F   18   SD *Enter . . . head*] Q (*against 18 and 19*); Enter Louell
and Ratcliffe, with Hastings Head. F (*following* 18)   19   O . . . Catesby] Q; Be patient, they are friends: *Ratcliffe, and Louell*
F   23   man] Q; Creature F   24   this] Q; the F   24–6   Christian – / Look ye, my Lord Mayor – / Made] Q; Christian.
/ Made F   *31   lived] F; laid Q   suspect] Q; suspects F   33   have imagined] Q; imagine F

Or almost believe, wert not by great preservation
We live to tell it you? The subtle traitor   35
Had this day plotted in the Council House
To murder me – and my good Lord of Gloucester.

MAYOR What! Had he so?

GLOUCESTER What? Think you we are Turks or Infidels?
Or that we would, against the form of law,   40
Proceed thus rashly to the villain's death,
But that the extreme peril of the case,
The peace of England, and our person's safety,
Enforced us to this execution?

MAYOR Now fair befall you, he deserved his death.   45
And you, my good lords both, have well proceeded
To warn false traitors from the like attempts.
I never looked for better at his hands
After he once fell in with Mistress Shore.

BUCKINGHAM Yet had not we determined he should die   50
Until your lordship came to see his death,
Which now the longing haste of these our friends
Somewhat against our meaning have prevented,
Because, my lord, we would have had you heard
The traitor speak, and timorously confess   55
The manner and the purpose of his treason,
That you might well have signified the same
Unto the citizens, who happily may
Misconster us in him and wail his death.

MAYOR But my good lord, your Grace's word shall serve   60
As well as I had seen or heard him speak.
And doubt you not, right noble Princes both,
But I'll acquaint your duteous citizens
With all your just proceedings in this cause.

GLOUCESTER And to that end we wished your lordship here   65
To avoid the carping censures of the world.

BUCKINGHAM But since you come too late of our intents
Yet witness what we did intend. And so, my lord, adieu.
                                        Exit Mayor [and Catesby]

34 not] Q; not, that F   35   you] Q; that F   36   Had this day plotted] Q; This day had plotted F   38   What . . . so?] Q;
Had he done so? F   41   to] Q; in F   46   you, my good lords] Q; your good Graces F   48–9   I . . . Shore] Q; *spoken by*
Buckingham in F   *50   SH BUCKINGHAM] *this edn; Dut.* Q; *part of Buckingham's speech starting at 48 in* F   not we] Q; we
not F   51   death] Q; end F   52   longing] Q; louing F   53   Somewhat] Q; Something F   meaning] Q; meanings F
54   we] Q; I F   56   treason] Q; Treasons F   60   Grace's word] Q (graces); Graces words F   61   or] Q; and F
62   doubt you not] Q; doe not doubt F   63   your] Q; our F   64   cause] Q1–5; case Q6; case F   66   carping censures of
the] Q; Censures of the carping F   67   But] Q; Which F   intents] Q; intent F   68   what] Q; what you heare F
And . . . adieu] Q; And so, my good Lord Maior, we bid farewell F   *68   SD *Exit . . . Catesby*] *this edn; Exit Maior* Q, F

GLOUCESTER After, after, cousin Buckingham!
      The Mayor towards Guildhall hies him in all post;   70
      There at your meet'st advantage of the time,
      Infer the bastardy of Edward's children;
      Tell them how Edward put to death a citizen
      Only for saying he would make his son
      Heir to the Crown – meaning (indeed) his house,   75
      Which by the sign thereof was termed so.
      Moreover, urge his hateful luxury
      And bestial appetite in change of lust,
      Which stretched to their servants, daughters, wives,
      Even where his lustful eye or savage heart   80
      Without control listed to make his prey.
      Nay, for a need, thus far come near my person;
      Tell them, when that my mother went with child
      Of that unsatiate Edward, noble York
      My princely father then had wars in France,   85
      And by just computation of the time
      Found that the issue was not his begot –
      Which well appeared in his lineaments,
      Being nothing like the noble Duke, my father;
      But touch this sparingly, as it were far off,   90
      Because you know, my lord, my mother lives.
BUCKINGHAM Fear not, my lord, I'll play the orator
      As if the golden fee for which I plead
      Were for myself.
GLOUCESTER If you thrive well, bring them to Baynard's Castle,   95
      Where you shall find me well accompanied
      With reverend fathers and well-learned bishops.
BUCKINGHAM About three or four o'clock look to hear
      What news Guildhall affordeth; and so, my lord, farewell.   *Exit*
GLOUCESTER Now will I in to take some privy order   100
      To draw the brats of Clarence out of sight,
      And to give notice that no manner of person
      At any time have recourse unto the Princes.   *Exit*

---

69 After, after] Q; Goe after, after F **71** meet'st advantage] Q; meetest vantage F **79** stretched to] Q; stretcht vnto F
80 lustful] Q; raging F **81** listed] Q; lusted F his] Q; a F **86** just] Q; true F **90** But] Q; Yet F **91** you know, my
lord] Q; my Lord, you know F **92** Fear] Q; Doubt F **94** myself.] Q; my selfe: and so, my Lord, adue. F (68 *in* Q)
98–9 About . . . farewell] Q; I goe, and towards three or foure a Clocke / Looke for Newes that the Guild-Hall affoords.
F **99** SD *Exit*] *Exit Buc.* Q (*right margin of* 100); *Exit Buckingham.* F (*following* 99) **100** *preceded in* F *by*: *Rich. Goe*
Louell with all speed to Doctor *Shaw*, / Goe thou to Fryer *Peuker*, bid them both / Meet me within this houre at Baynards
Castle. *Exit* **100** in] Q; goe F **102** notice] Q; order F of person] Q; person F **103** At any time have] Q; Haue any
time F

[3.6] *Enter a* SCRIVENER *with a paper in his hand*

SCRIVENER This is the indictment of the good Lord Hastings,
          Which in a set hand fairly is engrossed
          That it may be this day read over in Paul's.
          And mark how well the sequel hangs together.
          Eleven hours I spent to write it over,   5
          For yesternight by Catesby was it brought me;
          The precedent was full as long a-doing,
          And yet within these five hours lived Lord Hastings,
          Untainted, unexamined, free, at liberty.
          Here's a good world the while! Why, who's so gross   10
          That sees not this palpable device?
          Yet who's so blind but says he sees it not?
          Bad is the world and all will come to naught
          When such bad dealing must be seen in thought.   *Exit*

[3.7] *Enter* GLOUCESTER *at one door,* BUCKINGHAM *at another*

GLOUCESTER How now, my lord, what say the citizens?
BUCKINGHAM Now by the holy Mother of our Lord,
          The citizens are mum and speak not a word.
GLOUCESTER Touched you the bastardy of Edward's children?
BUCKINGHAM I did, with the insatiate greediness of his desires,   5
          His tyranny for trifles, his own bastardy,
          As being got, your father then in France.
          Withal, I did infer your lineaments –
          Being the right idea of your father,
          Both in your form and nobleness of mind –   10
          Laid open all your victories in Scotland,
          Your discipline in war, wisdom in peace,
          Your bounty, virtue, fair humility;

0 SD *Enter . . . hand*] Q; *Enter a Scriuener* F (*Scr.*); *om.* Q   1 This] Q; Here F   3   this] Q; to F
over] Q; o're F   5 spent] Q; haue spent F   6 brought] Q; sent F   8 lived Lord Hastings] Q; *Hastings* liu'd F
10 Why . . . gross] Q; Who is so grosse F (*begins* 11)   11 sees not] Q; cannot see F   12 who's] Q (whoes); whose Q2;
who Q3–6, F blind] Q; bold F   13 naught] Q1–2; nought Q3–6, F   14 bad] Q; ill F   0   SD *Enter . . . another*] Q; *Enter
Richard and Buckingham at seuerall Doores.* F   1 How now, my lord] Q; How now, how now F   3 and speak] Q; say F
5–8 I did . . . lineaments,] Q; F *has*:
          I did, with his Contract with Lady *Lucy,*
          And his Contract by Deputie in France,
          Th'vnsatiate greedinesse of his desire,
          And his enforcement of the Citie Wiues,
          His Tyrannie for Trifles, his owne Bastardie,
          As being got, your Father then in France,
          And his resemblance, being not like the Duke.
          Withall, I did inferre your Lineaments,

Indeed, left nothing fitting for the purpose
Untouched, or slightly handled in discourse.   15
And when mine oratory grew to an end,
I bid them that did love their country's good,
Cry, 'God save Richard, England's royal King!'

GLOUCESTER Ah – and did they so?

BUCKINGHAM No, so God help me,   20
But like dumb statues or breathing stones
Gazed each on other and looked deadly pale,
Which when I saw, I reprehended them,
And asked the Mayor what meant this wilful silence.
His answer was, the people were not wont   25
To be spoke to but by the Recorder.
Then he was urged to tell my tale again.
'Thus saith the Duke; thus has the Duke inferred' –
But nothing spake in warrant from himself.
When he had done, some followers of mine own   30
At the lower end of the Hall, hurled up their caps,
And some ten voices cried, 'God save King Richard!'
'Thanks loving citizens and friends,' quoth I,
'This general applause and loving shout
Argues your wisdoms and your love to Richard.'   35
And so brake off and came away.

GLOUCESTER What tongueless blocks were they! Would they not speak?

BUCKINGHAM No, by my troth, my lord.

GLOUCESTER Will not the Mayor then and his brethren come?

BUCKINGHAM The Mayor is here at hand. Intend some fear;   40
Be not spoken withal but with mighty suit,
And look you get a prayer book in your hand,
And stand betwixt two churchmen, good my lord,
For on that ground I'll build a holy descant.
Be not easily won to our request: 45
Play the maid's part: say 'No' – but take it.

GLOUCESTER Fear not me; if thou canst plead as well for them
As I can say nay to thee for myself,
No doubt we'll bring it to a happy issue.

14 the] Q; your F   16 mine] Q1–2; my Q3–6, F   grew to an] Q1–2, 4; grew to Q3, 5, 6; drew toward F   19 Ah – and]
Q (A and); And F   20 me,] Q; me, they spake not a word, F   22 Gazed] Q; Star'd F   25 wont] Q; vsed F   29 spake]
Q; spoke F   31 the lower] Q; lower F   32–3 Richard!' / 'Thanks] Q; *Richard: / And thus I tooke the vantage of those
few. / Thankes* F   33 loving] Q; gentle F   34 loving] Q; chearefull F   35 wisdoms] Q1–2 (wisedomes); wisedome Q3–
6, F   36 so] Q; euen here F   38 BUCKINGHAM . . . lord.] Q; *not in* F   •40 SH BUCKINGHAM] Q3–8, F; *Glo.* Q1–2
•hand. Intend] F (hand: intend); hand, and intend Q   41 Be . . . suit] Q; Be not you spoke with, but by mightie suit F
43 betwixt] Q; betweene F   44 build] Q; make F   45 Be] Q; And be F   request] Q; requests F   46 say 'No' – but]
Q; still answer nay, and F   47 Fear . . . canst] Q; I goe: and if you F   •48 myself] F (my selfe,); my selfe? Q   *Setting in
Simmes's house ends here and that in Short's begins*   49 we'll] Q; we F

BUCKINGHAM You shall see what I can do: get you up to the leads. 50

Exit [*Gloucester*]

[*Enter the* MAYOR *and* CITIZENS]

Now my Lord Mayor, I dance attendance here.
I think the Duke will not be spoke withal.

Enter CATESBY [*above*]

Here comes his servant. How now, Catesby, what says he?
CATESBY My lord, he does intreat your Grace
To visit him tomorrow – or next day. 55
He is within, with two right reverend fathers,
Divinely bent to meditation,
And in no worldly suit would he be moved
To draw him from his holy exercise.
BUCKINGHAM Return, good Catesby, to thy lord again, 60
Tell him myself, the Mayor and citizens,
In deep designs and matters of great moment,
No less importing than our general good,
Are come to have some conference with his Grace.
CATESBY I'll tell him what you say my lord. *Exit* 65
BUCKINGHAM Ah ha, my lord! This Prince is not an Edward.
He is not lulling on a lewd day-bed,
But on his knees at meditation;
Not dallying with a brace of courtesans,
But meditating with two deep divines; 70
Not sleeping to engross his idle body,
But praying to enrich his watchful soul.
Happy were England would this gracious Prince
Take on himself the sovereignty thereon,
But sure, I fear we shall never win him to it. 75
MAYOR Marry, God forbid his Grace should say us nay!
BUCKINGHAM I fear he will –

Enter CATES[BY]

– how now, Catesby,
What says your lord?
CATESBY My lord, he wonders to what end you have assembled

---

50 You . . . leads] Q; Go, go vp to the Leads, the Lord Maior knocks F   50 SD *Exit* [*Gloucester*]] Q (*Exit. at right margin of* 51); *om.* F   *SD *Enter . . . CITIZENS*] F; *om.* Q   51 Now my Lord Mayor] Q; Welcome, my Lord F   *52 SD *Enter . . . above*] *this edn; Enter Catesby.* Q, F   53 Here . . . he] Q; Now *Catesby,* what sayes your Lord to my / request? F   54 My . . . Grace] Q; He doth entreat your Grace, my Noble Lord, F   58 suit] Q; suites F   60 thy lord again] Q; the gracious Duke F   61 citizens] Q; Aldermen F   62 and matters] Q; in matter F   65 I'll . . . lord] Q; Ile signifie so much vnto him straight F   67 day-bed] Q; Loue-Bed F   73 gracious] Q; vertuous F   74 himself] Q; his Grace F thereon] Q; thereof F   75 never] Q; not F   76 forbid] Q; defend F   77–8 will . . . lord?] Q; will: here *Catesby* comes againe. / *Enter Catesby.* / Now *Catesby,* what says his Grace? F   79 My lord, he] Q; He F

Such troops of citizens to speak with him,   80
His Grace not being warned thereof before.
My lord, he fears you mean no good to him.
BUCKINGHAM Sorry I am my noble cousin should
    Suspect me that I mean no good to him.
    By heaven, I come in perfect love to him,   85
    And so once more return and tell his Grace.

                                                Exit Catesby

    When holy and devout religious men
    Are at their beads, 'tis hard to draw them thence,
    So sweet is zealous contemplation.

     Enter GLOUCESTER *with two bishops, aloft* [*with* CATESBY]

MAYOR See where he stands between two clergymen!   90
BUCKINGHAM Two props of virtue for a Christian Prince
    To stay him from the fall of vanity.
    Famous Plantagenet, most gracious Prince,
    Lend favourable ears to our request
    And pardon us the interruption   95
    Of thy devotion and right Christian zeal.
GLOUCESTER My lord, there needs no such apology.
    I rather do beseech you pardon me,
    Who, earnest in the service of my God,
    Neglect the visitation of my friends.   100
    But leaving this, what is your Grace's pleasure?
BUCKINGHAM Even that, I hope, which pleases God above,
    And all good men of this ungoverned isle.
GLOUCESTER I do suspect I have done some offence
    That seems disgracious in the City's eyes,   105
    And that you come to reprehend my ignorance.
BUCKINGHAM You have, my lord: would it please your Grace
    At our entreaties to amend that fault?
GLOUCESTER Else wherefore breathe I in a Christian land?
BUCKINGHAM Then know it is your fault that you resign   110
    The supreme seat, the throne majestical,
    The sceptred office of your ancestors,
    The lineal glory of your royal house,
    To the corruption of a blemished stock;

---

80 speak with] Q; come to F 82 My lord, he fears] Q; He feares, my Lord F 85 I] Q; we F in . . . him] Q; to him in
perfit loue F 88 hard] Q; much F *89 SD *Enter . . . *CATESBY] *Enter Rich. with two bishops a loste.* Q (*aloft* Q2–6);
Enter Richard aloft, betweene two Bishops. F 90 he] Q; his Grace F between] Q; tweene F 92–3 vanity. / Famous] Q;
Vanitie: / And see a Booke of Prayer in his hand, / True Ornaments to know a holy man. / Famous F 94 ears] Q; eare
F request] Q; requests F 98 I . . . you] Q; I doe beseech your Grace to F 100 Neglect] Q; Deferr'd F 105 eyes] Q;
eye F 107 please] Q; might please F 108 At] Q; On F that] Q; your F 110 Then know] Q; Know then F 112–
13 ancestors, / The lineal] Q; Ancestors, / Your State of Fortune, and your Deaw of Birth, / The Lineall F

Whilst, in the mildness of your sleepy thoughts,   115
Which here we waken to our country's good,
This noble isle doth want her proper limbs,
Her face defaced with scars of infamy
And almost shouldered in the swallowing gulf
Of blind forgetfulness and dark oblivion;   120
Which to recure we heartily solicit
Your gracious self to take on you the sovereignty thereof,
Not as Protector, Steward, Substitute,
Or lowly factor for another's gain,
But as successively, from blood to blood,   125
Your right of birth, your empery, your own.
For this, consorted with the citizens,
(Your very worshipful and loving friends,
And by their vehement instigation),
In this just suit come I to move your Grace.   130
GLOUCESTER I know not whether to depart in silence,
Or bitterly to speak in your reproof,
Best fitteth my degree or your condition.
Your love deserves my thanks, but my desert
Unmeritable shuns your high request.   135
First, if all obstacles were cut away,
And that my path were even to the crown
As my ripe revenue and due by birth,
Yet so much is my poverty of spirit,
So mighty and so many my defects,   140
As I had rather hide me from my greatness,
Being a bark to brook no mighty sea,
Than in my greatness covet to be hid
And in the vapour of my glory smothered.
But God be thanked, there's no need of me –   145
And much I need to help you if need were.
The royal tree hath left us royal fruit,
Which, mellowed by the stealing hours of time,
Will well become the seat of majesty,
And make, no doubt, us happy by his reign.   150
On him I lay what you would lay on me:
The right and fortune of his happy stars,
Which God defend that I should wring from him.

115 Whilst] Q; Whiles F   117 This] Q; The F   her] Q1–2; his Q3–6, F   118 Her] Q; His F   118–19 infamy / And] Q; Infamie, / His Royall Stock grafft with ignoble Plants, / And F   120 blind] Q; darke F   dark] Q; deepe F   122–3 sovereignty thereof / Not] Q; charge / And Kingly Gouernment of this your Land: / Not F   130 suit] Q; Cause F   131 know not whether] Q; cannot tell, if F   133–4 condition. / Your] Q; Condition. / If not to answer, you might haply thinke, / [*eight lines*] / Definitiuely thus I answer you. / Your F   138 my ripe . . . by] Q; my right . . . by Q2–6; the ripe . . . of F   141 As I had] Q; That I would F   146 if need were] Q; were there need F   151 what] Q; that F

BUCKINGHAM My lord, this argues conscience in your Grace,
        But the respects thereof are nice and trivial,   155
        All circumstances well considered.
        You say that Edward is your brother's son;
        So say we too – but not by Edward's wife;
        For first he was contract to Lady Lucy –
        Your mother lives, a witness to that vow;   160
        And afterward by substitute betrothed
        To Bona, sister to the King of France.
        These both put by, a poor petitioner,
        A care-crazed mother of a-many children,
        A beauty-waning and distressed widow,   165
        Even in the afternoon of her best days,
        Made prize and purchase of his lustful eye,
        Seduced the pitch and height of all his thoughts
        To base declension and loathed bigamy.
        By her, in his unlawful bed, he got   170
        This Edward, whom our manners term the Prince.
        More bitterly could I expostulate,
        Save that for reverence to some alive
        I give a sparing limit to my tongue.
        Then, good my lord, take to your royal self   175
        This proffered benefit of dignity,
        If not to bless us and the land withall,
        Yet to draw out your royal stock
        From the corruption of abusing time
        Unto a lineal, true, derived course.   180
MAYOR Do, good my lord: your citizens entreat you!
BUCKINGHAM Refuse not, mighty lord, this proffered love!
CATESBY O, make them joyful! Grant their lawful suit!
GLOUCESTER Alas, why would you heap these cares on me?
        I am unfit for state and dignity.   185
        I do beseech you, take it not amiss.
        I cannot, nor I will not, yield to you.
BUCKINGHAM If you refuse it, as in love and zeal
        Loath to depose the child, your brother's son –
        As well we know your tenderness of heart   190
        And gentle, kind, effeminate remorse,
        Which we have noted in you to your kin,
        And equally indeed to all estates –

*158 too] Q2–6, F; to Q1   159   he was] Q; was he F   160   that] Q; his F   163   by] Q; off F   164   of a-many children]
Q; to a many Sonnes F   167   lustful] Q; wanton F   168   all his thoughts] Q; his degree F   171   term] Q; call F
178   out . . . stock] Q; forth your Noble Ancestrie F   179   time] Q; times F   *182   Refuse . . . love!] F; *om.* Q
184   these cares] Q; this Care F   185   dignity] Q; Maiestie F   192   kin] Q; Kindred F

Yet whether you accept our suit or no,
You brother's son shall never reign our king,   195
But we will plant some other in the throne
To the disgrace and downfall of your house;
And in this resolution, here we leave you.
Come citizens! Zounds, I'll entreat no more!
GLOUCESTER O do not swear, my Lord of Buckingham!   200
     [Buckingham, Mayor, and Citizens exit slowly;
    Buckingham, Mayor, and two Citizens still on-stage at 206]
CATESBY Call them again, my lord, and accept their suit.
A CITIZEN *[Off]* Do, good my lord, lest all the land do rue it!
GLOUCESTER Would you enforce me to a world of care?
  Well, call them again. I am not made of stones,
  But penetrable to your kind entreats,   205
  Albeit against my conscience and my soul.
  Cousin of Buckingham, and you sage grave men,
  Since you will buckle fortune on my back
  To bear her burden whether I will or no,
  I must have patience to endure the load.   210
  But if black scandal or foul-faced reproach,
  Attend the sequel of your imposition,
  Your mere enforcement shall acquittance me
  From all the impure blots and stains thereof.
  For God he knows, and you may partly see,   215
  How far I am from the desire thereof.
MAYOR God bless your Grace: we see it, and will say it.
GLOUCESTER In saying so you shall but say the truth.
BUCKINGHAM Then I salute you with this kingly title:
  Long live Richard, England's royal king!   220
MAYOR Amen!
BUCKINGHAM Tomorrow will it please you to be crowned?
GLOUCESTER Even when you will, since you will have it so.
BUCKINGHAM Tomorrow then we will attend your Grace.
GLOUCESTER Come, let us to our holy task again.   225
  Farewell good cousin, farewell gentle friends.

            Exeunt

194 whether] Q; know, where F   **199** Zounds, I'll] Q; we will F   **200** GLOUCESTER . . . Buckingham !] Q; *not in* F
***200** SD *Buckingham . . . at 206*] *this edn; no exit, no entrance in* Q; *Exeunt. (after* 199), *Enter Buckingham, and the rest. (after*
206) F   **201** them] Q; him F   my lord, and] Q; sweet Prince F   ***202** A CITIZEN . . . it] Q (.*Ino.; this edn*); If you denie
them, all the Land will rue it (*attributed to Catesby*) F   **203** Would] Q; Will F   care] Q; Cares F   **204** Well, call] Q; Call
F   **205** entreats] Q; entreaties F   **207** you sage] Q; sage F   **209** whether] Q; where F   ***211** foul-faced] F (foule-
fac'd); foule-fac't Q1–2; so foule fac't Q3–5; so foulefac't Q6   **215** he knows] Q; doth know F   **216** thereof] Q; of this
F   **219** kingly] Q; Royall F   **220** Richard] Q; King *Richard* F   royal] Q; worthie F   ***221** SH MAYOR] Q (*Mʳyor.*); .*All.*
F   **222** will] Q; may F   **223** will, since] Q; please, for F   **224–5** Grace. / GLOUCESTER Come] Q; Grace. / And so
most ioyfully we take our leaue. / *Rich.* Come F   **225** task] Q; Worke F   **226** good cousin] Q; my Cousins F

[**4.1**] *Enter* QUEE[N ELIZABETH], DUCHESS OF YORK, MARQUESS [OF] DORSET
at one door; [ANNE] DUCHESS OF GLOUCEST[ER] *at another door*

DUCHESS Who meets us here? My niece Plantagenet?
ELIZABETH Sister, well met. Whither away so fast?
ANNE No farther than the Tower, and as I guess,
      Upon the like devotion as yourselves –
      To gratulate the tender Princes there.   5
ELIZABETH Kind sister, thanks. We'll enter all together.

Enter LIEUTENANT

      And in good time, here the Lieutenant comes.
      Master Lieutenant, pray you by your leave:
      How fares the Prince?
LIEUTENANT Well, madam, and in health, but by your leave   10
      I may not suffer you to visit him.
      The King hath straightly charged the contrary.
ELIZABETH The King? Why, who's that?
LIEUTENANT I cry you mercy, I mean the Lord Protector.
ELIZABETH The Lord protect him from that kingly title!   15
      Hath he set bounds betwixt their love and me?
      I am their mother: who should keep me from them?
DUCHESS I am their father's mother: I will see them.
ANNE Their aunt I am in law, in love their mother:
      Then fear not thou, I'll bear thy blame   20
      And take thy office from thee on my peril.
LIEUTENANT I do beseech your Graces all to pardon me;
      I am bound by oath, I may not do it.   [*Exit*]

Enter DERBY

DERBY Let me but meet you, ladies, an hour hence,
      And I'll salute your Grace of York as mother   25
      And reverend looker-on of two fair Queens.
      [*To Anne*] Come, madam, you must go with me to Westminster,
      There to be crowned Richard's royal Queen.

Many of the compositorial errors in this scene are listed on p.8; they are not repeated here. **0** SD *Enter . . . door*] Q (*Enter Quee.*
mother, Duchesse of Yorke, Marques Dorset, at / *one doore, Duchesse of Glocest. at another doore.*); *Enter the Queene, Anne*
Duchesse of Gloucester, the / *Duchesse of Yorke, and Marquesse Dorset.* F **1–3** Plantagenet? . . . No farther] Q; *Plantagenet,*
/ *Led in the hand of her kind Aunt of Gloster?* / *Now, for my Life, shee's wandring to the Tower,* / *On pure hearts loue,*
to greet the tender Prince. / *Daughter, well met.* / *Anne.* God giue your Graces both, a happie / And a ioyfull time of day.
/ *Qu.* As much to you, good Sister: whither away? / *Anne.* No farther F **5** tender] Q; gentle F **9** fares the Prince?] Q;
doth the Prince, and my young Sonne of Yorke? F **10** Well . . . leave] Q; Right well, deare Madame: by your patience F
11 him] Q; them F **12** straightly] Q; strictly F **13** Why, who's] Q (whose); who's F **14** I . . . I mean] Q; I meane
F **16** betwixt] Q; betweene F **17** should keep] Q; shall barre F **20** fear not thou] Q; bring me to their sights F
22–3 I do . . . not do it] Q; No, Madame, no; I may not leaue it so: / I am bound by Oath, and therefore pardon me F
*23 SD *Exit*] *Exit Lieutenant.* F; *om.* Q **24** an] Q; one F **27** go with me] Q; straight F

ELIZABETH O, cut my lace in sunder, that my pent heart
     May have some scope to beat, or else I sound   30
     With this dead-killing news.
DORSET Madam, have comfort. How fares your Grace?
ELIZABETH O Dorset, speak not to me! Get thee hence!
     Death and destruction dog thee at thy heels:
     Thy mother's name is ominous to children.   35
     If thou wilt outstrip death, go cross the seas
     And live with Richmond, from the reach of hell.
     Go, hie thee! Hie thee from this slaughter-house,
     Lest thou increase the number of the dead
     And make me die the thrall of Margaret's curse,   40
     Nor mother, wife, nor England's counted Queen.
DERBY Full of wise care is this your counsel, madam.
     [*To Dorset*] Take all the swift advantage of the time;
     You shall have letters from me to my son
     To meet you on the way and welcome you.   45
     Be not ta'en tardy by unwise delay.
DUCHESS O ill-dispersing wind of misery,
     O my accursed womb, the bed of death!
     A cockatrice hast thou hatched to the world,
     Whose unavoided eye is murderous.   50
DERBY Come madam; I in all haste was sent.
ANNE And I in all unwillingness will go.
     I would to God that the inclusive verge
     Of golden metal that must round my brow
     Were red-hot steel to sear me to the brain.   55
     Anointed let me be with deadly poison,
     And die, ere men can say, 'God save the Queen!'
ELIZABETH Alas, poor soul, I envy not thy glory;
     To feed my humour, wish thyself no harm.
ANNE No? When he that is my husband now,   60
     Came to me as I followed Henry's corse
     When scarce the blood was well-washed from his hands
     Which issued from my other angel-husband,
     And that dead saint, which then I weeping followed.
     O, when I say I looked on Richard's face,   65
     This was my wish: 'Be thou', quoth I, 'accursed
     For making me, so young, so old a widow;

29 in sunder] Q; asunder F 30 sound] Q; swoone F 31–2 news. / Madam] Q; newes. / *Anne.* Despightful tidings, O vnpleasing newes. / *Dors.* F 32 Madam, have comfort] Q; Be of good cheare: Mother F 33 hence] Q; gone F 34 dog] Q; dogges F *43 SD *To Dorset*] NCS; *not in* Q, F 43 time] Q; howres F 45 To meet . . . you] Q; In your behalfe, to meet you on the way Q 51 madam;] Q; Madame, come, F *52 SH ANNE] F; *Duch.* Q 52 in] Q; with F 53 I] Q; O F 55 brain] Q; Braines F 56 poison] Q; Venome F 58 Alas] Q; Goe, goe F 60 No?] Q; No: why ? F *61 corse] F; course Q1–6 64 dead] Q; deare F

And when thou wed'st, let sorrow haunt thy bed,
And be thy wife, if any be so mad,
As miserable by the death of thee   70
As thou hast made me by my dear lord's death.
Lo, ere I can repeat this curse again,
Even in so short a space, my woman's heart
Grossly grew captive to his honey words,
And proved the subject of my own soul's curse,   75
Which ever since hath kept my eyes from sleep.
For never yet one hour in his bed
Have I enjoyed the golden dew of sleep,
But have been waked by his timorous dreams.
Besides, he hates me for my father Warwick,   80
And will, no doubt, shortly be rid of me.
ELIZABETH Alas, poor soul, I pity thy complaints.
ANNE No more than from my soul I mourn for yours.
DORSET Farewell, thou woeful welcomer of glory!
ANNE Adieu, poor soul, thou tak'st thy leave of it.   85
DUCHESS [*To Dorset*] Go thou to Richmond, and good fortune guide thee;
          [*To Anne*] Go thou to Richard, and good angels guard thee;
          [*To Elizabeth*] Go thou to sanctuary, good thoughts possess thee;
          I to my grave, where peace and rest lie with me.
          Eighty-odd years of sorrow have I seen   90
          And each hour's joy wracked with a week of teen.   [*Exeunt*]

[4.2] *The Trumpets sound. Enter* RICHARD *crowned,* BUCKINGHAM, CATESBY *with other Nobles* [*and a* PAGE]

RICHARD Stand all apart! Cousin of Buckingham!
          Give me thy hand –
                              Here he ascends the throne
                    Thus high by thy advice
          And thy assistance is King Richard seated.
          But shall we wear these honours for a day,
          Or shall they last, and we rejoice in them?   5

70 As] Q; More F death] Q; Life F 71 As] Q; Then F 73 Even in so short a space] Q; Within so small a time F
75 my] Q; mine F 76 ever . . . sleep] Q; hitherto hath held mine eyes from rest F 78 Have I enjoyed] Q; Did I enioy
F 79 have . . . dreams] Q; with his timorous Dreames was still awak'd F 82 Alas, pour soul] Q; Poore heart adieu F
complaints] Q; complaining F 83 from] Q; with F 84 SH DORSET] Q, F; *Qu.* Q2–6 85 thou] Q; that F *86, 87,
88 SDS] F4; *not in* Q, F 87 guard] Q; tend F 88 good] Q; and good F *91 of teen] F; ofteene Q; F *follows with: Qu.*
Stay, yet looke backe with me vnto the Tower. / [*five lines*] / So foolish Sorrowes bids your Stones farewell. /
Exeunt. 0 SD *The Trumpets . . . a* PAGE] *This edn; The Trumpets . . . Nobles* Q; *Sound a Sennet. Enter Richard in pompe,
Buc-* / *kingham, Catesby, Ratcliffe, Louel.* F *1 SH RICHARD] F; *King.* Q; *and hereon* 1–2 Buckingham ! / Give] Q;
Buckingham. / *Buck.* My gracious Soueraigne. / *Rich.* Giue F 2 SD *Here . . . throne*] Q (*ascendeth*); *Sound.*
F 4 honours] Q; Glories F

BUCKINGHAM Still live they, and for ever may they last!
RICHARD O Buckingham, now do I play the touch
       To try if thou be current gold indeed.
       Young Edward lives: think now what I would say.
BUCKINGHAM Say on, my gracious sovereign.   10
RICHARD Why, Buckingham, I say I would be King.
BUCKINGHAM Why, so you are, my thrice-renowned liege.
RICHARD Ha! Am I King? 'Tis so – but Edward lives.
BUCKINGHAM True, noble Prince.
RICHARD   O bitter consequence!
       That Edward still should live – true noble Prince!   15
       Cousin, thou wert not wont to be so dull.
       Shall I be plain? I wish the bastards dead
       And I would have it suddenly performed.
       What say'st thou? Speak suddenly, be brief.
BUCKINGHAM Your Grace may do your pleasure.   20
RICHARD Tut, tut, thou art all ice, thy kindness freezeth.
       Say, have I thy consent that they shall die?
BUCKINGHAM Give me some breath, some little pause, my lord,
       Before I positively speak herein;
       I will resolve your Grace immediately.   *Exit*   25
CATESBY The King is angry. See, he bites the lip.
RICHARD [*To himself*] I will converse with iron-witted fools
       And unrespective boys; none are for me
       That look into me with considerate eyes.
       Boy!   30
       High-reaching Buckingham grows circumspect.
PAGE My lord?
RICHARD Knowest thou not any whom corrupting gold
       Would tempt unto a close exploit of death?
PAGE My lord, I know a discontented gentleman   35
       Whose humble means match not his haughty mind.
       Gold were as good as twenty orators
       And will, no doubt, tempt him to anything.
RICHARD What is his name?
PAGE His name, my lord, is Tyrrel.   40
RICHARD Go call him hither presently.
                                                              [*Exit Page*]

---

6 may they] Q; let them F   **9** say] Q; speake F   **10** gracious sovereign] Q; louing Lord F   **12** liege] Q; Lord F
16 wert] Q; wast] F   **19** thou] Q; thou now F   **21** freezeth] Q; freezes F   **23** breath] Q; litle breath F little pause,
my] Q; some pawse, deare F   **24** herein] Q; in this F   **25** your Grace immediately] Q; you herein presently F   **26** bites
the] Q; gnawes his F   •**27** SD *To himself*] *this edn; not in* Q, F   **30** Boy ! / High-] Q; High- F   **31** circumspect.] Q;
circumspect. / Boy. F   **34** Would] Q; Will F   **35** My lord, I] Q; I F   **36** mind] Q; spirit F   **41** Go . . . presently] Q;
I partly know the man: goe call him hither, / Boy F   •**41** SD *Exit Page*] *Exit.* F; *not in* Q

[*To himself*] The deep-revolving, witty Buckingham
No more shall be the neighbour to my counsel.
Hath he so long held out with me untired,
And stops he now for breath?   45

Enter DERBY

How now, what news with you?
DERBY My lord, I hear the Marquess Dorset is fled
      To Richmond, in those parts beyond the seas where he abides.
RICHARD Catesby!
CATESBY   My lord?
RICHARD   Rumour it abroad
      That Anne, my wife, is sick and like to die;   50
I will take order for her keeping close.
Enquire me out some mean-born gentleman
Whom I will marry straight to Clarence' daughter –
The boy is foolish and I fear not him.
Look how thou dream'st! I say again, give out   55
That Anne, my wife, is sick and like to die.
About it, for it stands me much upon
To stop all hopes whose growth may damage me.
                                    [*Exit Catesby*]
[*To himself*] I must be married to my brother's daughter,
Or else my kingdom stands on brittle glass,   60
Murder her brothers, and then marry her.
Uncertain way of gain! But I am in
So far in blood that sin will pluck on sin.
Tear-falling pity dwells not in this eye!

Enter TYRREL

Is thy name Tyrrel?   65
TYRREL James Tyrrel, and your most obedient servant.
RICHARD Art thou indeed?
TYRREL   Prove me, my gracious sovereign.
RICHARD Darest thou resolve to kill a friend of mine?
TYRREL Ay, my lord, but I had rather kill two enemies.
RICHARD Why, there thou hast it: two deep enemies.   70
      Foes to my rest, and my sweet sleep's disturbers

•42 SD *To himself*] *this edn; not in* Q, F 43 counsell] Q; counsailes F 45 breath ?] Q; breath ? Well, be it so. F
46 what . . . you] Q; Lord *Stanley*, what's the newes F 47 My . . . the] Q; Know my louing Lord, the F •47–8 is fled
/ To Richmond . . . abides] *lineation this edn*; Dorset / Is . . . he / abides Q; *Dorset* / As I . . . *Richmond*, / In the . . . abides
F 48 those parts beyond the seas] Q; the parts F 49 Catesby !. . . Rumour] Q; Come hither *Catesby*, rumor F
50 sick and like to die] Q; very grieuous sicke F 52 mean-borne] Q (meane borne); meane poore F 56 wife] Q;
Queene F 58 SD *Exit Catesby*] *om.* Q, F 63 will pluck] Q1, F; plucke Q2–5; pluck(e)s Q6–8 67 sovereign] Q; Lord
F 69 Ay, my lord,] Q (I); Please you: F 70 there] Q; then F •71 disturbers] F; disturbs Q

Are they that I would have thee deal upon.
Tyrrel, I mean those bastards in the Tower.
TYRREL Let me have open means to come to them
And soon I'll rid you from the fear of them.   75
RICHARD Thou singest sweet music. Come hither, Tyrrel. [*Tyrrel kneels*]
Go by that token. Rise, and lend thine ear.

                                        He whispers in his ear

'Tis no more but so: say, is it done?
And I will love thee – and prefer thee too.
TYRREL 'Tis done, my gracious lord.   80
RICHARD Shall we hear from thee, Tyrrel, ere we sleep?
TYRREL You shall, my lord.   [*Exit*]

                    Enter BUCKINGHAM

BUCKINGHAM My lord, I have considered in my mind
The late demand that you did sound me in.
RICHARD Well, let that pass. Dorset is fled to Richmond.   85
BUCKINGHAM I hear that news, my lord.
RICHARD Stanley, he is your wife's son: well, look to it.
BUCKINGHAM My lord, I claim your gift, my due by promise,
For which your honour and your faith is pawned:
The Earldom of Hereford and the moveables,   90
The which you promised I should possess.
RICHARD Stanley: look to your wife. If she convey
Letters to Richmond, you shall answer it.
BUCKINGHAM What says your Highness to my just demand?
RICHARD As I remember, Henry the Sixth   95
Did prophesy that Richmond should be King,
When Richmond was a little peevish boy.
A King – perhaps – perhaps.
BUCKINGHAM   My lord!
RICHARD How chance the prophet could not, at that time,
Have told me, I being by, that I should kill him?   100
BUCKINGHAM My lord: your promise for the Earldom?
RICHARD Richmond! When last I was at Exeter,
The Mayor, in courtesy, showed me the Castle
And called it Rougemont, at which name I started,
Because a bard of Ireland told me once   105

76 Come] Q; Hearke, come F   77 that] Q; this F   77 SD *He whispers in his ear*] Q; *Whispers.* F   78 'Tis] Q; There is F   is it] Q; it is F   79 too] Q; for it F   80–2 'Tis . . . shall, my lord.] Q; I will dispatch it straight. F   *82 SD *Exit*] F (*after* 80); *om.* Q   82 SD *Enter* BUCKINGHAM] Q (*rt margin of* 81); F (*follows* 82)   84 demand] Q; request F   85 pass] Q; rest F   86 that] Q; the F   *87 son] Q4–8, F; sonnes Q1–3   to] Q; vnto F   88 your] Q; the F   90 The Earldom] Q; Th'Earledome F   *Hereford] Q (Herford); Hertford F   91 The which you] Q; Which you haue F   should] Q; shall F   94 demand] Q; request F   95 As I remember] Q; I doe remember me F   98–118 King – perhaps – perhaps . . . Why then] Q; King perhaps. / *Buck.* May it F

    I should not live long after I saw Richmond.
BUCKINGHAM My lord –
RICHARD Ay? What's o'clock?
BUCKINGHAM I am thus bold to put your Grace in mind of what you
    promised me.   110
RICHARD Well, but what's o'clock?
BUCKINGHAM Upon the stroke of ten.
RICHARD Well – let it strike.
BUCKINGHAM Why let it strike?
RICHARD Because that, like a jack, thou keepest the stroke   115
    Betwixt thy begging and my meditation.
    I am not in the giving vein today.
BUCKINGHAM Why then, resolve me whether you will or no!
RICHARD Tut, tut, thou troublest me. I am not in the vein.
                             [*Exeunt all but Buckingham*]
BUCKINGHAM Is it even so? Rewardest he my true service   120
    With such deep contempt? Made I him king for this?
    O let me think on Hastings and be gone
    To Brecknock while my fearful head is on.   *Exit*

[4.3] *Enter* SIR JAMES TYRREL

TYRREL The tyrannous and bloody deed is done;
    The most arch act of piteous massacre
    That ever yet this land was guilty of.
    Dighton and Forrest, whom I did suborn
    To do this ruthless piece of butchery,   5
    Although they were fleshed villains, bloody dogs,
    Melting with tenderness and kind compassion,
    Wept like two children, in their deaths' sad stories.
    'Lo, thus', quoth Dighton, 'lay those tender babes';
    'Thus, thus', quoth Forrest, 'girdling one another   10
    Within their innocent alabaster arms;
    Their lips were four red roses on a stalk,
    Which in their summer beauty kissed each other.
    A book of prayers on their pillow lay,
    Which once', quoth Forrest, 'almost changed my mind.   15

118 Why then . . . or no!] Q; May it please you to resolue me in my suit. F   119   Tut, tut, thou] Q; Thou F   *119   SD *Exeunt . . . Buckingham*] *Exit.* Q, F   120   Is . . . service] Q; And is it thus ? repayes he my deepe seruice F   121   deep contempt] Q; contempt F   *0   SD *Enter . . .* TYRREL] this edn; *Enter Sir Francis Tirrell.* Q; *Enter Tyrrel.* F   1   deed] Q; Act F   2   act] Q; deed F   4   whom] Q; who F   5   ruthless piece of] Q1–2; ruthfull peece of Q3–6; peece of ruthfull F; piece of ruthless *Pope*   6   Although] Q; Albeit F   7   Melting] Q; Melted F   kind] Q; milde F   8   two] Q; to F   stories] Q; Story F   9   Lo] Q; O F   those tender] Q; the gentle F   *10   one] F; on Q   11   innocent alabaster] Q (alablaster); Alablaster innocent F   13   Which] Q; And F   15   once] Q; one F

But O, the Devil –'. There the villain stopped
Whilst Dighton thus told on: 'We smothered
The most replenished sweet work of Nature
That from the prime creation ever she framed.'
Thus both are gone with conscience and remorse;   20
They could not speak; and so I left them both
To bring this tidings to the bloody King.

Enter RICHARD

And here he comes. All hail, my sovereign liege.
RICHARD Kind Tyrrel, am I happy in thy news?
TYRREL If to have done the thing you gave in charge   25
Beget your happiness, be happy then,
For it is done, my lord.
RICHARD   But didst thou see them dead?
TYRREL I did, my lord.
RICHARD   And buried, gentle Tyrrel?
TYRREL The chaplain of the Tower hath buried them,
But how, or in what place, I do not know.   30
RICHARD Come to me, Tyrrel, soon – at after-supper –
And thou shalt tell the process of their death.
Meantime, but think how I may do thee good
And be inheritor of thy desire.
Farewell till soon.   35

Exit Tyrrel

The son of Clarence have I pent up close;
His daughter meanly have I matched in marriage;
The sons of Edward sleep in Abraham's bosom,
And Anne, my wife, hath bid the world goodnight.
Now, for I know that Breton Richmond aims   40
At young Elizabeth, my brother's daughter,
And by that knot looks proudly o'er the crown,
To her I go, a jolly, thriving, wooer.

Enter CATESBY

CATESBY My lord –
RICHARD Good news or bad that thou comest in so bluntly?   45
CATESBY Bad news, my lord. Ely is fled to Richmond,

*16 There] F (there); their Q   17 Whilst] Q; When F   *19 ever she] F (ere); euer he Q   20 Thus] Q; Hence F
22 bring] Q; beare F   23 hail] Q; health F   liege] Q (leige); Lord F   *25 gave] Q3–6, F; giue Q1–2   27 done, my
lord] Q; done F   30 how . . . place] Q; where (to say the truth) F   *31 SH RICHARD] F; *Tir.* Q   *Tyrrel] Q2–6, F; *Tirre!*
Q1 at] Q; and F   32 And] Q; When F   33 thee] Q; the F   35–6 soon. / The son] Q; then, / *Tir.* I humbly take my
leaue. / *Rich.* The Sonne F   35 SD *Exit Tyrrel*] Q (*after* 34); *om.* F   39 the] Q; this F   *40 Breton] Brittaine Q; Britaine
F   42 o'er] Q (ore); on F   43 I go] Q; go I F   43 SD *Enter* CATESBY] Q; *Enter Ratcliffe.* F   44, 46 SHS CATESBY] Q
(*Cat., Cates.*); *Rat.* F   45 news or bad] Q; or bad newes F   46 Ely] Q; *Mourton* F

And Buckingham, backed with the hardy Welshmen,
Is in the field and still his power increaseth.
RICHARD Ely with Richmond troubles me more near
    Than Buckingham and his rash-levied army.   50
    Come: I have heard that fearful commenting
    Is leaden servitor to dull delay.
    Delay leads impotent and snail-paced beggary.
    Then, fiery expedition be my wing,
    Jove's Mercury, and herald for a King.   55
    Come, muster men. My counsel is my shield.
    We must be brief when traitors brave the field.

                                            Exeunt

[4.4] *Enter* QUEEN MARGARET

MARGARET So now prosperity begins to mellow
    And drop into the rotten mouth of death.
    Here in these confines slyly have I lurked
    To watch the waning of mine adversaries.
    A dire induction am I witness to   5
    And will to France, hoping the consequence
    Will prove as bitter, black, and tragical.
    Withdraw thee, wretched Margaret: who comes here?

      Enter QUEEN ELIZABETH *and the* DUCHESS OF YORK

ELIZABETH Ah, my young Princes! Ah, my tender babes,
    My unblown flowers, new-appearing sweets!   10
    If yet your gentle souls fly in the air
    And be not fixed in doom perpetual,
    Hover about me with your airy wings
    And hear your mother's lamentation.
MARGARET [*Aside*] Hover about her! Say that right for right   15
    Hath dimmed your infant morn to aged night.
ELIZABETH Wilt thou, O God, fly from such gentle lambs
    And throw them in the entrails of the wolf?
    When didst thou sleep when such a deed was done?
MARGARET [*Aside*] When holy Harry died, and my sweet son.   20
DUCHESS Blind sight, dead life, poor mortal living ghost;
    Woe's scene, world's shame, grave's due by life usurped.

---

50 army] Q; Strength F 51 heard] Q; learn'd F 56 Come] Q; Go F 0 SD *Enter* QUEEN MARGARET] *Enter Queene*
Margaret sola. Q; *Enter old Queene Margaret.* F 4 adversaries] Q; enemies F 8 SD *Enter . . .* YORK] *Enter the Qu. and the*
Dutchesse of Yorke. Q; *Enter Dutchesse and Queene.* F 9 young] Q; poore F 10 unblown] Q; vnblowed F 21 Blind
sight, dead life] Q; Dead life, blind sight F 22–3 usurped. / Rest] Q; vsurpt, / Breefe abstract and record of tedious
dayes, / Rest F

Rest thy unrest [*sitting*] on England's lawful earth,
Unlawfully made drunk with innocents' blood.
ELIZABETH O, that thou wouldst as well afford a grave   25
As thou canst yield a melancholy seat,
Then would I hide my bones, not rest them here [*sitting*].
O who hath any cause to mourn but I?
DUCHESS So many miseries have crazed my voice
That my woe-wearied tongue is mute and dumb.   30
Edward Plantagenet, why art thou dead?
MARGARET [*Comes forward*] If ancient sorrow be most reverend,
Give mine the benefit of seigniory
And let my woes frown on the upper hand.
If sorrow can admit society,   35
Tell over your woes again by viewing mine.
I had an Edward, till a Richard killed him;
I had a husband, till a Richard killed him.
Thou hadst an Edward, till a Richard killed him;
Thou hadst a Richard, till a Richard killed him.   40
DUCHESS I had a Richard too, and thou didst kill him;
I had a Rutland too, thou holpst to kill him.
MARGARET Thou hadst a Clarence too, and Richard killed him.
From forth the kennel of thy womb hath crept
A hell-hound that doth hunt us all to death.   45
That dog, that had his teeth before his eyes,
To worry lambs and lap their gentle bloods,
That foul defacer of God's handiwork,
Thy womb let loose, to chase us to our graves.
O, upright, just, and true-disposing God!   50
How do I thank thee, that this carnal cur,
Preys on the issue of his mother's body,
And makes her pew-fellow with others' moan.
DUCHESS O Harry's wife, triumph not in my woes,
God witness with me, I have wept for thine.   55
MARGARET Bear with me. I am hungry for revenge
And now I cloy me with beholding it.
Thy Edward, he is dead that stabbed my Edward;
Thy other Edward dead to quit my Edward;
Young York, he is but boot, because both they   60
Match not the high perfection of my loss.

---

24 innocents'] Q (innocents); innocent F **25** as well] Q; assoone F **28** I] Q; wee F **29–31** DUCHESS So many . . . dead ?] Q; *after* 16 *in* F **30** mute and dumb] Q; still and mute F **34** woes] Q; greefes F **36** Tell . . . mine.] Q; *om.* F •**38** husband] F; Richard Q •**Richard**] F; Ricard Q •**41** too] Q2–6, F; to Q1 •**42** too] Q2–6, F; to Q1 •holpst] Q2–6; hopst Q1; hop'st F **47** bloods] Q; blood F **48–9** handiwork, / Thy] Q; handy worke: / That reignes in gauled eyes of weeping soules: / That excellent grand Tyrant of the earth, / Thy F •**54** wife] Q2–6, F; wifes Q **58** stabbed] Q; kill'd F **59** Thy] Q; The F **61** Match] Q; Matcht F

Thy Clarence, he is dead that killed my Edward;
And the beholders of this tragic play,
The adulterate Hastings, Rivers, Vaughan, Grey,
Untimely smothered in their dusky graves.   65
Richard yet lives, hell's black intelligencer,
Only reserved their factor to buy souls
And send them thither. But at hand, at hands,
Ensues his piteous and unpitied end.
Earth gapes, hell burns, fiends roar, saints pray,   70
To have him suddenly conveyed away.
Cancel his bond of life, dear God, I pray,
That I may live to say, 'The dog is dead!'
ELIZABETH O thou didst prophesy the time would come
That I should wish for thee to help me curse,   75
That bottled spider, that foul, bunch-backed toad.
MARGARET I called thee then, vain flourish of my fortune;
I called thee then, poor shadow, painted Queen,
The presentation of but what I was;
The flattering index of a direful pageant;   80
One heaved a-high to be hurled down below;
A mother only mocked with two sweet babes;
A dream of which thou wert a breath, a bubble;
A sign of dignity, a garish flag
To be the aim of every dangerous shot;   85
A Queen in jest, only to fill the scene.
Where is thy husband now? Where be thy brothers?
Where are thy children? Wherein dost thou joy?
Who sues to thee and cries 'God save the Queen!'?
Where be the bending peers that flattered thee?   90
Where be the thronging troops that followed thee?
Decline all this, and see what now thou art:
For happy wife, a most distressed widow;
For joyful mother, one that wails the name;
For Queen, a very caitiff, crowned with care;   95
For one being sued to, one that humbly sues;
For one commanding all, obeyed of none;
For one that scorned at me, now scorned of me.
Thus hath the course of justice wheeled about
And left thee but a very prey to time,   100

---

62 killed] Q; stab'd F   63 tragic] Q; franticke F   68 at hand, at hands] Q; at hand, at hand F   *69 Ensues] F (Insues);
ensues Q   71 away] Q; from hence F   73 to] Q; and F   82 sweet] Q; faire F   83–5 A dream . . . shot] Q; A dreame
of what thou wast, a garish Flagge / To be the ayme of euery dangerous Shot; / A signe of Dignity, a Breath, a Bubble F
88 are thy children] Q1–2; be thy children Q3–8; be thy two Sonnes F   89 sues . . . cries] Q; sues, and kneeles, and sayes
F   *92 Decline] Q2–6, F; decline Q1   94–99 *Order in* F: 94, 96, 95, 98 / *line omitted from* Q: For she being feared of all,
now fearing one: / 97, 99   98 one] Q; she F   99 wheeled] Q (whe'eld); whirl'd F

Having no more but thought of what thou wert
To torture thee the more, being what thou art.
Thou didst usurp my place, and dost thou not
Usurp the just proportion of my sorrow?
Now thy proud neck bears half my burdened yoke,   105
From which, even here, I slip my weary neck
And leave the burden of it all on thee.
Farewell, York's wife, and Queen of sad mischance.
These English woes will make me smile in France.

ELIZABETH O thou, well skilled in curses, stay awhile   110
And teach me how to curse mine enemies.

MARGARET Forbear to sleep the nights, and fast the days;
Compare dead happiness with living woe;
Think that thy babes were fairer than they were,
And he that slew them fouler than he is: 115
Bettering thy loss makes the bad causer worse;
Revolving this will teach thee how to curse.

ELIZABETH My words are dull, O quicken them with thine!

MARGARET Thy woes will make them sharp and pierce like mine.   *Exit*

DUCHESS Why should calamity be full of words?   120

ELIZABETH Windy attorneys to your client-woes,
Airy succeeders of intestate joys,
Poor breathing orators of miseries.
Let them have scope, though what they do impart
Help not at all, yet do they ease the heart.   125

DUCHESS If so, then be not tongue-tied; go with me
And in the breath of bitter words let's smother
My damned son, which thy two sweet sons smothered.
I hear his drum; be copious in exclaims.

Enter RICHARD *marching with drums and trumpets*

RICHARD Who intercepts my expedition?   130

DUCHESS Ah! She that might have intercepted thee –
By strangling thee in her accursed womb –
From all the slaughters, wretch, that thou hast done.

ELIZABETH Hidest thou that forehead with a golden crown
Where should be graven, if that right were right,   135
The slaughter of the Prince that owed that crown,
And the dire death of my two sons and brothers?

101 wert] Q1–2; art Q3–6; wast F   106 weary neck] Q; wearied head F   109 will] Q; shall F   112 nights] Q1–2; night Q3–6, F   days] Q1–2; day Q3–6, F   114 fairer] Q; sweeter F   121 your client-woes] Q1–3, 5–6 (Client woes); your clients woes Q4; their Clients Woes F   122 intestate] Q; intestine F   124 do] Q; will F   125 not at all] Q; nothing els F   128 which] Q; that F   129 I hear his drum] Q; The Trumpet sounds F   129 SD *Enter . . . trumpets*] Q; *Enter King Richard, and his Traine.* F   130 my] Q; me in my F   135 Where] Q; Where't F   graven] Q; branded F   137 two] Q; poore F

Tell me, thou villain-slave, where are my children?
DUCHESS Thou toad! Thou toad! Where is thy brother Clarence –
  And little Ned Plantagenet, his son?   140
ELIZABETH Where is kind Hastings, Rivers, Vaughan, Grey?
RICHARD A flourish! Trumpets! Strike alarum drums!
  Let not the heavens hear these tell-tale women
  Rail on the Lord's anointed. Strike, I say!
               The trumpets [and drums sound]
  Either be patient and entreat me fair,   145
  Or with the clamorous report of war
  Thus will I drown your exclamations.
DUCHESS Art thou my son?
RICHARD Ay, I thank God, my father and yourself.
DUCHESS Then patiently hear my impatience.   150
RICHARD Madam, I have a touch of your condition,
  Which cannot brook the accent of reproof.
DUCHESS I will be mild and gentle in my speech.
RICHARD And brief, good mother, for I am in haste.
DUCHESS Art thou so hasty? I have stayed for thee,   155
  God knows, in anguish, pain, and agony.
RICHARD And came I not at last to comfort you?
DUCHESS No, by the holy Rood, thou knowest it well:
  Thou camest on earth to make the earth my hell.
  A grievous burden was thy birth to me;   160
  Tetchy and wayward was thy infancy;
  Thy schooldays frightful, desperate, wild, and furious;
  Thy prime of manhood, daring, bold, and venturous;
  Thy age confirmed, proud, subtle, bloody, treacherous.
  What comfortable hour canst thou name   165
  That ever graced me in thy company?
RICHARD Faith, none but Humphrey hour, that called your Grace
  To breakfast once, forth of my company.
  If I be so disgracious in your sight,
  Let me march on and not offend your Grace.   170
DUCHESS O hear me speak, for I shall never see thee more!
RICHARD Come, come, you are too bitter.
DUCHESS Either thou wilt die by God's just ordinance

141–2 Where . . . A flourish] Q; Where is the gentle *Riuers, Vaughan, Gray* ? / *Dut.* Where is kinde *Hastings* ? / *Rich.* A flourish F *144 SD *The trumpets . . . sound*] *this edn*; The trumpets Q; *Flourish. Alarums.* F 152 Which] Q; That F 152–3 reproof. / I will] Q; reproofe. / *Dut.* O let me speake. / *Rich.* Do then, but Ile not heare. / *Dut.* I will F 153 speech] Q; words F 156 anguish, pain and agony] Q; torment and in agony F 164 bloody, treacherous] Q; slye, and bloody F 164–5 treacherous. / What] Q; bloody, / More milde, but yet more harmfull; Kinde in hatred: / What F 166 in] Q; with F 167 Humphrey hour] Q (houre); *Humfrey Hower* F 169 sight] Q; eye F 170–3 your Grace . . . Either thou] Q; you Madam. / Strike vp the Drumme. / *Dut.* I prythee heare me speake. / *Rich.* You speake too bitterly. / *Dut.* Heare me a word: / For I shall neuer speake to thee againe. / *Rich.* So. / *Dut.* Either thou F

Ere from this war thou turn a conqueror,
Or I with grief and extreme age shall perish,   175
And never look upon thy face again.
Therefore take with thee my most heavy curse,
Which in the day of battle tire thee more
Than all the complete armour that thou wearest.
My prayers on the adverse party fight,   180
And there the little souls of Edward's children
Whisper the spirits of thine enemies
And promise them success and victory.
Bloody thou art, bloody will be thy end.
Shame serves thy life and doth thy death attend.   *Exit*   185

ELIZABETH Though far more cause, yet much less spirit to curse
    Abides in me. I say 'Amen' to all.
RICHARD Stay, madam. I must speak a word with you.
ELIZABETH I have no more sons of the royal blood
    For thee to murder. For my daughters, Richard,   190
    They shall be praying nuns, not weeping queens,
    And therefore level not to hit their lives.
RICHARD You have a daughter called Elizabeth,
    Virtuous and fair, royal and gracious.
ELIZABETH And must she die for this? O let her live,   195
    And I'll corrupt her manners, stain her beauty,
    Slander myself as false to Edward's bed,
    Throw over her the veil of infamy;
    So she may live unscarred from bleeding slaughter
    I will confess she was not Edward's daughter.   200
RICHARD Wrong not her birth: she is of royal blood.
ELIZABETH To save her life I'll say she is not so.
RICHARD Her life is only safest in her birth.
ELIZABETH And only in that safety died her brothers.
RICHARD Lo, at their births good stars were opposite.   205
ELIZABETH No, to their lives bad friends were contrary.
RICHARD All unavoided is the doom of destiny.
ELIZABETH True, when avoided grace makes destiny.
    My babes were destined to a fairer death,
    If grace had blest thee with a fairer life.   210
RICHARD Madam, so thrive I in my dangerous attempt of hostile arms,

---

*174 Ere] F; Eeare Q   176 look upon] Q; more behold F   177 heavy] Q; greeuous F   187 all] Q; her F   188 speak]
Q; talke F   190 murder] Q; slaughter F   199 from] Q; of F   201 of royal blood] Q; a Royall Princesse F   203 only
safest] Q; safest onely F   205 births] Q; Birth F   206 bad] Q; ill F   210–11 life. / Madam, so] Q; life. / *Rich.* You
speake as if that I had slaine my Cosins ? / *Qu.* Cosins indeed, and by their Vnckle couzend, / [*11 lines*] / Rush all to peeces
on thy Rocky bosome. / *Rich.* Madam, so F   211–14 I   in . . . What good] Q; I in my enterprize / And dangerous
successe of bloody warres, / As I intend more good to you and yours, / Then euer you and yours by me were harm'd. /
Qu. What good F

As I intend more good to you and yours
Than ever you or yours were by me wronged.
ELIZABETH What good is covered with the face of heaven,
    To be discovered that can do me good.   215
RICHARD The advancement of your children, mighty lady.
ELIZABETH Up to some scaffold, there to lose their heads.
RICHARD No, to the dignity and height of honour,
    The high imperial type of this earth's glory.
ELIZABETH Flatter my sorrows with report of it.   220
    Tell me what state, what dignity, what honour?
    Canst thou demise to any child of mine?
RICHARD Even all I have, yea, and myself and all
    Will I withal endow a child of thine.
    So in the Lethe of thy angry soul   225
    Thou drown the sad remembrance of those wrongs
    Which thou supposest I have done to thee.
ELIZABETH Be brief, lest that the process of thy kindness
    Last longer telling than thy kindness do.
RICHARD Then know that from my soul I love thy daughter.   230
ELIZABETH My daughter's mother thinks it with her soul.
RICHARD What do you think?
ELIZABETH That thou dost love my daughter from thy soul;
    So from thy soul's love didst thou love her brothers,
    And from my heart's love I do thank thee for it.   235
RICHARD Be not so hasty to confound my meaning.
    I mean that with my soul I love thy daughter,
    And mean to make her Queen of England.
ELIZABETH Say then, who dost thou mean shall be her king?
RICHARD Even he that makes her Queen, who should be else?   240
ELIZABETH What, thou?
RICHARD I, even I; what think you of it, madam?
ELIZABETH How canst thou woo her?
RICHARD   That would I learn of you,
    As one that are best acquainted with her humour.
ELIZABETH And wilt thou learn of me?
RICHARD   Madam, with all my heart!   245
ELIZABETH Send to her, by the man that slew her brothers,
    A pair of bleeding hearts; thereon engrave
    'Edward' and 'York'. Then haply she will weep.

---

*214 the] Q2–6, F; rhe Q1   216 mighty] Q; gentle F   218 No, to] Q; Vnto F   honour] Q; Fortune F   220 sorrows]
Q; sorrow F   223 yea] Q; I F   *228 the] Q2–6, F; thc Q1   229 do] Q; date F   238 mean] Q; do intend F   239 Say]
Q; Well F   thou] Q; yᵘ F   240 should be else] Q1; should else Q2–6; else should bee F   242 I, even . . . madam] Q; Euen
so: How thinke you of it F   243 would I] Q1–2; I would Q3–6, F   244 that are] Q1–2; that were Q3–6; being F
*248 haply] F; happelie Q   she will] Q; will she F

Therefore present to her – as sometimes Margaret
Did to thy father – a handkercher steeped in Rutland's blood,   250
And bid her dry her weeping eyes therewith.
If this inducement force her not to love,
Send her a story of thy noble acts.
Tell her thou madest away her uncle Clarence,
Her uncle Rivers, yea, and for her sake   255
Madest quick conveyance with her good aunt Anne.

RICHARD   Come, come, you mock me; this is not the way
    To win your daughter.

ELIZABETH   There is no other way
    Unless thou couldst put on some other shape
    And not be Richard that hath done all this.   260

RICHARD   Infer fair England's peace by this alliance.

ELIZABETH   Which she shall purchase with still-lasting war.

RICHARD   Say that the King, which may command, entreats.

ELIZABETH   That, at her hands, which the King's King forbids.

RICHARD   Say she shall be a high and mighty Queen.   265

ELIZABETH   To wail the title as her mother doth.

RICHARD   Say I will love her everlastingly.

ELIZABETH   But how long shall that title 'ever' last?

RICHARD   Sweetly in force unto her fair life's end.

ELIZABETH   But how long – fairly – shall her sweet life last?   270

RICHARD   So long as heaven and nature lengthens it.

ELIZABETH   So long as hell and Richard likes of it.

RICHARD   Say I, her sovereign, am her subject-love.

ELIZABETH   But she, your subject, loathes such sovereignty.

RICHARD   Be eloquent in my behalf to her.   275

ELIZABETH   An honest tale speeds best being plainly told.

RICHARD   Then in plain terms tell her my loving tale.

ELIZABETH   Plain and not honest is too harsh a style.

RICHARD   Madam, your reasons are too shallow and too quick.

ELIZABETH   O no, my reasons are too deep and dead: 280
    Too deep and dead, poor infants, in their grave.

RICHARD   Harp not on that string, madam; that is past.

ELIZABETH   Harp on it still shall I, till heartstrings break.

RICHARD   Now by my George, my Garter, and my Crown –

249 sometimes] Q1–2; sometime Q3–6, F   **250–2** a handkercher . . . If] Q; steept in Rutlands blood, / A hand-
kercheefe, which say to her did dreyne / The purple sappe from her sweet Brothers body, / And bid her wipe her weeping
eyes withall. / If F   **252** force] Q; moue F   **253** story] Q; Letter F   acts] Q; deeds F   **255** yea] Q; I F   **257** Come,
come, you] Q; You F   me] Q; me Madam F   this is] Q; this F   **260–1** all this. / RICHARD Infer] Q; all this. / Ric. Say
that I did all this for loue of her. / [48 lines] / Qu. What were I best to say, her Fathers Brother / [4 lines] / Can make seeme
pleasing to her tender yeares ? / Rich. Inferre F   **263** Say that] Q; Tell her F   which] Q; that F   **266** wail] Q; vaile
F   **271, 272** So] Q; As F   **273** love] Q; low F   **277** in plain terms tell her] Q; plainly to her, tell F   **279** Madam,
your] Q; Your F   too quick] Q; to quicke F   *280 too] F; to Q   281 grave] Q; graves F   *282 on] F; one
Q   282 *follows* 283 *in* F

ELIZABETH Profaned, dishonoured, and the third usurped.   285
RICHARD I swear by nothing –
ELIZABETH   By nothing, for this is no oath,
    The George, profaned, hath lost his holy honour;
    The Garter, blemished, pawned his knightly virtue;
    The Crown, usurped, disgraced his kingly dignity.
    If something thou wilt swear to be believed,   290
    Swear then by something that thou hast not wronged.
RICHARD Now, by the world –
ELIZABETH   'Tis full of thy foul wrongs.
RICHARD My father's death –
ELIZABETH   Thy life hath that dishonoured.
RICHARD Then by my self –
ELIZABETH   Thyself thyself misusest.
RICHARD Why then, by God –
ELIZABETH   God's wrong is most of all.   295
    If thou hadst feared to break an oath by Him,
    The unity the King my husband made
    Had not been broken, nor my brother slain,
    If thou hadst feared to break an oath by Him,
    The imperial metal circling now thy brow   300
    Had graced the tender temples of my child,
    And both the Princes had been breathing here,
    Which now, two tender playfellows for dust,
    Thy broken faith hath made a prey for worms.
    What canst thou swear by now?
RICHARD   By the time to come.   305
ELIZABETH That thou hast wronged in time o'erpast.
    For I myself have many tears to wash,
    Hereafter time, for time, by the past wronged.
    The children live whose parents thou hast slaughtered:
    Ungoverned youth, to wail it in their age;   310
    The parents live, whose children thou hast butchered:
    Old withered plants, to wail it with their age.
    Swear not by time to come, for that thou hast
    Misused, ere used, by time misused o'erpast.
RICHARD As I intend to prosper and repent,   315

---

286 I swear by nothing] Q; I sweare F   287, 288, 289 The] Q; Thy F   289 dignity] Q; Lordly F   287 holy] Q; Lordly F   289 dignity] Q; Glory F   290 wilt] Q; would'st F   292–4 *as* 294, 292, 293 *in* F   293 that] Q; it F   294 thyself misusest] Q; is selfe-misvs'd F   295 God] Q; Heauen F   God's] Q; Heanens F   296 hadst feared] Q; didd'st feare F   by] Q; with F   *297 husband] F; brother Q   298 Had not been] Q; Thou had'st not F   brother slain] Q; Brothers died F   300 brow] Q; head F   303 playfellows] Q; Bed-fellowes F   304 a] Q; the F   *305 What ... now ?] F; *om.* Q   305 By] Q; *om.* F   308 by the past wronged] Q; past, wrong'd by thee F   309 parents] Q; Fathers F   310 in their] Q1–4; with their Q5, F; with her Q6   312 withered] Q; barren F   314 time misused o'erpast] Q; times ill-vs'd repast F

So thrive I in my dangerous attempt
Of hostile arms. Myself myself confound.
Day, yield me not thy light, nor night thy rest!
Be opposite, all planets of good luck,
To my proceedings, if with pure heart's love,   320
Immaculate devotion, holy thoughts,
I tender not thy beauteous, princely daughter.
In her consists my happiness and thine.
Without her follows to this land and me,
To thee, herself, and many a Christian soul,   325
Sad desolation, ruin, and decay.
It cannot be avoided but by this:
It will not be avoided but by this.
Therefore, good mother – I must call you so –
Be the attorney of my love to her.   330
Plead what I will be, not what I have been;
Not by deserts, but what I will deserve.
Urge the necessity and state of times,
And be not peevish, fond in great designs.

ELIZABETH Shall I be tempted of the devil thus?   335
RICHARD Ay, if the devil tempt thee to do good.
ELIZABETH Shall I forget myself to be myself?
RICHARD Ay, if your self's remembrance wrong yourself.
ELIZABETH But thou didst kill my children!
RICHARD But in your daughter's womb I buried them,   340
   Where in that nest of spicery they shall breed,
   Selves of themselves, to your recomforture.
ELIZABETH Shall I go win my daughter to thy will?
RICHARD And be a happy mother by the deed.
ELIZABETH I go. Write to me very shortly.   345
RICHARD Bear her my true love's kiss. [*Kisses her*] Farewell.

             Exit [*Elizabeth*]

Relenting fool – and shallow, changing woman.

     Enter RAT[CLIFFE *and* CATESBY]

RATCLIFFE My gracious sovereign, on the western coast
   Rideth a puissant navy. To the shore

316   attempt] Q; Affayres F   317–18   confound. / Day] Q; confound: / Heauen, and Fortune barre me happy houres. / Day F   320   proceedings] Q; proceeding F   pure] Q; deere F   324–5   this land . . . herself] Q; my selfe, and thee; / Her selfe, the Land F   326   Sad] Q; Death F   •328   by] Q2–6, F; *om.* Q1   329   good] Q; deare F   332   by] Q; my F   334   peevish, fond] Q; peeuish found F   336   thee] Q; you F   339   But] Q; Yet F   340   buried] Q1–2; bury Q3–8, F   341   shall] Q; will F   345–6   shortly. / Bear] Q; shortly, / And you shal vnderstand from me her mind. *Exit Q. / Rich.* Beare F   •346   kiss. [*Kisses her*] Farewell.] Q (*with editorial* SD); kisse, and so farewell. F   346   SD *Exit Elizabeth*] *Exit.* Q; *Exit Q.* F (*end of* F's *preceding line*)   347–8   woman. . . sovereign] *this edn*; woman. *Enter Rat./ Rat.* My gracious Souereigne] Q; Woman. / How now, what newes ? / *Enter Ratcliffe. / Rat.* Most mightie Soueraigne F   •347   SD *and* CATESBY] *this edn*; *om.* Q, F   349   the shore] Q; our Shores F

Throng many doubtful, hollow-hearted friends,   350
Unarmed, and unresolved to beat them back.
'Tis thought that Richmond is their admiral,
And there they hull, expecting but the aid
Of Buckingham to welcome them ashore.
RICHARD Some lightfoot friend, post to the Duke of Norfolk.   355
  Ratcliffe thyself – or Catesby: where is he?
CATESBY Here, my lord.
RICHARD Fly to the Duke. [*To Ratcliffe*] Post thou to Salisbury,
  When thou comest there – [*To Catesby*] dull, unmindful villain,
  Why standst thou still and goest not to the Duke?   360
CATESBY First, mighty sovereign, let me know your mind,
  What from your Grace I shall deliver him.
RICHARD O, true, good Catesby! Bid him levy straight
  The greatest strength and power he can make
  And meet me presently at Salisbury.   365

                            [*Exit Catesby*]
RATCLIFFE What is it your Highness pleasure I shall do at Salisbury?
RICHARD Why? What wouldst thou do there before I go?
RATCLIFFE Your Highness told me I should post before.
RICHARD My mind is changed, sir, my mind is changed.
  How now, what news with you?   370

                Enter DERBY

DERBY None good, my lord, to please you with the hearing,
  Nor none so bad but it may well be told.
RICHARD Hoyday, a riddle! Neither good nor bad –
  Why dost thou run so many miles about
  When thou mayest tell thy tale a nearer way?   375
  Once more: what news?
DERBY   Richmond is on the seas.
RICHARD There let him sink, and be the seas on him –
  White-livered runagate! What doth he there?
DERBY I know not, mighty sovereign, but by guess –
RICHARD Well, sir, as you guess, as you guess?   380
DERBY Stirred up by Dorset, Buckingham, and Ely,

---

357 lord] Q; good Lord F   358–9 Fly . . . villain] Q; *Catesby*, flye to the Duke. / *Cat.* I will, my Lord, with all conuenient haste. / *Rich. Catesby* come hither, poste to Salisbury: / When thou com'st thither: Dull vnmindful Villaine F *358, 359 SDS] *this edn*; *not in* Q, F   360 standst thou still] Q; stay'st thou here F   361 sovereign . . . mind] Q; Liege, tell me your Highnesse pleasure F *362 him] Q3–6; them Q1–2; to him F   364 he] Q; that he F   365 presently] Q; suddenly F *365 Salisbury.] Q (*om. Exit*); Salisbury. / *Cat.* I goe. *Exit.* F   366 is it . . . shall] Q; may it please you, shall I F   369 changed . . . changed] Q; chang'd F   370 How . . . you ? / *Enter* DERBY] Q; *Enter Lord Stanley.* / *Stanley,* what newes with you ?* F   371 lord] Q; Liege F   372 it may well be told] Q; well may be reported F   374 Why dost] Q; What need'st F   * miles] F; mile Q   375 a nearer] Q; the neerest F   380 Well . . . guess] Q; Well, as you guesse F 381 Ely] Q; *Morton* F

He makes for England, there to claim the crown.

RICHARD Is the chair empty? Is the sword unswayed?
Is the King dead? The empire unpossessed?
What heir of York is there alive but we?   385
And who is England's King but great York's heir?
Then tell me, what doth he upon the sea?

DERBY Unless for that, my liege, I cannot guess.

RICHARD Unless for that he comes to be your liege,
You cannot guess wherefore the Welshman comes.   390
Thou wilt revolt and fly to him, I fear.

DERBY No, mighty liege, therefore mistrust me not.

RICHARD Where is thy power then to beat him back?
Where are thy tenants? – and thy followers?
Are they not now upon the western shore,   395
Safe-conducting the rebels from their ships?

DERBY No, my good lord, my friends are in the north.

RICHARD Cold friends to Richard: what do they in the north
When they should serve their sovereign in the west?

DERBY They have not been commanded, mighty sovereign.   400
Please it your Majesty to give me leave,
I'll muster up my friends and meet your Grace
Where and what time your Majesty shall please.

RICHARD Ay, ay, thou wouldst be gone to join with Richmond.
I will not trust you, sir.

DERBY   Most mighty sovereign,   405
You have no cause to hold my friendship doubtful.
I never was, nor never will be, false.

RICHARD Well, go muster men. But hear you: leave behind
Your son, George Stanley. Look your faith be firm,
Or else his head's assurance is but frail.   410

DERBY So deal with him as I prove true to you.   [*Exit*]

Enter a MESSENGER

1 MESSENGER   My gracious sovereign, now in Devonshire –
As I by friends am well advertised –
Sir William Courtney and the haughty prelate,
Bishop of Exeter, his brother there,   415
With many more confederates, are in arms.

Enter another MESSENGER

382 there] Q; here F   •387 doth] Q3–6; doeth Q1–2; makes F   sea] Q; Seas F   392 mighty liege] Q; my good Lord F
394 are] Q; be F   398 Richard] Q; me F   400 sovereign] Q; King F   401 Please it] Q; Pleaseth F   404 Ay, ay,] Q
(I, I,); I, F   405 I] Q; But I F   you, sir] Q; thee F   408 Well, go] Q; Goe then F   But hear you] Q; but F   409 faith]
Q; heart F   •411 SD *Exit*] *Exit Stanley*. F; *om.* Q   •412, 417, 420, 423, 431, 432 SHS I, 2, 3, 4 MESSENGER] *Mes.* Q; *Mess.*
F   414 William] Q; *Edward* F   415 brother there] Q; elder Brother F

2 MESSENGER   My liege, in Kent the Guildfords are in arms
　　　　　　　And every hour more competitors
　　　　　　　Flock to their aid, and still their power increaseth.

Enter another MESSENGER

3 MESSENGER   My lord, the army of the Duke of Buckingham –   420
RICHARD   Out on you, owls! Nothing but songs of death?
　　　　　　　Richard strikes him
　　　　　　　Take that until thou bring me better news.
3 MESSENGER   Your Grace mistakes. The news I bring is good.
　　　　　　　My news is that by sudden flood and fall of water,
　　　　　　　The Duke of Buckingham's army is dispersed and scattered   425
　　　　　　　And he himself fled, no man knows whither.
RICHARD   O, I cry you mercy, I did mistake.
　　　　　　　Ratcliffe, reward him for the blow I gave him.
　　　　　　　Hath any well-advised friend given out
　　　　　　　Rewards for him that brings in Buckingham?   430
3 MESSENGER   Such proclamation hath been made, my liege.

Enter another MESSENGER

4 MESSENGER   Sir Thomas Lovell and Lord Marquess Dorset,
　　　　　　　'Tis said, my liege, are up in arms.
　　　　　　　Yet this good comfort bring I to your Grace:
　　　　　　　The Breton navy is dispersed; Richmond in Dorset   435
　　　　　　　Sent out a boat to ask them on the shore
　　　　　　　If they were his assistants: yea or no.
　　　　　　　Who answered him they came from Buckingham
　　　　　　　Upon his party. He, mistrusting them,
　　　　　　　Hoist sail and made away for Bretagne.   440
RICHARD   March on, march on! Since we are up in arms,
　　　　　　　If not to fight with foreign enemies,
　　　　　　　Yet to beat down these rebels here at home.

Enter CATESBY

CATESBY   My liege, the Duke of Buckingham is taken:
　　　　　　　That's the best news. That the Earl of Richmond   445

417   My liege, in Kent] Q; In Kent, my Liege F   419   their . . . increaseth] Q; the Rebels, and their power growes strong
F   420   the Duke of Buckingham] Q; great *Buckingham* F   421   SD *Richard strikes him*] *He striketh him.* Q (*after* 420),
F   422   Take . . . me] Q; There, take thou that, till thou bring F   423–4   Your Grace . . . news] Q; The newes I haue to
tell your Maiestie F   424   flood] Q; Floods F   water] Q; Waters F   425   The Duke of Buckingham's] Q; *Buckinghams* F
426   fled] Q; wandred away alone F   427   O, I] Q; I F   mercy, I did mistake] Q; mercie F   428   Ratcliffe . . . him] Q;
There is my Purse, to cure that Blow of thine F   429   given out] Q; proclaym'd F   430   Rewards for] Q; Reward to F   in
Buckingham] Q; the Traytor in F   431   liege] Q; Lord F   433   are up] Q; in Yorkeshire are F   434   Yet] Q; But F
Grace] Q; Highnesse F   •435   Breton] Brittaine Q, F   435–7   dispersed . . . If they] Q (Dorshire); dispers'd by Tempest.
/ *Richmond* in Dorsetshire sent out a Boat / Vnto the shore, to aske those on the Banks, / If they F   440   away] Q; his
course againe F   •*Bretagne*] Brittaine Q, F   445   That's] Q; That is F

Is with a mighty power landed at Milford
Is colder tidings, yet they must be told.
RICHARD Away towards Salisbury! While we reason here
A royal battle might be won and lost.
Someone take order Buckingham be brought   450
To Salisbury; the rest march on with me.

Exeunt

[4.5] *Enter* DERBY [*and*] SIR CHRISTOPHER [URSWICK]

DERBY Sir Christopher, tell Richmond this from me:
That in the sty of this most bloody boar
My son, George Stanley, is franked up in hold.
If I revolt, off goes young George's head;
The fear of that withholds my present aid.   5
But tell me, where is princely Richmond now?
URSWICK At Pembroke, or at Ha'rfordwest in Wales.
DERBY What men of name resort to him?
URSWICK Sir Walter Herbert, a renowned soldier;
Sir Gilbert Talbot, Sir William Stanley,   10
Oxford, redoubted Pembroke, Sir James Blunt,
Rhys ap Thomas, with a valiant crew,
With many more of noble fame and worth;
And towards London they do bend their course,
If by the way they be not fought withal.   15
DERBY Return unto thy lord; commend me to him;
Tell him the Queen hath heartily consented
He shall espouse Elizabeth, her daughter.
These letters will resolve him of my mind.
Farewell.   20

Exeunt

[5.1] *Enter* BUCKINGHAM *to execution* [*attended by* RATCLIFFE *and a guard*]

BUCKINGHAM Will not King Richard let me speak with him?
RATCLIFFE No, my lord, therefore be patient.

447 tidings,] Q; Newes, but F   **451** SD Exeunt] Q; Florish. Exeunt F   **0** SD Enter . . . URSWICK] Entee Darbie, Sir
Christopher. Q; Enter Derby, and Sir Christopher. F   **2** this most bloody] Q; the most deadly F   **5** withholds] Q; holds off
F   **7** Pembroke] Q; Penbroke F   Ha'rfordwest] Q (Harford-west); Hertford West F   **12** Rhys ap] Q (Rice vp); And Rice
ap F   **13** With . . . fame] Q; And many other of great name F   **14** they . . . course] Q; do they bend their power F
15 withal.] Q; F follows with: Der. Well hye thee to thy Lord: I kisse his hand,   **16–18** Return . . . daughter.] Q; follow
line 5 in F   **16–17** Return . . . the Queen] Q; So get thee gone: commend me to thy Lord. / Withall say, that the Queene
F (lines 6–7)   **18** shall] Q; should F (line 8)   **19** These letters] Q; My Letter F   **•0** SD Enter . . . guard] this edn; Enter
Buckingham to execution. Q; Enter Buckingham with Halberds, led / to Execution. F   **2** SH RATCLIFFE] Q (Rat.); Sher.
F   lord] Q; good Lord F

BUCKINGHAM Hastings, and Edward's children, Rivers, Grey,
        Holy King Henry, and thy fair son Edward,
        Vaughan, and all that have miscarried   5
        By underhand, corrupted, foul injustice –
        If that your moody, discontented souls
        Do through the clouds behold this present hour,
        Even for revenge, mock my destruction.
        This is All Souls' Day, fellows, is it not?   10
RATCLIFFE It is, my lord.
BUCKINGHAM Why then, All Souls' Day is my body's doomsday.
        This is the day that, in King Edward's time,
        I wished might fall on me when I was found
        False to his children – or his wife's allies.   15
        This is the day wherein I wished to fall
        By the false faith of him I trusted most.
        This, this All Souls' Day, to my fearful soul
        Is the determined respite of my wrongs:
        That high All-Seer that I dallied with   20
        Hath turned my feigned prayer on my head
        And given in earnest what I begged in jest.
        Thus doth he force the swords of wicked men
        To turn their own points on their master's bosom.
        Now Margaret's curse is fallen upon my head   25
        'When he', quoth she, 'shall split thy heart with sorrow,
        Remember Margaret was a prophetess.'
        Come sirs, convey me to the block of shame;
        Wrong hath but wrong, and blame the due of blame.
                                                        Exeunt

[5.2] *Enter* RICHMOND [*attended by three* LORDS] *with drums and trumpets*

RICHMOND Fellows in arms and my most loving friends,
        Bruised underneath the yoke of tyranny,
        Thus far into the bowels of the land
        Have we marched on without impediment;
        And here receive we from our father, Stanley,   5
        Lines of fair comfort and encouragement.
        The wretched, bloody, and usurping boar,

3 Rivers, Grey] Q; *Gray & Riuers* F   10 fellows] Q; (Fellow) F   11 RATCLIFFE It is, my lord] Q; *Sher.* It is F
13 that] Q; which F   15 or] Q; and F   17 I trusted most] Q; whom I most trusted F   20 that] Q; which F
*23 doth] F; doeth Q   24 on] Q; in F   bosom] Q; bosomes F   25 Now] Q; Thus F   is fallen upon my head] Q; falles
heauy on my necke F   *26 quoth] Q2–6, F; quorh Q1   28 sirs, convey me] Q; leade me Officers F   *29 SD *Exeunt*]
Exeunt Buckingham with Officers. F; *om.* Q   *0 SD *Enter . . . trumpets*] *this edn*; *Enter Richmond with drums and trumpets.* Q;
Enter Richmond, Oxford, Blunt, Herbert, and / others, with drum and colours. F

That spoiled your summer fields and fruitful vines,
Swills your warm blood like wash, and makes his trough
In your embowelled bosoms; this foul swine   10
Lies now even in the centre of this isle,
Near to the town of Leicester, as we learn.
From Tamworth thither is but one day's march;
In God's name, cheerly on, courageous friends,
To reap the harvest of perpetual peace   15
By this one bloody trial of sharp war.

1 LORD Every man's conscience is a thousand swords
To fight against that bloody homicide.

2 LORD I doubt not but his friends will fly to us.

3 LORD He hath no friends but who are friends for fear,   20
Which in his greatest need will shrink from him.

RICHMOND All for our vantage; then in God's name march!
True hope is swift and flies with swallows' wings;
Kings it makes gods and meaner creatures kings.

Exeunt

[5.3] *Enter* RICHARD, NORFOLK, RATCLIFFE, CATESBY *with* [*two soldiers*]

RICHARD Here pitch our tents, even here in Bosworth field.
Why, how now Catesby? Why lookst thou so bad?

CATESBY My heart is ten times lighter than my looks.

RICHARD Norfolk, come hither.
Norfolk, we must have knocks, ha!, must we not?   5

NORFOLK We must both give and take, my gracious lord.

RICHARD Up with my tent there!

[*They start to erect Richard's tent at one side of the stage*]

Here will I lie tonight –
But where tomorrow? Well, all is one for that.
Who hath descried the number of the foe?

NORFOLK Six or seven thousand is their utmost number.   10

RICHARD Why, our battalia trebles that account!
Besides, the King's name is a tower of strength,

11 Lies] Q; Is F centre] Q; Centry F 17 SH 1 LORD] Q; *Oxf.* F 17 swords] Q; men F 18 that bloody] Q; this
guilty F 19 SH 2 LORD] Q; *Her.* F 19 fly] Q; turne F 20 SH 3 LORD] Q; *Blunt.* F 20 who] Q; what F
21 greatest] Q; deerest F shrink] Q; flye F •24 makes] Q6, F; make Q1–5 24 SD Exeunt] *Exit.* Q; *Exeunt Omnes.* F
•0 SD Enter . . . soldiers] this edn; Enter King Richard, Norffolke, Ratcliffe, / Catesbie, with others. Q; Enter King Richard in
Armes, with Norfolke, Ratcliffe, / and the Earle of Surrey. F 1 tents] Q; Tent F 2 Why . . . bad] Q; My Lord of Surrey,
why looke you so sad F 3 SH CATESBY] Q; *Sur.* F 4–5 Norfolk . . . we] Q; My Lord of Norfolke. / Nor. Heere most
gracious Liege. / Rich. Norfolke, we F 6 gracious] Q; louing F 7 tent there] Q; Tent F 8 all is] Q; all's F 9 foe]
Q; Traitors F 10 utmost number] Q (*but one copy has* greatest); vtmost power F •11 battalia] F; battalion Q

Which they upon the adverse party want.
Up with my tent there! Valiant gentlemen,
Let us survey the vantage of the field.   15
Call for some men of sound direction;
Let's want no discipline, make no delay,
For lords, tomorrow is a busy day.

                                                                    Exeunt

Enter RICHMOND *with* [BLUNT *and two soldiers who erect a*
tent on the opposite side of the stage to Richard's tent]

RICHMOND The weary sun hath made a golden set,
          And by the bright track of his fiery car   20
          Gives signal of a goodly day tomorrow.
          Where is Sir William Brandon? He shall bear my standard.
          The Earl of Pembroke keep his regiment –
          Good Captain Blunt, bear my good night to him,
          And by the second hour in the morning,   25
          Desire the Earl to see me in my tent.
          Yet one thing more, good Blunt, before thou goest:
          Where is Lord Stanley quartered? Dost thou know?
BLUNT   Unless I have mista'en his colours much,
          Which well I am assured I have not done,   30
          His regiment lies half a mile at least
          South from the mighty power of the King.
RICHMOND If without peril it be possible,
          Good Captain Blunt, bear my good night to him,
          And give him from me this most needful scroll.   35
BLUNT   Upon my life, my lord, I'll undertake it.
RICHMOND Farewell, good Blunt.

                                                              [*Exit Blunt*]

          Give me some ink and paper in my tent.
          I'll draw the form and model of our battle,
          Limit each leader to his several charge,   40
          And part in just proportion our small strength.
          Come, let us consult upon tomorrow's business –

---

13 party] Q; Faction F want] Q; went *some copies of* F 14 my tent there! Valiant] Q; the Tent: Come Noble F
15 field] Q; ground F 17 want] Q; lacke F *18 SD *Enter . . . tent*] *this edn*; Enter Richmond with the Lordes, &c. Q;
Enter Richmond, Sir William Brandon, Ox- / ford, and Dorset. F *19 sun] Q2–6, F; sonne Q1 *set] F; sete Q1 *seate
Q2–5; seat Q6 20 track] Q; Tract F 21 signal] Q; token F 22 Where . . . He] Q; Sir *William Brandon,* you F Q *omits
before* 23, F's My Lord of Oxford, you Sir *William Brandon,* / And your Sir *Walter Herbert* stay with me: 23 keep] Q;
keepes F 27 good Blunt . . . goest] Q; (good Captaine) do for me F 28 Dost thou] Q (doest); do you F
34 Good . . . him] Q; Sweet *Blunt,* make some good meanes to speak with him F 35 scroll] Q;
Note F 36–7 it . . . Blunt] Q; it. / And so God giue you quiet rest to night. / *Richm.* Good night good Captaine *Blunt*
F *37 SD *Exit Blunt*] *this edn*; *om.* Q, F 38–41 Give . . . strength] Q; *follow line 22 in* F 41 strength] Q; Power
F 42 Come] Q; Come Gentlemen F

Into our tent! The air is raw and cold.

                                    [They withdraw into the tent]

        Enter RICHARD, NORFOLK, RATCLIFFE, CATESBY [*and two soldiers*]

RICHARD What is o'clock?
CATESBY It is six of clock, full supper time.   45
RICHARD I will not sup tonight. Give me some ink and paper.
       What? Is my beaver easier than it was?
       And all my armour laid into my tent?
CATESBY It is, my liege, and all things are in readiness.
RICHARD Good Norfolk, hie thee to thy charge.   50
       Use careful watch; choose trusty sentinels.
NORFOLK I go, my lord.
RICHARD Stir with the lark tomorrow, gentle Norfolk.
NORFOLK I warrant you, my lord.   *[Exit]*
RICHARD Catesby!   55
CATESBY My lord?
RICHARD   Send out a pursuivant-at-arms
       To Stanley's regiment; bid him bring his power
       Before sun rising lest his son George fall
       Into the blind cave of eternal night.

                                [Exit Catesby]

       Fill me a bowl of wine. Give me a watch.   60
       Saddle white Surrey for the field tomorrow.
       Look that my staves be sound and not too heavy.
       Ratcliffe!
RATCLIFFE My lord?
RICHARD Sawest thou the melancholy Lord Northumberland?   65
RATCLIFFE Thomas the Earl of Surrey and himself,
       Much about cockshut time, from troop to troop
       Went through the army cheering up the soldiers.
RICHARD So; I am satisfied. Give me a bowl of wine!

                              [Exit soldier]

       I have not that alacrity of spirit   70
       Nor cheer of mind that I was wont to have.
             [Enter soldier with wine]
       Set it down. Is ink and paper ready?
RATCLIFFE It is, my lord.
RICHARD   Bid my guard watch. Leave me.

                              [Exit soldier]

---

43   our] Q; my F   air] Q; Dew F   QI is from here to the end the prime source; collations for F are only exceptionally given.   *43 SD *They . . . tent*] F; *om.* Q   *51   sentinels] Centinels F; centinell Q   *54 SD *Exit*] F; *om.* Q 55   Catesby] Q; *Ratcliffe* F

Ratcliffe, about the mid of night, come to my tent
And help to arm me. Leave me, I say.   75
                    Exit Ratcliffe. [Richard enters tent]

Enter DERBY *to* RICHMOND *in his tent [with two lords]*

DERBY Fortune and victory sit on thy helm!
RICHMOND All comfort that the dark night can afford
            Be to thy person, noble father-in-law.
            Tell me, how fares our loving mother?
DERBY I, by attorney, bless thee from thy mother,   80
            Who prays continually for Richmond's good.
            So much for that. The silent hours steal on
            And flaky darkness breaks within the east.
            In brief, for so the season bids us be,
            Prepare thy battle early in the morning,   85
            And put thy fortune to the arbitrement
            Of bloody strokes and mortal staring war.
            I, as I may – that which I would I cannot –
            With best advantage will deceive the time
            And aid thee in this doubtful shock of arms.   90
            But on thy side I may not be too forward,
            Lest, being seen, thy brother, tender George,
            Be executed in his father's sight.
            Farewell! The leisure and the fearful time
            Cuts off the ceremonious vows of love   95
            And ample interchange of sweet discourse,
            Which so long-sundered friends should dwell upon.
            God give us leisure for these rights of love!
            Once more adieu: be valiant and speed well.
RICHMOND Good lords, conduct him to his regiment.   100
            I'll strive with troubled thoughts to take a nap
            Lest leaden slumber peise me down tomorrow
            When I should mount with wings of victory.
            Once more, good night, kind lords and gentlemen.
                            Exeunt [Stanley and lords]
            [*Kneels*] O Thou, whose captain I account myself,   105
            Look on my forces with a gracious eye.
            Put in their hands Thy bruising irons of wrath
            That they may crush down with a heavy fall
            The usurping helmets of our adversaries.
            Make us Thy ministers of chastisement,   110
            That we may praise Thee in the victory.

●97   long-sundered] *this edn*; long sundried Q1–2; long sundired Q3–4; long sundered Q5–6; long sundred F

To Thee I do commend my watchful soul
Ere I let fall the windows of mine eyes.
Sleeping and waking, O defend me still!   [*Enters tent; sleeps*]

Enter the ghost of young PRINCE EDWARD, *son to Harry the Sixth*

EDWARD'S GHOST [*To Richard*] Let me sit heavy on thy soul tomorrow.   115
  Think how thou stabb'dst me in my prime of youth
  At Tewkesbury: despair therefore, and die!
  [*To Richmond*] Be cheerful Richmond for the wronged souls
  Of butchered princes fight in thy behalf.
  King Henry's issue, Richmond, comforts thee.   [*Exit*]   120

Enter the ghost of HENRY THE SIXTH

HENRY'S GHOST [*To Richard*] When I was mortal, my anointed body
  By thee was punched full of deadly holes.
  Think on the Tower and me. Despair and die!
  Harry the Sixth bids thee despair and die.
  [*To Richmond*] Virtuous and holy, be thou conqueror.   125
  Harry, that prophesied thou shouldst be King,
  Doth comfort thee in thy sleep. Live and flourish!   [*Exit*]

Enter the ghost of CLARENCE

CLARENCE'S GHOST [*To Richard*] Let me sit heavy in thy soul tomorrow,
  I that was washed to death with fulsome wine,
  Poor Clarence, by thy guile betrayed to death.   130
  Tomorrow in the battle think on me,
  And fall thy edgeless sword. Despair and die!
  [*To Richmond*] Thou offspring of the House of Lancaster,
  The wronged heirs of York do pray for thee;
  Good angels guard thy battle. Live and flourish!   [*Exit*]   135

Enter the ghosts of RIVERS, GREY, [*and*] VAUGHAN

RIVERS'S GHOST [*To Richard*] Let me sit heavy in thy soul tomorrow,
  Rivers, that died at Pomfret. Despair and die!
GREY'S GHOST [*To Richard*] Think upon Grey, and let thy soul despair.
VAUGHAN'S GHOST [*To Richard*] Think upon Vaughan, and with guilty fear
  Let fall thy lance. Despair and die!   140
ALL [*To Richmond*] Awake, and think our wrongs in Richard's bosom
  Will conquer him. Awake, and win the day!
          [*Exeunt ghosts of Rivers, Grey, Vaughan*]

Enter the ghosts of the two young PRINCES

122 deadly] Q; *om.* Q2–8, F   *136 SH RIVERS'S GHOST] *Riu* Q3–8, F; *King* Q1–2   *142 Will] Q2–6, F; Wel Q1   143–
50 *The Ghosts of the two young princes appear before that of Hastings*, 151–5, *in* Q: *see Introduction, p. 29.*

PRINCES' GHOSTS [*To Richard*] Dream on thy cousins, smothered
    in the Tower.
    Let us be lead within thy bosom, Richard,
    And weigh thee down to ruin, shame, and death.   145
    Thy nephews' souls bid thee despair and die!
    [*To Richmond*] Sleep, Richmond, sleep in peace and wake in joy.
    Good angels guard thee from the boar's annoy.
    Live and beget a happy race of kings!
    Edward's unhappy sons do bid thee flourish.   150

                        [*Exeunt ghosts of Princes*]

        Enter the ghost of HASTINGS

HASTINGS'S GHOST [*To Richard*] Bloody and guilty, guiltily awake,
    And in a bloody battle end thy days.
    Think on Lord Hastings! Despair and die!
    [*To Richmond*] Quiet untroubled soul; awake, awake!
    Arm, fight, and conquer for fair England's sake!   [*Exit*]   155

        Enter the ghost of LADY ANNE, *his wife*

ANNE'S GHOST [*To Richard*] Richard, thy wife, that wretched Anne, thy wife,
    That never slept a quiet hour with thee,
    Now fills thy sleep with perturbations.
    Tomorrow in the battle think on me
    And fall thy edgeless sword. Despair and die!   160
    [*To Richmond*] Thou quiet soul, sleep thou a quiet sleep.
    Dream of success and happy victory.
    Thy adversary's wife doth pray for thee.   [*Exit*]

        Enter the ghost of BUCKINGHAM

BUCKINGHAM'S GHOST [*To Richard*] The first was I that helped thee to the
    crown;
    The last was I that felt thy tyranny.   165
    O, in the battle, think on Buckingham
    And die in terror of thy guiltiness.
    Dream on, dream on, of bloody deeds and death.
    Fainting, despair; despairing, yield thy breath!
    [*To Richmond*] I died for hope ere I could lend thee aid,   170
    But cheer thy heart and be thou not dismayed;
    God and good angels fight on Richmond's side,
    And Richard falls in height of all his pride.   [*Exit*]

        RICHARD *starts up out of a dream*

143 SH PRINCES' GHOSTS [*To Richard*]] Q (*Ghost to Ri*); *Ghosts.* F (*six lines later*) 144 lead] Q1; laid Q2–6,
F *156 SH ANNE'S GHOST [*To Richard*]] *this edn; Ghost to Rich.* F; *om.* Q1–6 *158 perturbations] Q2–6, F;
preturbations Q1 *164 SH BUCKINGHAM'S GHOST [*To Richard*]] *this edn; Ghost to Rich.* F; *om.* Q1–6 173 SD
RICHARD . . . *dream*] Q (*starteth*); *Richard starts out of his dreame.* F

RICHARD   Give me another horse! Bind up my wounds!
        Have mercy, Jesu! Soft, I did but dream.   175
        O coward conscience! How dost thou afflict me!
        The lights burn blue; it is now dead midnight.
        Cold fearful drops stand on my trembling flesh.
        What do I fear? Myself? There's none else by.
        Richard loves Richard – that is I and I.   180
        Is there a murderer here? No! Yes, I am.
        Then fly. What, from myself? Great reason, why?
        Lest I revenge? What, myself upon myself?
        Alack, I love myself. Wherefore? For any good
        That I myself have done unto myself?   185
        O no! Alas, I rather hate myself
        For hateful deeds committed by myself.
        I am a villain – yet I lie, I am not!
        Fool, of thyself speak well! Fool, do not flatter;
        My conscience hath a thousand several tongues,   190
        And every tongue brings in a several tale,
        And every tale condemns me for a villain:
        Perjury – perjury in the highest degree;
        Murder – stern murder in the direst degree;
        All several sins, all used in each degree,   195
        Throng to the bar, crying all, 'Guilty! Guilty!'
        I shall despair! There is no creature loves me,
        And if I die, no soul will pity me –
        And wherefore should they, since that I myself
        Find in myself no pity to myself?   200
        Methought the souls of all that I had murdered
        Came to my tent, and every one did threat
        Tomorrow's vengeance on the head of Richard.

              Enter RATCLIFFE

RATCLIFFE   My lord!
RICHARD   Zounds! Who is there?   205
RATCLIFFE   Ratcliffe, my lord, 'tis I. The early village cock
        Hath twice done salutation to the morn;
        Your friends are up and buckle on their armour.
RICHARD   O Ratcliffe, I have dreamed a fearful dream.
        What thinkst thou? Will our friends prove all true?   210
RATCLIFFE   No doubt, my lord.
RICHARD   O Ratcliffe, I fear, I fear!

177   now] Q1; not Q2–6, F   193   Perjury – perjury] Q1–2; Periurie Q3–6, F   205   Zounds] Q; *om.* F   209–
11   RICHARD . . . my lord.] Q; *om.* F

RATCLIFFE Nay, good my lord, be not afraid of shadows.
RICHARD By the Apostle Paul, shadows tonight
     Have struck more terror to the soul of Richard
     Than can the substance of ten thousand soldiers,   215
     Armed in proof, and led by shallow Richmond.
     'Tis not yet near day; come, go with me.
     Under our tents I'll play the eavesdropper
     To see if any mean to shrink from me.

                                                Exeunt

                Enter the LORDS *to* RICHMOND

LORDS Good morrow, Richmond.   220
RICHMOND Cry mercy, lords and watchful gentlemen
     That you have ta'en a tardy sluggard here.
I LORD How have you slept my Lord?
RICHMOND The sweetest sleep and fairest-boding dreams
     That ever entered in a drowsy head   225
     Have I since your departure had, my lords.
     Methought their souls whose bodies Richard murdered
     Came to my tent and cried on victory.
     I promise you, my soul is very jocund
     In the remembrance of so fair a dream.   230
     How far into the morning is it, lords?
2 LORD Upon the stroke of four.
RICHMOND Why, then 'tis time to arm and give direction.
             His oration to his soldiers
     More than I have said, loving countrymen,
     The leisure and enforcement of the time   235
     Forbids to dwell upon. Yet remember this:
     God, and our good cause, fight upon our side;
     The prayers of holy saints and wronged souls,
     Like high-reared bulwarks, stand before our faces.
     Richard except, those whom we fight against   240
     Had rather have us win than him they follow.
     For what is he they follow? Truly, gentlemen,
     A bloody tyrant and a homicide;
     One raised in blood and one in blood established;
     One that made means to come by what he hath,   245
     And slaughtered those that were the means to help him;
     A base, foul stone, made precious by the foil
     Of England's chair, where he is falsely set;

•218 eavesdropper] ease dropper Q1, F; ewse dropper Q2; ewse-dropper Q3; eawse-dropper Q4; ewese-dropper Q5–6
•226 departure] F; depature Q 229 soul] Q1–6; Heart F •240 Richard except,] Q3–6 (*Richard* Q6); Richard, except
Q1–2; (*Richard* except) F

One that hath ever been God's enemy.
Then, if you fight against God's enemy,   250
God will, in justice, ward you as his soldiers.
If you do sweat to put a tyrant down,
You sleep in peace, the tyrant being slain;
If you do fight against your countries foes,
Your country's fat shall pay your pains the hire;   255
If you do fight in safeguard of your wives,
Your wives shall welcome home the conquerors;
If you do free your children from the sword,
Your children's children quits it in your age.
Then, in the name of God and all these rights,   260
Advance your standards, draw your willing swords!
For me, the ransom of my bold attempt
Shall be this cold corpse on the earth's cold face;
But if I thrive, the gain of my attempt,
The least of you shall share his part thereof.   265
Sound drums and trumpets boldly and cheerfully!
God and Saint George! Richmond and victory!

> [*Exeunt Richmond and his lords*]

> *Enter* RICHARD, RATCLIFFE [*and lords*]

RICHARD   What said Northumberland as touching Richmond?
RATCLIFFE   That he was never trained up in arms.
RICHARD   He said the truth. And what said Surrey, then?   270
RATCLIFFE   He smiled and said, 'The better for our purpose.'
RICHARD   He was in the right, and so indeed it is.

> *The clock strikes*

Tell the clock there! Give me a calendar –
Who saw the sun today?
RATCLIFFE   Not I, my lord.
RICHARD   Then he disdains to shine, for by the book   275
He should have braved the east an hour ago.
A black day will it be to somebody. Ratcliffe!
RATCLIFFE   My lord?
RICHARD   The sun will not be seen today.
The sky doth frown and lour upon our army.
I would these dewy tears were from the ground!   280
Not shine today? Why, what is that to me
More than to Richmond? For the self-same heaven

**263, **293 Shall] F; shall Q   267 SD *Enter . . . lords*] *Enter King Richard, Rat. &c.* Q; *Enter King Richard, Ratcliffe, and Catesby.* F   272 SD *The clock strikes*] Q (*striketh*); *Clocke strikes.* F   **277 somebody. Ratcliffe!] *Johnson;* some bodie Rat. Q; somebody. "" *Ratcliffe.* F

That frowns on me looks sadly upon him.

Enter NORFOLK

NORFOLK Arm, arm, my lord! The foe vaunts in the field!
RICHARD Come! Bustle, bustle! Caparison my horse!   285
                    [RICHARD *arms*]
Call up Lord Stanley: bid him bring his power.
I will lead forth my soldiers to the plain
And thus my battle shall be ordered :
My foreward shall be drawn out all in length,
Consisting equally of horse and foot;   290
Our archers shall be placed in the midst.
John, Duke of Norfolk, Thomas, Earl of Surrey,
Shall have the leading of this foot and horse;
They thus directed, we will follow
In the main battle, whose puissance on either side   295
Shall be well winged with our chiefest horse.
This – and Saint George to boot! What thinkst thou, Norfolk?
NORFOLK A good direction, warlike sovereign.
                    He shews him a paper
This found I on my tent this morning.
RICHARD [*reads*] *Jockey of Norfolk be not so bold,*   300
          For Dickon thy master is bought and sold.
A thing devised by the enemy.
Go gentlemen! Every man unto his charge.
Let not our babbling dreams affright our souls.
Conscience is but a word that cowards use,   305
Devised at first to keep the strong in awe.
Our strong arms be our conscience, swords our law.
March on! Join bravely! Let us to it pell-mell –
If not to heaven, then hand in hand to hell!
                    His oration to his army
What shall I say more than I have inferred?   310
Remember whom you are to cope withal:
A sort of vagabonds, rascals, and runaways,
A scum of Bretons and base lackey-peasants,
Whom their o'er-cloyed country vomits forth
To desperate adventures and assured destruction.   315
You, sleeping safe, they bring to you unrest;
You, having lands and blest with beauteous wives,
They would restrain the one, distain the other.
And who doth lead them but a paltry fellow –

---

*297 boot] Q3–6, F; bootes Q1–2   *300 SH RICHARD [*reads*]] *Capell; King* Q *(but at* 302*),* F   309 SD *His . . . army*] Q;
om. F

Long kept in Bretagne at our brother's cost?   320
A milksop! One that never in his life
Felt so much cold as overshoes in snow.
Let's whip these stragglers o'er the seas again!
Lash hence these overweening rags of France,
These famished beggars weary of their lives,   325
Who, but for dreaming on this fond exploit,
For want of means, poor rats, had hanged themselves.
If we be conquered, let men conquer us
And not these bastard Bretons, whom our fathers
Have in their own land beaten, bobbed, and thumped,   330
And in record left them the heirs of shame.
Shall these enjoy our lands, lie with our wives,
Ravish our daughters?
                    [*Drum afar off*]
                    Hark, I hear their drum.
Fight, gentlemen of England! Fight bold yeomen!
Draw archers, draw your arrows to the head!   335
Spur your proud horses hard and ride in blood!
Amaze the welkin with your broken staves!

                    [*Enter a* MESSENGER]

What says Lord Stanley? Will he bring his power?
MESSENGER My lord, he doth deny to come.
RICHARD Off with his son George's head!   340
NORFOLK My lord, the enemy is past the marsh;
        After the battle let George Stanley die.
RICHARD A thousand hearts are great within my bosom.
        Advance our standards! Set upon our foes!
        Our ancient word of courage, fair Saint George,   345
        Inspire us with the spleen of fiery dragons!
        Upon them! Victory sits on our helms!
                                                    Exeunt

[5.4] *Alarum, excursions. Enter* CATESBY

CATESBY Rescue, my Lord of Norfolk! Rescue! Rescue!
        The King enacts more wonders than a man,
        Daring an opposite to every danger.
        His horse is slain and all on foot he fights,

•**320** brother's] mothers Q, F   •**333** SD *Drum afar off*] F; *om.* Q   •**337** SD *Enter a* MESSENGER] F; *om.* Q   **347** SD
Exeunt] Q; *om.* F

Seeking for Richmond in the throat of death.   5
Rescue, fair lord, or else the day is lost!

[*Alarums*] *Enter* RICHARD

RICHARD A horse! A horse! My kingdom for a horse!
CATESBY Withdraw, my lord! I'll help you to a horse.
RICHARD Slave! I have set my life upon a cast
And I will stand the hazard of the die.   10
I think there be six Richmonds in the field;
Five have I slain today in stead of him.
A horse! A horse! My kingdom for a horse!

[*Exeunt*]

[5.5] *Alarum. Enter* RICHARD *and* RICHMOND; *they fight.* RICHARD *is slain.*

Then retreat being sounded, enter RICHMOND, DERBY *bearing the crown, with other lords* [*and soldiers*]

RICHMOND God and your arms be praised, victorious friends!
The day is ours: the bloody dog is dead!
DERBY Courageous Richmond, well hast thou acquit thee.
Lo! Here this long-usurped royalty [*offers crown*]
From the dead temples of this bloody wretch   5
Have I plucked off to grace thy brows withal.
Wear it, enjoy it, and make much of it!
RICHMOND Great God of Heaven, say 'Amen to all!'
But tell me, is young George Stanley living?
DERBY He is, my lord, and safe in Leicester town,   10
Whither, if it please you, we may now withdraw us.
RICHMOND What men of name are slain on either side?
[*A document is given to* RICHMOND]
John, Duke of Norfolk; Walter, Lord Ferrers;
Sir Robert Brakenbury; and Sir William Brandon.
Inter their bodies as become their births.   15
Proclaim a pardon to the soldiers fled
That in submission will return to us;
And then, as we have ta'en the sacrament,
We will unite the white rose and the red.
Smile heaven upon this fair conjunction   20
That long have frowned upon their enmity.
What traitor hears me and says not 'Amen'?

---

*5.4.6 SD *Alarums*] F; *om.* Q   5.5.7   enjoy it,] Q1–2; *om.* Q3–6, F   11   if it please you] Q; (if you please) F

England hath long been mad and scarred herself.
The brother blindly shed the brother's blood;
The father rashly slaughtered his own son;   25
The son compelled, been butcher to the sire.
All this divided York and Lancaster –
Divided in their dire division.
O now let Richmond and Elizabeth,
The true succeeders of each royal house,   30
By God's fair ordinance conjoin together,
And let their heirs – God, if thy will be so –
Enrich the time to come with smoothfaced peace,
With smiling plenty and fair prosperous days.
Abate the edge of traitors, gracious Lord,   35
That would reduce these bloody days again,
And make poor England weep in streams of blood.
Let them not live to taste this land's increase
That would with treason wound this fair land's peace.
Now civil wounds are stopped: peace lives again!   40
That she may long live here, God say 'Amen'!

                 [*Exeunt*]

FINIS

32 their] Q1–2; thy Q3–6, F

TEXTUAL NOTES

1.1.0 SD GLOUCESTER In Q as *Gloucester* until crowned then *King*; speech headings similarly as *Glo.* (with occasional variants, e.g. *Gl.*) until *King.*; *Ri.* or *Rich.* appears occasionally in SDs. In F, *Richard*, or abbreviations thereof, throughout in directions and SHs. In this edition, GLOUCESTER is used until Richard is crowned and then RICHARD.

1.1.13 love F has 'Lute', which makes more obvious sense and which modern editors follow. The old principle of *difficilior lectio* prompts the thought that 'love' was what the actor intended (and it persists through the later Quartos). The meaning that the loved one is lasciviously pleased is, perhaps, more pointed and less commonplace than that the lute is lasciviously pleasing. It ties in with the idea of strutting before 'a wanton ambling nymph' (17). It is possibly significant that at 3.7.67 F has Buckingham claim that Richard is 'not lulling on a lewd Loue-Bed' (which the actor recalls as 'day-bed' in Q). For a 'love' as a paramour, compare *Wiv.*, 3.5.78: 'to search the house for his wife's love'. The opening of the play is particularly accurately reported and, in the light of 26, this might be an authorial revision.

1.1.26 spy Authorial revision for F's 'see' (and accepted as such by editors, e.g. Dover Wilson and Hammond; see Arden, 26n).

1.1.42 days The greeting, 'good days', is not recorded in *OED* and appears nowhere else in Shakespeare. Editors understandably emend to 'good day', as in F. However, no later quarto emends and possibly it was understood not as a salutation but in the sense in *Shr.*, 'my fortune lives for me, / And I do hope good days and long to see' (1.2.191–2). This would be appropriately ironic and in accord with Richard's 'We are not safe' (70).

1.1.50 shall be Memorial substitution for F's 'should be'; for further substitutions see 138n and Collation 52, 61, 75, 83, 87, 100, 124, 133, 142.

1.1.65 tempers As Hammond puts it, 'Q1 is patently correct', having been developed from 'Clarence' in *The Mirror for Magistrates* (Arden, 65n). F's 'tempts' was introduced by Q2. For a selection of F's readings which derive from later quartos, see Introduction, p. 26.

1.1.71 is secured F's 'secure' (which avoids doubling 'is') is attractive. However, the stress on no man having been made safe, and the hypermetric line (which memorial reconstruction might here be expected to smooth out), may indicate that Q's reading is intentional.

1.1.84 SH BRAKENBURY As *Bro.* in Q; *Bra.* in F. The form, *Brokenbury*, recurs at 88 and 105. As the name of the historical character was spelt with an 'a' (though historically he was not at the time of Clarence's incarceration yet Constable of the Tower), 'Brakenbury' has been preferred here.

1.1.101–2 What one . . . betray me? Omitted from surviving copies of Q1. Q2 may have been printed from a corrected copy of Q1 that is not represented in any of the surviving copies, or it may itself have been amended. The lines indicate that they have been squeezed in. A2ᵛ of Q2 has an extra line and room is made for the inclusion of a second line of text by running back 'pointed' under the end of 44. From this it would seem that it was realised that the compositor had accidentally omitted these two lines, probably because he jumped to the speech head for Brakenbury at 103 instead of setting that speech head at 101. See also 2.1.5n and 5.3.10n.

1.1.114–16 For Richard's action here, see Introduction, p. 25.

1.1.115 or lie Possibly revised from F's 'or else lye', so allowing the stress to fall on the ambiguous 'lie' enabling Richard, as Vice, to 'moralize two meanings in one word', as he puts it at 3.1.83.

1.1.132 eagle F has 'Eagles' which might reasonably refer to Clarence and Hastings, but Clarence is more properly described as a royal bird than Hastings, and only Clarence is now in prison; decorum is better served by the singular so this might be a revision.

1.1.138 Saint Paul The actor may have recalled the name of the saint (for F's Saint John) mentioned by Richard on four later occasions. Alternatively, the manuscript underlying F may go back to a time before Shakespeare had settled on the saint that Richard, according to More, invoked, in which case Q would be an authorial revision.

1.2.0 SD *Enter* . . . ATTENDANTS F is much more descriptive than Q. Both entries are incomplete. Anne addresses Tressel and Berkeley at 209 and they then exit with her (though only so directed in F as '*Exit two with Anne*'). A Gentleman and a Servant are each required to speak one line (36 and 214 – as Halberdier and Attendant in this edition). As Tressel and Berkeley are otherwise mute in Q/F it might be thought one of them could speak the line assigned in Q and F to a Gentleman, but he obviously carries a halberd (38) which is unusual for a private gentleman: see 36n. In addition to Richard, Anne, Tressel, and Berkeley, the scene requires at least two Halberdiers and from two to four men to manage the hearse – eight to ten in all. On tour, the company could conveniently find nine actors from its complement of twelve. They could draw on one or two backstage hands to swell out the scene with mutes, but their assistance is never relied on for the doubling pattern suggested in figure 2.

1.2.1 load Q has 'lo', expanded to 'lord' in Q2 and as 'load' in F. See Introduction, p. 8.

1.2.11 hands . . . holes Possibly memorial substitutions for F's 'hand' and 'wounds'; 'hand' suggests an individual as well as stabbing using a single hand; 'holes' anticipates the last word of 14. See 104n and 224n.

1.2.14 fatal Memorial exaggeration; see Collation 127; contrast 199n below.

1.2.15–16 do it. / More direful F has a third curse between these lines: 'Cnrsed [*sic*] the Blood, that let this blood from hence:' which the boy-actor playing Anne skipped and F's compositor misspelt. See also 23–4n.

1.2.18 adders Authorial revision for F's 'Wolues, to', so avoiding the awkwardness of a second 'to' and selecting a creature that goes better with spiders and toads than does the wolf?

1.2.23–4 view. / If ever Between these lines F has 'And that be Heyre to his vnhappinesse'. D. L. Patrick considered the omission of this line an oversight by the actor, arguing that it is necessary in order to direct Anne's curse to Richard (and see Arden, 1.2.25n). However, Anne's reference to abortive birth (20) harks back to Richard's own reference to his being born before his time, sent into the world deformed, unfinished, scarce half made up (1.1.20–1), so the association is clear.

1.2.25–6 As . . . As Q memorially weakens F's 'More . . . Then'; see below 156n and Collation 58, 76.

1.2.26 poor Substitution for F's 'young'; see below 74n, 91n, 104n, 135n, 137n, 156n, 167–9n, 186n, 191n, 194n, 222n, 224n, 234n, and 238n; and Collation 29, 58, 68, 77, 84, 86, 87, 93, 97, 99, 116, 120, 122, 124, 127, 128, 129, 141, 148, 154, 159, 163, 173, 177, 198, 199, 200, 244.

1.2.34 Villain F has 'Villaines', the singular of Q probably reflecting a smaller cast and simplified staging on tour.

1.2.36 SH HALBERDIER The speech headings in Q and F refer to a Gentleman but it is clear from 38 that a halberd is 'advanced' towards Richard and Halberdier is, in this context, a clearer representation of what is happening on-stage. It may be objected that Gentlemen did not carry halberds but there is an important exception. The Company of Gentlemen at Arms was formed as a royal escort in 1539 (Shakespeare may well have thought it was older) and to this day, on ceremonial occasions, is armed with partisans – virtually identical with halberds. The officer in command carries a sword. To avoid confusion, the speech heading is here given as Halberdier.

1.2.74 evils Substitution for F's 'Crimes'; the actor may have been influenced by 'devils' at 71 or Anne's 'evils' at 77. It is just possible that this is an authorial change to enhance the stress on the two epithets: 'supposed evils' against 'known evils'.

1.2.78 to curse Q and F have the same reading; Arden amends (after Spedding) to 't'accuse', which is convincing, balancing with 'to excuse' two lines later. It is not, however, essential and Q's reading has been allowed to stand.

1.2.91 hand Q's singular may be no more than an actor's substitution, but it is more effective than F's 'hands'.

1.2.104 fitter F's 'better' has strong editorial support; 'fitter' here may anticipate its use at 107 and Anne's reversal of the sense at 108; further, as Arden points out, 104 may echo *King Leir*: 'You are fitter for the King of heauen' (F3ʳ) and 'to send us both to heauen, / Where, as I thinke, you neuer meane to come' (I4ʳ). The actor, possibly recalling *King Leir*, has anticipated 107; and see 1.4.90n and 92–3n. The repertoire of the Queen's Men included several plays closely associated with Shakespeare: *King Leir*, *The Famous Victories of Henry V*, and *The True Tragedy of Richard III*.

1.2.126 rend F erroneously has 'rent'.

1.2.135 you F has 'thee'. This seemingly slight change points to an important dramatic pattern in the use of 'thy', 'thee', and 'thou', as opposed to 'you', 'your', and 'ye', in Anne's and Richard's exchanges. Anne uses the second person singular, the appropriate usage by a superior to an inferior in rank (as by Richard to the Halberdier at 37–40 above) from 81 to 180 on some two dozen occasions. At 184, at a telling moment, she uses the second person plural, 'Well, well, put up your sword'; the contest is over: she has capitulated. Thereafter she uses 'you' five times, at 186 (changed in Q from F's 'thou'), 208, 210, and 211 (twice), before leaving the stage. Thus, very subtly, we *know* that she has accepted Richard's proposal of marriage. Richard, apart from 'thee' at 79 in Q and F (an oversight?) uses 'you', 'your', and 'ye' from 66 to 128 in Q and F. Then, as he shifts from defence to wooing he, too, uses the second person singular, in F from 135 (where Q has 'you'), in Q from 138 (but with 'you' at 141; at 167, where the actor confuses his part, 'your husband' replaces F's 'King *Henrie*'). Then, at 204 in Q (198 in F) Richard reverts to 'you'. It is unsurprising that the actor should have difficulty in recalling the precise moments of change, but the correction to the pattern at 186 is surely deliberate. Shakespeare makes the same kind of distinction in 1.4; see 1.4.225n, and, for a general discussion of 'thou' and 'you' and the usages of Shakespeare's time, see Abbott, section 231.

1.2.137 slew The boy playing Anne recalls his part well so 'slew' could be an authorial change for F's 'kill'd'; 'slewest' appears in Q for F's 'killd'st' at 1.3.118 (in Margaret's part); see note.

1.2.141 Go to Not in F; Burbage has 'improved' his part in a manner suggestive of the jocularity of his playing of Richard. See 175n and Introduction, pp. 21–2.

1.2.154–5 drops. / I never Twelve lines of F are omitted in Q here. It is impossible to be certain whether they were revised out by Shakespeare for the production in London, cut for the touring version, or forgotten by the actor.

1.2.156 soothing words Weakened substitution of F's 'smoothing [=flattering] word'.

1.2.167–9 that killed your husband ... killed King Henry The actor carelessly recalls F, inverting the order of the murders and repeating 'killed' for F's 'did kill King *Henrie* ... stabb'd yong *Edward*'. See Collation 183 for another inversion.

1.2.175 Tush Burbage 'improves' his part in Q.

1.2.179 accessary The legal spelling of 'accessory' is found in Q and F.

1.2.186 shall you Q modernises F's 'shalt thou': see 135n.

1.2.190 ANNE To take ... give Omitted from F – a compositorial oversight?

1.2.191 this ring The actor substitutes for F's 'my Ring', perhaps following stage business.

1.2.194 suppliant Q's reading may be an authorial revision of F's 'Seruant'. Whilst the latter might readily have been substituted by the actor for 'suppliant', the reverse substitution is less likely. 'Suppliant' is particularly in accord with the tone of Richard's requests and, possibly, with stage business: he might kneel here.

1.2.198 thee F reverts to 'you' here; Q makes the change at the next opportunity, 204. See 135n.

1.2.199 more If F's 'most' had originated in Q, and 'more' had appeared in F, 'most' would have been rejected as a typical memorial exaggeration, a particularly common class of error. Both words may be authorial, Q's more limiting word being a revision; contrast 14n above.

1.2.222 her Q's 'her' is more logical (as Hammond has argued) than F's 'my' and the change might be authorial. However, Henry VI's corpse must seem to Anne cause for her hatred of Richard (supporting 'my') and 'her' could have been recalled by the actor, or set by the compositor, under the influence of the use of 'her' eight times from 218–23 in addition to this reading. Revision is thus by no means certain.

1.2.224 nothing Possibly in anticipation of 'nothing' at 226 (for F's 'no Friends').

1.2.234 debase Q's reading is superior to F's 'abase' (and so Arden, 1.2.251n). The change may stem from the actor, not Shakespeare.

1.2.238 halt ... unshapen F has 'halts ... mishapen', and at first sight Q may seem a product of memorial error, but 'halt' (as in the 'halt and blind') is more pointed and the line has possibly been authorially revised. Q accords with the practice of omitting 'do' in negative and interrogative sentences, characteristics of this and the preceding line. Thus, 'On me, that do halt, and am unshapen thus?' See Abbott, section 306.

1.3.5 words Weakened substitution for F's 'eyes'; see also 193n.

1.3.6 of Substitution for F's 'on'. For further substitutions see also 43n, 54n, 58n, 67n, 68–9n, 77n, 118n, 130n, 146n, 193n, 196n, 317n, 318n, 323n, 329n, 337n; and Collation 8, 17, 21, 27, 32, 33, 36, 37–8, 47, 53, 63, 66, 80, 90, 97, 106, 111, 124, 130, 131, 142, 149, 160, 168, 172, 190, 195, 196, 200, 209, 222, 231, 241, 242, 268, 274, 278, 283, 285, 298, 300, 301, 306, 311, 319, 320, 323, 326, 333, 340, 348, and 349.

1.3.6 If ... me? F repeats this line with the error 'Ifhe' (unspaced).

1.3.7 SH RIVERS F allocates to Grey; Q is possibly a deliberate revision. Compare 30n and see Collation 54.

1.3.16 SD *Enter ... DERBY* Stanley was not created Earl of Derby until after the Battle of Bosworth. Here and in F Shakespeare calls him Derby and that title is used elsewhere, but he is also referred to as Stanley in SDs and SHs (e.g. in 3.2). Derby is used throughout for directions in this edition.

1.3.17 come ... Lords F's 'comes' was erroneously introduced via Q3; F's compositor B then corrected the grammar, making 'Lords' singular even though this produced nonsense.

1.3.30 SH RIVERS F allocates to the Queen; Arden suggests F is in error but revision is possible.

1.3.41 at the highest Exaggeration of F's 'at the height'. Contrast 1.2.199n.

1.3.43 are they that complains F has 'is it that complaines' and Q8, 'are they that complain', but Q1's reading was reprinted by Q2–7. Q probably represents the northern English third person plural in *-s*, which Abbott finds extremely common but generally altered by modern editors (section 333). Compare 66n.

1.3.54 whom Q is grammatically correct; also at 323. The error in F is often found in Shakespeare, for example at 4.3.4, where Q again corrects; see Abbott, section 274. Possibly the scribe or the actor was punctilious.

1.3.58 His royal person F's 'Grace' for 'person' is formally more correct and the obvious reading; 'person' for 'Grace' is, however, an improbable error: 'his royal

Grace' would surely trip off the tongue automatically. The change might, therefore, be deliberate (and subtly insulting).

1.3.66 actions Q1's plural, for F's 'action', might be by attraction to the next word, 'shows'. F's 'action' stands in contrast to 'hatred', one outward, one inward. Lack of concord is found in the work of each of the three compositors who set Q1, so the source might go back to copy showing the influence of the grammatical form described in 43n.

1.3.67 kindred, brother Q's 'kindred' is, perhaps deliberately, more all-embracing than F's 'Children'; the singular form of F's 'Brothers' points directly, and correctly, at Rivers. This could either be attributed to authorial revision or the actor.

1.3.68–9 Makes him . . . to remove it F has only one line, 'Makes him to send, that he may learne the ground'; Pope combined F with an amended second line of Q: 'Of your ill will, and thereby to remove it'. This is more felicitous but Q's report, though ungainly, is clear.

1.3.77 we The actor may be anticipating the use of the royal plural for F's 'I' or echoing the Duchess at 76; it is possible that, as Richard refers not only to himself but to Clarence and the nobility, the change is deliberate. See also 269n and 328n.

1.3.92 She may, my lord – F's 'She may my Lord, for——' indicates that Shakespeare planned an overlap of dialogue in order that Richard could break in and stop Rivers giving his interpretation of events. The memorial reconstruction need not indicate this – Q simply has 'my Lord' – once the overlap had been rehearsed. See 229n.

1.3.98 yea F has the equivalent, 'I' (=ay). The Folio compositors, A and B, may have both regularly substituted 'I' when they found 'yea' in the manuscript of F, but Q may represent, in the main, the way the actors pronounced this syllable or the company's scribe(s) wrote it down. See also 120, 125, and 135; but at 2.1.82 Q and F have 'I' for 'Yea'.

1.3.101 a handsome It looks as if Shakespeare thought of 'bachelor' as disyllabic but that Burbage in Q gave it three syllables and compensated by omitting 'and'. See 117n and Collation 80.

1.3.109 thus . . . baited Reversal and substitution of F's 'so baited, scorn'd, and stormed'. See below 227n and 287n; also Collation 36, 106, 152, 272, 325, 333.

1.3.111 This line, and all Margaret's lines to 156, are usually marked and acted as asides. Following 156, 'I can no longer hold me patient', she is directed to come forward. The comedic technique of successive asides is appropriate to the mixed genre of *Richard III* but even more dramatic might be the disregarding by others of her grumbling interjections leading to her bursting out in anger with 'Hear me'. This makes more effective the incongruity of her claiming to have been patient and her use of asides in 4.4.

1.3.114–15 Tell him . . . of the King Both Q and F make sense but more appears to be at issue than the vagaries of actor's recall. F reads disjointedly and Q may represent, if not authorial revision, the actor's recall of a revised passage.

1.3.117 I remember F has 'I do remember'. This suggests that here Shakespeare considered 'devil' monosyllabic but that the actor playing Margaret gave it two syllables and compensated accordingly. Hammond, though generally following F, omits 'do' and points out that in half the instances in this play, 'devil' is unmistakably disyllabic.

1.3.118 slewest This may be a memorial substitution for F's 'killd'st' but it is possible the change was made deliberately, either by Shakespeare or the actor. The conjunction of consonants in 'killd'st' is awkward if the past tense is to be made clear. See 1.2.137n for a similar substitution.

1.3.130 yours As Richard addresses the company and not only Margaret, Q offers a slight improvement on F's 'you'; this may derive from the actor (or even the scribe).

1.3.146 lawful Substitution for F's 'Soueraigne', possibly prompted by the sound of the immediately preceding 'lord' (as 'Lo.' in Q).

1.3.154 A Q and F are identical; Arden argues for 'Ay'.

1.3.165–6 thee go. / A husband Between these lines F has Richard's question, 'Wert thou not banished, on paine of death?', and the first two lines of Margaret's response: 'I was: but I doe find more paine in banishment, / Then death can yeeld me here, by my abode.' As Burbage is very reliable in his recall, and as this exchange involves two actors, it would be surprising if Q were wrong. It helps preserve a unity of thought that F, with Richard's interjection, disrupts. F causes unnecessary confusion in the minds of members of the audience. Thus, Q probably represents Shakespeare's revision.

1.3.172 drewst F's 'drew'st' acknowledges the elided 'e'. In his paradigms of Late Middle English and Modern English, Henry Sweet brackets this 'e' in, for example, 'her(e)st' and 'call(e)st' (*A Short Historical Grammar*, pp. 147 and 155).

1.3.180 ever Q might have been expected to reproduce F's elided form, 'ere', but Q, with few exceptions, expands ellipses. This was, presumably, a scribal characteristic. If – and these are bold assumptions – the elided forms in F derive from Shakespeare's manuscript, then he could hardly have acted as a scribe producing the memorial reconstruction where non-elided forms appear. However, though this must be borne in mind, to sustain such a hypothesis means overlooking the intervention of compositors.

1.3.193 If A weakening of F's 'Though' which suggests (as Hammond points out) that though the Yorkists have been victorious, 'an ignominious death may yet strike Edward'; 'If' leaves this open; 'Though' reinforces Margaret's sense of defeat which 'informs her entire jeremiad'.

1.3.196 my Editors often prefer Q's 'my' to F's 'our'. Margaret's speech is remarkably accurate. Apart from the variants listed, there are only such slight changes as 'could' for 'should' (190), and 'which' for 'that' (195 and 196).

1.3.227 mother's heavy womb Q and F are both represented in modern editions. Q, the more logical of the two – it is the womb that makes the mother heavy – may be an authorial revision but could simply be an actor's inversion.

1.3.229 &c. '&c.' probably indicates that Margaret's cursing is to continue indistinctly as Richard breaks in with 'Margaret!' F has two short dashes here. Doris Fenton, *The Extra-Dramatic Moment in Elizabethan Plays before 1616* (Philadelphia,

1930), lists 26 plays with this indication, designed to prompt legitimate ad-libbing (p. 19, n. 28). See 92n above.

1.3.242 that Possibly a memorial substitution for F's 'this'; it may have been prompted by an appropriate gesture.

1.3.255 blasts Q1's 'blast' is probably a compositorial error; Q2–8 and F have 'blasts'.

1.3.269 Have done Buckingham anticipates his repeated 'Haue done' in F, six lines later (said only once at that point in Q). The reporting from here to the end of the scene is less accurate than that for the first 268 lines.

1.3.276 I will Presumably a scribal expansion of F's 'Ile' (which accords better with the metre). But compare 'I'll' (Q, Ile) for F's 'I will' 283.

1.3.278 princely Repetition from two lines earlier for F's 'Noble'.

1.3.287 rankle thee to death Inversion of F's 'rankle to the death'. Q1 misprints as 'rackle'; corrected in Q2.

1.3.299 yours Q1 has 'your' which Q2 sensibly emends to 'you'. As emendation is necessary, F's 'yours' is preferred. The error was probably the compositor's or scribe's, not the actor's.

1.3.300 SH HASTINGS F gives this line to Buckingham. The touring version does not itself require that Hastings speak this line – doubling is not involved. A change of speaker was probably made deliberately because it would be illogical for Buckingham to speak of his hair standing on end when he has very recently shown such equanimity (e.g. 281–2 and 292). He might, perhaps, be attempting irony or sarcasm. The only other occurrence of 'hair' in *Richard III* is at 1.4.50 when it is mentioned by Clarence. There are thus no textual grounds, and no patterns of imagery, to indicate who should speak the line. Q's recording of what happened onstage, coupled with the illogicality of having Buckingham speak the line, suggests this is an authorial revision.

1.3.301 wonder Probably memorial substitution for 'muse why' but it is possible that the flowery style of F was deemed unsuitable and revised.

1.3.304 that I have done F continues with 'to her', which is metrically sound.

1.3.315 SD *To himself* Q omits F's direction; had a scribe added this indication he might be expected to use the usual word, 'Aside'; this looks, therefore, like Shakespeare's own instruction. In F it is given a line of its own between 314 and 315. **cursed, now** F punctuates as 'curst now', and possibly Q represents Burbage's phrasing.

1.3.317 and you my noble lords Q has 'Lo:' which can be singular or plural, the latter being required here. F has 'and yours my gracious Lord'. At first sight this seems appropriate as Buckingham, like Gloucester (earlier referred to as 'your Grace' (54)), is entitled to be addressed as 'your Grace'. However, there are several lords present so Q's 'noble lords' is more appropriate and may represent revision.

1.3.318 we . . . us F avoids a possible royal plural: 'I . . . mee.'

1.3.323 laid Prompted by 'lay' in the preceding line, Burbage may have substituted 'laid' for F's 'cast'; 'laid' has already occurred thrice in Richard's speeches: 1.1.32, 1.2.97, and 1.3.170.

1.3.328 believe me Q anticipates 'me' from the end of the line for F's 'it'.

1.3.329 Vaughan F has *Dorset*, a more important figure, but Vaughan will be executed with Rivers and Grey, and as in Q he is, except as a Ghost, mute (even in 3.3 when he is executed), this helps place him in the audience's mind. Dorset and Vaughan could have been played by the same actor in the touring version.

1.3.337 deed Were F's 'thing' to be found in Q and 'deed' in F, 'thing' would be taken to be a memorial weakening. Conversely, 'deed' may be an authorial, not an actor's substitution.

1.3.346–8 In Q and F no distinction is made between the actors who shall deliver the two speeches allotted in this scene to the Executioner (or, in F, Villain). Some editors give the speech to the Second Executioner/Murderer. This might be justified in Q because at 1.4.80–1 it is he who says 'O sir, it is better to be brief than tedious. . . . Talk no more'; if that is the justification, then editors following F should give the speech to the First Executioner, who has the equivalent speech in Folio 1.4. In the conjectural doubling suggested for touring, the Second Executioner also plays Catesby and he will quite recently have spoken (316–17), so there are grounds for giving both speeches to his companion on tour. See also 350n.

1.3.346 Tush . . . lord In Q, the actor 'improves' what is found in F: 'Tut, tut, my Lord'; see Introduction, p. 23.

1.3.348 come F's 'go' has here, paradoxically, the same sense.

1.3.350 your business In F, Richard continues: 'straight. / Go, go, dispatch' and he receives the response, 'We will my Noble Lord.' The speech head for this final line in F is *Vil.* Arden describes this line as 'a characteristic duet, a mumbled response of agreement' and refers to 1.4.149 (as numbered in this edition). But at that point, F gives the hesitant words to the First Executioner; only in Q (which does not have this final exchange of 1.3) is the speech heading *Am.* – BOTH. Those reporting Q probably did know what their business was about here. Richard's conclusion to the scene in Q is far more chilling and characteristic than the conventional obsequiousness of F.

1.4.0 SD Q spells Brakenbury as Brokenbury in 1.1 and 1.4; he is referred to only as 'Lieutenant' (of the Tower) in 4.1 in Q and F. The quarto combines the rôles of Keeper and Brakenbury, the latter not entering until 68 in F; see 69–76n.

1.4.3 ugly sights, of ghastly dreams Inversion with substitutions. For inversions in this scene, see also below 62n, 86n, and Collation 22; for substitutions, 8n, 12n, 24n, 47n, 66n, 77n, 128n, 131n, 133n, 136n, 191n, 229n; and Collation 13, 17, 21, 23, 27, 30, 33, 35, 36, 38, 39, 40, 42, 43, 50, 56, 60, 61, 63, 64, 73, 75, 79, 80, 81, 85, 87, 88, 89, 90, 91, 92, 98, 99, 101–3, 113, 116, 118, 123, 130, 132, 157, 159, 170, 171, 172, 173, 175, 184, 186, 189, 190, 193, 199, 200, 201, 203, 205, 214, 217, 218, 219, 223, 224, 225, 227, 228, 230, 232, 235, 239, 240, 241, 243, 244, 249, 250, 251, 252.

1.4.8 What was . . . tell it The uncertainty of the actor playing Brakenbury, who has taken over the Keeper's lines, is reflected here in his resort to paraphrase for F's 'What was your dream my Lord, I pray you tel me'; see 62n and Introduction, p. 25.

1.4.9 Methoughts . . . Burgundy Clarence makes one line of F's two: 'Me thoughts that I had broken from the Tower, / And was embark'd to crosse to Burgundy.' The audience has just been made aware of Clarence's situation in the preceding dialogue at the end of 1.3 and it is possible that this directness in Q is an authorial simplification. See 24n, 26–7n, 34n, and Introduction, p. 33.

1.4.12 thence Q is superior to F's 'There', which may derive from Q6; compare 21, where Q6/F have 'water' against Q1–5 'waters', but contrast at 12, 'toward' in Q1–5, F with Q6's 'towards'.

1.4.13 fearful This is unlikely to be a revision of F's 'heauy'; it is probably an anticipation by the actor of 'fearful' at 23. See 114n.

1.4.20 Lord, Lord, Actor's 'improvement' of F's 'O Lord'; see also 40, 189, 201.

1.4.24 Ten thousand This could easily be taken to be a careless exaggeration of F's 'A thousand', typical of memorial reconstruction and scribal transcription. Editors regularly take F to be in error. See Introduction, p. 9.

1.4.26–7 jewels. / Some lay Between these lines F has 'All scattred in the bottome of the Sea'. The absence of this line from Q has been variously interpreted as a memorial omission by the actor, an omission by the compositor, or (by Smidt) as an authorial cut to avoid anticipating 'bottom' and 'scattered' at 30 and 31. Suggestions for authorial revision elsewhere in this passage (9, 24, 34), may support the argument that this, too, is authorial. See also 34n, 65–6n, 99–100n, 231–2n, 237–8n; and for minor omissions, see Collation 109, 112, 119, 124, 127, and 135.

1.4.34 Methought . . . flood Hammond suggests the omission of F's 'and often did I striue / To yeeld the Ghost' after 'had' may be deliberate alteration to make the sense more intelligible, attributing this to the actor rather than Shakespeare or the compositor. However, in the light of 9n, 24n, and 26–7n, this could be authorial.

1.4.47 cried F has the less dramatic 'spake'.

1.4.51 squeaked Q anticipated, through compositor's error, by two-and-a-half centuries the first use of the past participle 'squawked' (spelt 'squakt'), although the word appeared in the nineteenth century as an adjective. The omitted 'e' was rectified by Q2.

1.4.54 to your torments Actor's careless exaggeration; compare 24n and see 179n and Collation 121.

1.4.56 about Not found in F, 'howled' being given two syllables to make the line scan.

1.4.62 I promise you, I am afraid The actor, having added 'my' in the preceding line, now, in a kind of inversion, roughly approximates to F's 'I am affraid (me thinkes)'; compare 8n.

1.4.65–6 requites me. / I pray Q omits four lines of F here. They may have been forgotten by the actor, though some paraphrase of so passionate a prayer might have been expected to survive; they could be a late addition to F (as Patrick believed, p. 125), though there is not much evidence for that; or they may have been deliberately cut. Arden argues that the shift from mythological to Christian imagery is insufficient ground for cutting and that is surely correct, as is Hammond's and Smidt's argument that an Elizabethan audience would not be troubled by the fact that Clarence's wife was already dead; only the best-informed members of the audience would recall that she had died on 12 December 1476, before Clarence was imprisoned. However, the cut may have been made by Shakespeare on dramatic grounds: the change of direction – to prayer – shifts the focus of interest from Clarence's pathetic isolation; its omission brings together the references to himself. It is also possible that the lines were cut to avoid giving offence to the House of Tudor (especially as the Lord Chamberlain became the patron of Shakespeare's company in spring 1594).

1.4.66 I pray ... Keeper The change from F may be the work of the actor but it is more likely to be a deliberate revision. In F Clarence is addressing the Keeper; in Q Brakenbury, Lieutenant of the Tower, plays the Keeper's and his own rôle in this scene. See 69–76n and Collation 63.

1.4.69–76 Sorrow ... fame These lines are preceded by the entry in F: 'Enter Brakenbury the Lieutenant.' The Keeper does not speak again in F after 'I will, my lord. God give your Grace good rest' and there is no exit for him.

1.4.69 breaks Q's 'breake' probably lacks its final 's' because the compositor, reading the line over to himself in the course of setting, confused the various s's in this line. As the error is thus assumed to be compositorial, it has been amended here.

1.4.76 SD *The Murderers enter* The speech heads of Q refer to them (when named) as Executioners, the form used here.

1.4.77 In God's name ... hither? F precedes Brakenbury's demand (given as 'What would'st thou Fellow? And how camm'st thou hither?') with the First Murderer's, 'Ho, who's heere?'. As so much of 1.4 is 'improved' this cut is, at first sight, surprising, but the text has been skilfully modified in Q at this point, and this omission may be authorial. The silent approach of the executioners is far more chilling than their announcing themselves, as in F, with a loutish cry; Brakenbury's sudden shift from verse to prose in Q at 77 marks his shock and it signifies the beginning of the breakdown of order.

1.4.78 The First Executioner, having had his first line, found in F, cut, is given this line which, in F, was spoken by the Second Murderer. The Second Executioner first speaks at 80 in Q (his fellow's line in F).

1.4.86 Here ... asleep This is not simply a reverse of the F order. Q evidently allows for a very small stage on tour – Clarence sitting asleep rather than lying – and the order of Q is more logical.

1.4.90 shall I ... sleeps? *King Leir* has 'Now could I stab them brauely, while they sleepe' (1467). See 1.2.104n and below 92–3n.

1.4.92–3 When ... Day *King Leir* has 'thou art in a dreame, / And thou shalt neuer wake untill doomes day' (1616–17); see 1.2.104n. The use of 'fool' might point to the First Executioner's stupidity but it might confirm that the fools are playing these rôles. The Second Executioner's repetition of 'When he wakes' at 92 (here made a question) is typical of a two-clown act.

1.4.99–100 us. / Back Q omits F's elaboration of the Second Executioner's faint-heartedness: '1 I thought thou had'st bin resolute. / 2 So I am, to let him liue.' This omission, because it helps develop a distinction between the two Executioners, is unlikely to be authorial but rather a joint omission by Kemp and Cowley.

1.4.100 Back In Q, the First Executioner tells his fellow to take his qualms to Gloucester; in F, which has 'Ile back', he will play the informer. The change is slight but Q could be evidence of a two-clown act.

1.4.105 Faith An actor's interpolation which 'places' for the audience what follows; compare 'So' at 110; 'Zounds', 124; 'Tut', 128, 'I warrant thee', 129; and Clarence's 'Why sirs' at 189 and 'O' at 201.

1.4.114 it is a dangerous thing Q reports this speech fairly accurately but here anticipates 'for a dangerous thing' at 121, and omits F's parenthetical 'by chance' after 'purse of gold that' in 119. Q attempts vainly to set the speech as verse paying no regard to scansion.

1.4.124–5 it is . . . Duke Another clue that the murderers might have been played by the clowns: compare Launcelot Gobbo's monologue, *MV* 2.2.1–32, in which 'the fiend is at mine elbow' with, evidently, his conscience at the other one. Critics have complained that the murderers have been played excessively clownishly. Hankey notes of a Victorian production that 'the *Manchester Guardian* had to warn the murderers against "getting too much into the Dogberry and Verges vein" lest the murder should be "enacted to the accompaniment of a mirthful pit" (6 September 1870). Irving's murderers [1896] came "straight out of the pantomime of *The Babes in the Wood*" (Shaw, *Our Theatre in the Nineties*, 3 vols., 1948, II, 292). In Henry Cass's production at the Old Vic in 1936 "they comport themselves like the Gobbo family" (*Sunday Times*, 19 January 1936)'; Hankey, p. 125.

1.4.128 strong in fraud Possibly a deliberate variation by the actor (Kemp) of F's 'strong fram'd', but it could be a compositorial misreading. 'Framed' is used by Richard at 1.2.231 and by Tyrrel at 4.3.19.

1.4.131 to this gear See Introduction, p. 23.

1.4.133 chop him in the malmsey butt The vivid use of 'chop', peculiar to Q, is repeated by the First Executioner at 239.

1.4.136 stirs . . . strike In F, the First Murderer notes that Clarence 'wakes' and the Second Murderer gives the order 'Strike'. The quarto, in line with the Second Executioner's reluctance to kill, gives the proposal to strike to the First Executioner and his fellow then suggests reasoning with Clarence – in F, the First Murderer's line. This logical and thoughtful reversal of speeches is probably authorial rather than confused reporting. The Executioners' speeches are reversed until they both speak together at 148; see also 222–3, 224n.

1.4.146–7 speak. / Tell Q omits the line in F between these two: 'Your eyes do menace me: why looke you pale?' This is possibly an oversight but more probably a deliberate authorial omission to avoid the contradiction between the Second Executioner's humble looks at 144 and menacing eyes three lines later. From here to 150 the lines hover between prose and verse, settling to verse at 151.

1.4.159 evidence Used as collective noun for 'witnesses' (hence 'are'); *OED sb* 7.

1.4.165–6 to have redemption . . . sins F omits 166 and makes the end of 165 'for any goodnesse' in order to accord with the 1606 Statute to Restrain Abuses (3 Jac. I., c.21). See Collation 107 and 124 for omission of 'Zounds' from F and 2.1.38 for F's 'heauen' for 'God'.

1.4.177 throw F repeats 'hurle' from 176. Either Shakespeare or the actor may have initiated this variation.

1.4.179 holy The addition of 'holy' to Q causes a line break after 'sacrament', making 180 hypermetric.

1.4.191 revenged for this A memorial weakening of F's 'auenged for the'. Q omits the next line of F, which may be the actor's mistake, but, as so much is well reported here, it could be an authorial cut in order to simplify the sense.

1.4.199 the devil Either the scribe, the actor, or the compositor has thoughtlessly repeated these words from the preceding line.

1.4.222–3, 224 Q reverses the speakers assigned in F to deliver these lines. Apart from Q's 'world's' for F's 'earths', the reporting is good. It would be strange were Kemp and Cowley both to get the assignation of these lines wrong, so the change was probably deliberate. See 225n and Collation 148, 209, 215 for both actors speaking together instead of only one, as in F.

1.4.225 Hast thou In Q Clarence addresses only one Executioner, presumably the last speaker (Kemp), whereas in F he pleads with both: 'Haue you'. This may be a memorial slip and could be explained by the reversal of speakers in Q at 222–3 and 224. However, Clarence (in Q) is made to realise which is the more determined of the two. Thus, Shakespeare's hand may be suspected here. This may be supported by the singular forms 'thou', 'thy own soul', and 'thou' in Q at 227 and 228 as opposed to F's 'you', 'your owne soules' and 'you'. See Introduction, pp. 33–4.

1.4.229 he Q's singular (for F's 'they') pinpoints Gloucester.

1.4.231–2 souls. / Relent The sense in Q manages adequately without F's five lines of Clarence's further plea and the omission ensures that the First Executioner's 'Relent' 232, immediately takes up Clarence's 'Relent' five words earlier. The cut may be authorial. For text, see p. 32.

1.4.237–8 pities not. / Ay Q omits a warning given between these lines spoken in F by the Second Executioner: 'Looke behinde you, my Lord.' The actor would hardly have forgotten such a line. The deletion of this warning serves to ensure that the Second Executioner is not as kindly intentioned as some editors believe.

1.4.242 grievous guilty murder done Q fills out F's part-line: 'greeuous murther'. The alliteration in Q suggests this is the work of the actor.

2.1.1 So, now I have done Q omits F's 'Why' before 'So' and inverts F's 'haue I' resulting in irregular metre. For another omission, see 137.

2.1.5 now in peace . . . to heaven Three of the surviving copies of Q1 have 'to heauen' and two have 'from heauen'. It would not need consultation of copy used for setting this passage in order to correct this error but copy was certainly consulted at 5.3.10 (see note). Q's reporting of this line, as corrected, is more accurate than F's, F's 'to peace' seeming erroneously to anticipate 'to heauen'. Rowe emended to read 'more in peace' and Capell to 'more at peace'. The latter is preferable; its 't' possibly prompted F's 'to' so indicating how the error arose; 'at peace' recurs in the next line – which can be interpreted as mere repetition or as rhetorical balance.

2.1.6 set Q's reading for F's 'made' is unexpected from an actor or scribe and cannot be explained as a homoeograph. There are indications of revision in this scene (see notes to 7, 24–5, 39, 64, 79, 90, and 101) so 'set' may be authorial, offering in 'set at peace' an implied contrast with the conventional 'set at odds' (used by Shakespeare in *Lear*, 'sets us all at odds', 1.3.5); line 68 here has 'any jot at odds'.

2.1.7 Rivers and Hastings Q is correct against F's '*Dorset* and *Riuers*'. The initial error and the correction may have been Shakespeare's.

2.1.9 heart Rivers anticipates 'heart' in the next line for F's 'soule'. See 32n, 76n.

2.1.18 are . . . in Substitutions for F's 'is . . . from'; for further substitutions see also 39n, 43n, 76n, 90n, 101n; and Collation 19, 23, 38, 44, 48, 51, 52, 56, 73, 77, 82, 85, 87, 95, 96, 105, 109, 114, 128, 133, 137.

2.1.24–5 mine. / DORSET This Between these lines F has the King's '*Dorset*, imbrace him: / *Hastings*, loue Lord Marquesse.' This is unlikely to be a memorial omission because several actors are involved and they should have prompted recall. The compositor's eye may have skipped from 'Dorset' in the King's first line to the speech head at 25. The scene flows effectively without the speech and it is possible that a cut was made to enhance that.

2.1.27 my lord Hastings's addition may be an actor's 'improvement'.

2.1.32 On you or yours Buckingham (who is prone to error – but see 39n) anticipates 'you and yours' of the next line for F's 'Vpon your Grace'.

2.1.39 zeal Despite doubts about Buckingham's capacity for accurate recall, and although he twice elsewhere uses 'zeal' (3.7.96 and 188), 'zeal' might be an authorial revision for F's 'loue'. The word is not an obvious, nor a precise, substitute for 'love' – Shakespeare distinguishes 'love and zeal' at 3.7.188.

2.1.43 perfect period of this peace The actor is probably responsible for substituting 'perfect' for F's 'blessed', tempted by the opportunity to alliterate.

2.1.44 the noble Duke F requires Ratcliffe's entry here. Ratcliffe does not speak in this scene, nor is he specifically addressed, so the touring version (Q) can omit him.

2.1.54 unwittingly F's 'unwillingly' is a compositorial misreading, taking 'tt' to be a scribal crossed 'll'.

2.1.64 Of . . . of you F has 'Of you and you, Lord *Riuers* and of *Dorset*'. This line, and the omission from Q of the line in F that follows 65: 'Of you Lord *Wooduill*, and Lord *Scales* of you' (giving two of Rivers's titles as if they were two other people), indicate revision by Shakespeare.

2.1.76 thus scorned A weak substitution for F's 'so flowted', suggested by the anticipation of 'scorn' two lines on; see also 101n.

2.1.79 SH RIVERS This line is given to the King in F; the change – hardly an oversight because it involves two actors – may be authorial.

2.1.90 but The substitution of this antithesis (for F's 'and') starts a sequence of minor changes which, together, give a more dramatic effect. Though not beyond the actors, this may be authorial. Thus, 'grant' (followed by Edward angrily breaking in) for F's 'heare me' 95; 'speak' for 'say' and 'demand'st' for 'requests' 96. These changes may have been made for the London production – but contrast 101n.

2.1.94 I pray thee Q tends to use more literary forms and F the colloquial – 'I prethee'. A memorial text might be expected to be colloquial; it is likely that the scribe was responsible for the spelling out found in Q. See Introduction, pp. 7–8.

2.1.101 the same F has the more original-sounding 'that tongue'. Q has a number of memorial substitutions in the ensuing lines, suggesting, rather than revision (see 90n), that the actor playing Edward was prone to error: 'slew' for 'kill'd', 102; 'cruel' for 'bitter', 103; 'rage' for 'wrath', 104; and for 106, 'Who spoke of Brother-hood? who spoke of loue?'

2.1.132 O poor Clarence! As part of 129 in Q but a separate line in F. Inevitably the scribe taking down a memorially reconstructed text could find precise lineation difficult.

2.1.137 But come, let's in Q has been slightly reworked so that only Richard and Buckingham (and possibly Stanley) remain after the King leaves. This may have been a convenience for touring but could have been revised for the London production when '*some*' in the stage direction was clarified: the actors would have had to know who was to exit and who remain. In F, Ratcliffe would also have remained with Richard and Buckingham but he is not present in this scene in Q.

2.2.0 SD Enter . . . CLARENCE F's entry (given here) is clearer than Q's: *Enter Dutches of Yorke, with Clarence Children*, though the requirements are the same.

2.2.1 SH BOY F has *Edw.* for the first speech heading but *Boy.* thereafter. For Q's *Gerl.* it has *Daugh.* The children's names, historically, were Edward and Margaret.
Granam Q's spelling throughout for F's 'Grandam' indicates how the two boy-actors (or possibly the scribes) pronounced the word. But see 2.4.10n. See Introduction, p. 24.

2.2.3 you wring your hands Q (for F's 'do weepe so oft') may indicate stage action; see Introduction, p. 24.

2.2.6 wretches, orphans Memorial inversion; see Collation 12, 58, 100.

2.2.7 be Substitution for F's 'were'; for further substitutions see below 8n, 24n, 40–1n, 45n, 59n, 104n, 116n; and Collation 13, 15, 22, 23, 25, 26, 27, 39, 46, 49, 53, 55, 56, 57, 60, 61, 62, 70, 79, 80, 81, 82, 87, 88, 90, 94, 98, 104, 112, 119, and 122.

2.2.8 me much Alliterative substitution for F's 'me both'; see also Collation 11.

2.2.15 effect Q omits Clarence's Daughter's line, 'And so will I' following 'effect' in F; see Introduction, p. 25, and 87n and 109n; for a minor omission, see Collation 20.

2.2.23 hugged me in his arm See Introduction, pp. 22 and 25.

2.2.24 on . . . in F's 'on . . . on' strikes the modern ear as more correct, and 'in' may be an error. However, 'in' could be so used in Shakespeare's day (*OED* Rely v^1 6 and 7); possibly a subtle distinction is intended.

2.2.32 SD Enter . . . ears Q has here, in the right margin of 32 and 33, *Enter the / Quee.*; the entry for this edition draws on F's: *Enter the Queene with her haire about her ears*, which F follows with *Riuers & Dorset after her.* Rivers and Dorset are cut from this scene in Q (see Introduction, p. 14). This may indicate that the actors who played them were present in this scene already – as Clarence's children.

2.2.40–1 withered . . . gone Q's substitution of 'withered' for 'gone' in 40 is initially attractive but it merely anticipates 'wither' in the next line and misplaces 'gone'. The result is a typical memorial approximation of 'gone? / Why wither not the leaues that want their sap?' See below 116n, and 'Madam', Collation 88 (anticipation of 91).

2.2.45 perpetual rest Memorial substitution echoing Clarence's 'perpetual night', 1.4.44 (in Q and F). That might suggest the same actor played Clarence and Elizabeth. This would just be practicable, though demanding.

2.2.55 thee Added in Q, making the line hypermetric.

2.2.56 husband F is correct here; Q's 'children' could be an unthinking repetition from the preceding line by the actor (though the scribe might have been expected to pick up such an error) but it is much more likely to be a compositorial error. In the text as printed, 'thy children' is slightly to the right of 'my children' and that could easily have caught the compositor's eye if the manuscript was similarly arranged. On the basis that the error is compositorial, the text has been emended in this edition. Two errors are attributable to the scribe or compositor in 59: 'Then' for 'Thine' and the omission of 'a' before 'moiety'; for these, F's readings have been adopted.

2.2.59 Thine Q's 'Then' could be a compositorial error.

grief Substitution for F's 'moane'; the substitution is reversed at 79.

2.2.66 laments Repetition from the preceding line for F's 'complaints'.

2.2.68 moon Q's spelling, 'moane', was doubtless induced by the prevailing mood of tears and lamentation.

2.2.77, 78 a dearer On each occasion, F repeats Elizabeth's 'so deere'; in Q, the actors memorially exaggerate, prompted by the similarity of F's sound: 'so deere a'. See also 113n.

2.2.87 The Duchess's speech is followed in F by speeches of seven and five lines by Dorset and Rivers respectively, both of whom were cut from this scene on tour; see 32 SDn.

2.2.104 hearts F's 'hates' makes more obvious sense and this variant could derive from the scribe or compositor. However, the actor recalling the scene may have had in mind the overweening pride of all those at odds (note 'the Queen's proud kindred' 119) and 'hearts' could well be what he actually said here. Further, if 'splintered' in the next line means (as here) 'broken' (see 105n), then 'broken hearts' makes good sense.

2.2.105 splintered Q and F agree but it has been urged (e.g. by Hammond) that 'splinted' is intended. To splint, knit, and join *are* all of a piece, though the order should be join, splint, and knit. However, as it stands, Q/F are logical: broken, knit together, and finally united. 'Splintered' is well supported, being derived from a written and a spoken source and it is noteworthy that F did not pick up 'splinted' found in Q2–8.

2.2.109 Q cuts the ensuing eighteen lines after the Duchess's speech. This makes a convenient cut for the touring version, probably initiated by Rivers having been omitted from this scene.

2.2.111, 123 Ludlow F has 'London' – a good example of Compositor B's inattention.

2.2.113 weighty business Q exaggerates F's 'businesse' so making the line hypermetric.

2.2.116 behind Substitution for F's 'at home', perhaps anticipating 'behind' seven lines later.

2.3.0 SD *Enter two* CITIZENS　F's *Enter one Citizen at one doore, and another at / the other* is much more revealing of stage action than is Q's simple direction. F may reflect what happened on tour, at least at some venues, but that is not certain so F has not been adopted here. The opening of the scene as found in F may be arranged as rough verse but in Q the language is very prosaic and no attempt has been made to fashion verse out of it until the scene settles down at line 10. Comment is only made on the more interesting variants.

2.3.1 Neighbour, well met! Q's approximation of F's 'Good morrow Neighbour' might represent the actor's own customary greeting; compare 17n.

2.3.3 1 CITIZEN . . . **abroad** This is part of the Second Citizen's speech in F.

2.3.5 Bad Substitution for F's 'Ill'; for further substitutions see also Collation 7, 14, 18, 19, 23, 24, 25, 29, 32, 33, 34, 36, 39, 41, 42, 44, 45, 47, and compare 9n.

2.3.6 troublous Q anticipates 'troublous' of line 10 for F's 'giddy'.

2.3.9 It doth Q sharply abbreviates F's 'I sir, it is too true, God helpe the while.'

2.3.17 Harry Q's colloquial form (for F's 'Henry') is probably that used by the actor.

2.3.26 now, who shall Q inverts F's 'who shall now'; see 39n (Collation 40).

2.3.39 dread Q1–2 have 'bread', a compositorial error caused by faulty dissing of 'b' and 'd' (an easy error); Q3 corrects. The actor has memorially reversed 'dread' (in F at 41) for 'fear' (F's reading here). In line 40 the actor inverts F's 'reason (almost)'.

2.3.44 Ensuing Q is correct; see Introduction, p. 9.

2.4.0 SD *Enter* . . . YORK Q and F have substantially the same entry with the notable exception that in Q it is the Cardinal (the Archbishop of Canterbury) of 3.1 who appears instead of the Archbishop of York. Q's speech heads are altered to show that it is the Cardinal, not the Archbishop, who speaks. See Introduction pp. 27 and 28.

2.4.1–2 Northampton . . . **will they be** In F the order of the places is reversed, reflecting the backtracking historically forced on the Prince's party by Richard. As this is not explained in the play it must have seemed topographically erroneous and at some point the order was simplified. The prompter has been suspected (e.g. Arden) but the removal of this avoidable confusion more probably goes back to the play's first production. In Q, 'will they be' is substituted for F's 'they do rest'; for further substitutions, see 9n, 35n, 51n, 55n, 68n; and Collation 13, 21, 31, 33, 40, 41, 43, 45, 50, 52, 56, 76.

2.4.9 young This could be a memorial substitution for F's 'good' but as F has 'good' twice in the line it could be an authorial revision.

2.4.10 Grandam Except on this occasion, Q always uses the form 'Granam'; see 2.2.1n and Introduction, p. 24. The spelling here may be attributed to the compositor. (The same compositor set 2.2, 2.4, and 3.1.)

2.4.12 uncle F has 'Vnkle' and Q, 'Nnckle', which is probably a compositorial error, either caused by faulty dissing or, if 'mine Vncle' stood in his copy, the compositor may have 'heard' this as he carried the line in his head as 'my N[u]nckle'. It is possible that the familiar 'Nuncle', later found seventeen times in *Lear*, was intended – ironic in the circumstances.

2.4.20 this were a true rule Q inverts F's 'his rule were true'; see also 25n.

2.4.21 SH CARDINAL This line is intended to be spoken by the Archbishop of York in F (see 0 SDn) but, with two Yorks in the scene, it is mistakenly given to the young Duke. The error must lie in Shakespeare's draft underlying F because F normally distinguishes the speakers by *Arch.* and *Yor.*

2.4.25 That . . . mine Q inverts F's 'growth . . . toucht'.

2.4.26 pretty York Anticipation of 'pretty York' at 31 for F's 'yong Yorke'.

2.4.35 perilous This variant, for F's 'parlous', could have originated with the actor, the scribe who wrote down his part, or the compositor; 'perilous' and 'parlous' can both mean cunning, mischievous, shrewd. At 3.1.154 'perilous boy' is used by Richard in Q and F. The actor playing Elizabeth, or more probably the scribe, may have picked up this form from that scene; it is not likely to derive from doubling as only Richard, Buckingham, and Catesby are on-stage at 3.1.154 and Elizabeth could not be doubled with any of them.

2.4.37 SD DORSET As Messenger in F. Presumably in London two different actors played Dorset and the Messenger. The Archbishop of York's line in F (for 38–9 here), 'Heere comes a Messenger: What Newes?', is given to the Cardinal in Q and lengthened to ensure that the rôle the actor is playing is made clear to the audience by giving his name in its two forms.

2.4.51 lady This substitution, for F's 'Lord' (which refers to the relevant prelate), reflects that Elizabeth's son, Dorset, has replaced the Messenger and, appropriately, so addresses his mother.

2.4.54 jet F's 'Iutt' has the same meaning; compare 35n.

2.4.55 lawless Q's substitution for F's 'awelesse' is typical of memorial weakening; it makes good sense but lacks the individuality of the original.

2.4.65 blood against blood The actor's recall is faulty here. Q omits F's 'Brother to Brother', possibly prompted by an attempt to smooth F's hypermetric and rhythmically irregular line, 'Blood to blood, selfe against selfe: O preposterous'.

2.4.68 death Possibly a compositorial misreading of the scribe's secretary-hand letters (F has 'earth') perhaps prompted by 'die' earlier in the line.

2.4.69 sanctuary F follows, on a separate line, with 'Madam, farwell.' It was probably missed in the process of recall. The omission disturbs the rhythm; in F, with the Duchess's 'Stay, I will go with you', it made a line of verse. In Q, line 70 is distinctly prosaic: 'I'll go along with you.'

3.1.0 SD etc. Even with the later entries to this scene, four of the touring company of twelve were available as attendants – the *etc.* Actors 5 and 10 have been *conjecturally* assigned in the table of doublings, leaving 2 and 8 free, though these, too, could have been on-stage.

3.1.0 SD–165 Copy for F is derived from the quartos: see Collation. The omissions at 40 and 141, stemming initially from Q3 and Q2 respectively, are particularly indicative of F's dependence on the quartos.

3.1.78 all-ending Q2–6 and F have 'ending'; many editors follow, assuming that the last syllable of the preceding word, 'generall' in Q1, has been repeated. However, the rhythm of Q1 is to be preferred and the error is the compositor's of Q2.

3.1.82 formal Vice, Iniquity Q lacks the initial capitals found in F. Folio *1H4* uses capitals whereas Q *1H4* does not in similar circumstances: 'that reuerend Vice, that grey Iniquitie, that Father Ruffian, that Vanitie in yeeres' (Folio, TLN 1411–12; Riverside *1H4* 2.4.453–4 gives only 'Vice' and 'Iniquity' initial capitals). The implication that Richard, like Falstaff, is playing the rôle of Vice is thus made clear in the Folio editions of both plays.

3.1.120 heavy F's 'weightie' was introduced in Q2 (waightie). Were the readings of Q1 and F reversed the actor might be held responsible for introducing 'weightie' by association with 'weightier' in the preceding line and 'weigh' in the next. The error – also by association – was, however, made by the Q2 compositor.

3.1.150 SD Q includes Dorset among those required to exit but he was not specifically named at the start of the scene and he is given nothing to say, nor is he referred to. Because Q provides copy for F for this section of the text, F follows suit. Dorset may have appeared in an earlier version of the play but he could clearly be dispensed with, and presumably was not included in this scene on tour.

3.1.167 What will he? Inversion of F's 'Will not hee?' F is now independent of Q.

3.1.169–72 Well then . . . willing The lineation follows Q (and also F for 169–70). Neither Q nor F is strictly metrical and editors realign following Pope. Q omits Buckingham's three-line instruction to Catesby (following 'purpose', 172) to summon Hastings to the Tower 'To sit about the Coronation'. As Catesby does not carry such a message to Hastings in Q or F it looks as if the lines were omitted to remove this inconsistency, perhaps when the play was produced in London. The omission would not, therefore, be an oversight by the actors; the cut improves the logical consistency.

3.1.182 friend Probably a memorial substitution for F's 'Lord' but authorial revision cannot be ruled out; the irony of 'friend' is so characteristic of Richard. See also 185n, 191n, 196n, and Collation 173, 175, 188, 193, 194, 195.

3.1.184 effect Buckingham omits F's 'goe', which makes the line metrical. Contrast 190 where, in Q, he adds 'William' before 'Lord Hastings', making that line irregular. This anticipates 3.4.27, where Buckingham has 'William, Lord Hastings' in Q and F.

3.1.185 may Memorial substitution for F's 'can'. Discrimination between 'may' and 'can' is sometimes illuminating: 'may' here suggests greater reservation than 'can' – 'I may be able to' rather than 'I can do'. Memorialisation tends to flatten such distinctions so Q's more subtle reading is noteworthy. As there are signs of revision here, this may be another. See also 3.7.222n.

3.1.186–7 Shall we . . . my lord Richard and Tyrrel have this exchange at 4.2.81–2.

3.1.191 Somewhat we will do Probably a memorial substitution for F's 'Something wee will determine.' However, in Q Richard is marginally less decisive and as at 194 the run-of-the-mill 'was possest' of F becomes in Q the more interesting 'stood possessed', Shakespeare's revising hand, rather than the actor's memory, might here be involved.

3.1.196 all willingness Though the actor could be responsible, this again may be an authorial revision (of F's 'all kindnesse').

3.2.0 SD *Enter . . . door* The omission of a reference to a door in Q may simply be an oversight but, in the light of line 2 (see 1–3n), the word may not have appeared in the manuscript because the actors on tour could not rely on having an appropriate door on their touring stages. In such circumstances the knocking could have been done off-stage. See also 3.7.50n.

3.2.1–3 What ho . . . Stanley These lines are only roughly recalled by the actors. However, the second line ('Who knockes?' in F) may have had 'at the door' added to the touring version in order to make clear what might not have been readily apparent on touring stages.

3.2.3 SD *Enter* HASTINGS The entry in Q is two short lines earlier than in F. As the actors must have known when the entry was made, this may represent a production change, not necessarily for the touring version.

3.2.5 ff. Q's line 5, which has 'thy master', though not metrically perfect, is more rhythmical than F's, which has 'my Lord *Stanley*'; the change is not beyond the actor, but it may be authorial – and it is just possible that the actor who played Hastings was Shakespeare. The lines that follow may also show authorial revision: Q's 'should seem' for F's 'appeares', 6, is more sophisticated; Q's repeated 'And then' in 8, and the Messenger's direct response, are more rhetorically effective than is F; line 9 in Q is far more rhythmical than F and this is no mere matter of counting syllables; line 15 has the edge rhythmically over F. Later, 'my servant, Catesby,' (for F's 'my good friend *Catesby*'), 20, and 'wanting' for F's 'without', 23, may also suggest revision. Buckingham refers to Catesby as Richard's servant at 3.7.53 *in Q only*. For further substitutions in this scene, see 15n, 24n, 78n, 82n, 85n, 87–9n, 92 SDn, 119n; and Collation 7, 10, 18, 32, 42, 44, 50, 56, 59, 65, 71, 78, 93, 109, 113, 114, 115, and 117.

3.2.9 boar Q1–5 have 'beare' and this is taken by editors to be a compositorial error, especially as 'boare' appears four times in Hastings's next speech.

3.2.14 presently you will Inversion of F's 'you will presently'; see Collation 109.

3.2.15 into The author or actor omits F's needless repetition of 'with him' and substitutes 'into' for 'toward', making the line unmetrical.

3.2.24 fond In the light of revisions suggested above, this, for F's 'simple', might seem another. However, Hastings does speak of himself as 'too fond' at 3.4.83 in a passage where he refers back to this scene, in particular to the boar razing Stanley's helm, so anticipation may be adduced. See also 26n.

3.2.26 pursues us Q hypermetrically adds 'us', perhaps in anticipation of 'us' at the end of the next line. The error may be either the actor's or the compositor's.

3.2.44 Upon my life, my lord Catesby expands F's 'I, on my life'.

3.2.58 What my lord? In Q, Catesby breaks into Hastings's line with this question. Hastings and Ely employ the same ensemble technique at 3.4.30–4. See Introduction p. 24.

3.2.76 as you do yours Q and F have different meanings and this hypermetric line probably derives from the actor.

3.2.77 life Repeated from the preceding line (for F's 'dayes').

3.2.78 Was it . . . is now Presumably an approximation of F's 'Was it so precious to me, as 'tis now'. If Shakespeare played Hastings, 76–8 need to be considered as possibly authorially revised.

3.2.82 was sure Q's 'was' would be a curious error for the actor, who might be expected to say 'were'. Possibly the compositor, with the three s's of 'states' and 'sure' on either side to distract him, was responsible. However, the quartos uniformly accept 'was' and this may be an instance of what Abbott describes as 'a general predilection for . . . the northern E.E. third person plural in -*s*' (section 333), here akin to 'What manners is in this', *Romeo and Juliet*, 5.3.214.

3.2.85 scab F's 'stab' makes the more obvious sense and Q might easily be a compositorial error arising from foul case or a misreading of the manuscript. However, none of the quartos thought fit to amend it and the reading is more imaginative. *OED* gives an appropriate parallel: 'It is a scabbe of the world to be enuious at vertue' (W. Baldwin, *A Treatise of Morall Philosophie*, enlarged by T. Palfreyman (1564), 1565, (as *OED* bibliography), dated 1567 in *OED* reference), where scab means a moral or spiritual disease.

3.2.87–9 But come . . . beheaded This looks like revision in Q, arising partly from Derby's reference in F that 'the day is well spent' – it was only 4.00 am at line 4 – and the very ungainly 'Wot you what, my Lord', something which may have struck Shakespeare forcefully if he played Hastings.

3.2.92 SD Enter . . . Pursu[iv]ant F does not name the Pursuivant in the dialogue which Q does not once but twice. Possibly an over-zealous editor of F omitted the names he deemed to be 'obvious errors'. But it is no mistake; Hastings was the name of the Pursuivant and Halle records their meeting. If the name was not cut from F's text (and there are no grounds for believing it was), it must have been added in the course of production. It leads to a series of consequential verbal changes; see Collation 94, 95, 96, 97, 104, 104 SD, 105.

3.2.106–8 What . . . content you Q is quite differently arranged from F. In F, the Priest greets Lord Hastings. In Q, the Priest is reduced, in effect, to a mute having only to whisper in Hastings's ear (as the SD, peculiar to Q) directs. The Priest's second (and final) line in F, 'Ile wait vpon your Lordship' might have been cut because Hastings has that identical line as his last of the scene in F – but that too is not found in Q. Although a regular actor has been given the part of the Priest in the doubling table, this is solely to demonstrate that it can easily be managed; it could be that robbing the Priest of his lines was because the part was entrusted on tour to a back-stage worker unfitted to speak even such simple lines. See Collation 106–7, 108.

3.2.119 shall . . . along Buckingham approximates F's 'will you goe'; Hastings's response, 'Ile wait vpon your Lordship', is omitted.

3.3.0 SD F includes in its SD *with Halberds* (see Collation), meaning not the weapons but the Halberdiers who carried them. At first sight it might appear that the touring version dispensed with these supernumeraries, but Ratcliffe's order must be directed at some such (see 1n), so allowance has been made in the doubling pattern for a single Halberdier (all that the doubling pattern can afford) to accompany them; reinforcements, if required, could be supplied by back-stage workers (compare 3.2.106–8n).

3.3.1 Come . . . prisoners Ratcliffe's line (not in F) may have been added not for the tour but when the play was produced in London; though the prisoners may have visually looked such, Ratcliffe's line makes their situation immediately apparent. See also 21n.

3.3.5 keep Q's reading is more appropriate than F's 'blesse'. Revision?

3.3.6 bloodsuckers In F, Vaughan has a single line after 'bloodsuckers': 'You liue, that shall cry woe for this heere- / after'; its omission from Q reduces Vaughan to a mute (so economising on a speaking rôle) except for his lines as a Ghost in 5.3, which, being spoken in disguise, in effect could have been said by any available actor.

3.3.11 soul Substitution for F's more appropriate 'Seat'. See Collation 12, 17, 18, 19, 22, 23 (and 5n) for further substitutions.

3.3.13–14 heads, / For F has 'when shee exclaim'd on *Hastings*, you, and I'; Q's omission is probably a memorial error but as the speech makes good sense without the line, scholars have suggested that it was cut because it was inconsistent with Margaret's earlier cursing, e.g. at *3H6*, 5.5, where none of the three was present, or earlier in this play. However, it would take a listener with a singularly good memory to recall the precise content of Margaret's previous curses and these three can stand for many so cursed. See Hammond's note to this line.

3.3.15, 16 Q inverts the names 'Hastings' and 'Richard'.

3.2.21 Come . . . out Q combines two of Ratcliffe's lines in F into one. This could have been a deliberate re-arrangement, made when Ratcliffe was given his introductory line to the scene.

3.4.0 SD Enter . . . table This scene in the original production must have filled the stage. On tour it became, perforce, much more intimate; Lovell was excluded here (and throughout the play) to save a part on tour; Norfolk (mute in F) and 'others' were dropped. Catesby replaces Ratcliffe in Q, as he does in 3.5, changes that could have been made for the London production when it was realised Ratcliffe was at Pomfret in Yorkshire on this same day overseeing the execution of Rivers, Grey, and Vaughan. However, audiences might not then have noticed this breach of verisimilitude and it might not have been until adapting the play for touring that Catesby was substituted for Ratcliffe and then for the convenience of a smaller company rather than on grounds of logic. Although the Oxford Old-Spelling Shakespeare replaces Ratcliffe by Catesby in 3.4 and 3.5, other reputable modern editions (e.g. Riverside and Arden) follow F, in effect having Ratcliffe simultaneously in Yorkshire and London.

3.4.1 My lords, at once The first of many substitutions in this scene, here for 'Now Noble Peeres'. See 6n, 67n, 70n, 85n, 91–2n, 98–9n; Collation 3, 4, 6, 9, 11, 12, 18, 21, 23, 24, 27, 37, 38, 41, 42, 44, 46, 49, 50, 52, 61, 66, 69, 70, 72, 75, 77, 78, 81, 89, 96, 99, 100, and 105.

3.4.6 ELY . . . time Q gives this speech to Rivers, who has just been led away to execution. The error could have arisen from a compositor's misreading of his manuscript, but there is a more interesting possibility. The actor playing Rivers would easily have had time to throw a cope over his costume as Rivers and, if necessary, don a mitre, whilst a table was being set up, and then reappear as Ely. That would provide an explanation for the confusion in assigning the line when recording his recall of his two parts. Ely is a very timid character so a boy might well act his part. Neither Ely nor Rivers is anything like word-perfect; here he only approximates to F's 'To morrow then I iudge a happie day', picking up Buckingham's 'time' from two lines earlier.

3.4.10 Who I, my lord? Buckingham's protestation, a delightfully disingenuous improvement, throws out the lineation of 11 and 12 with consequential damage to the metre. See 59n.

3.4.17 gracious pleasure Q's 'Graces pleasure' is certainly an aural error but whose – actor's, scribe's, or compositor's – it is impossible to say. Q7 at 3.5.60 reproduces 'graces' as 'gracious' so the responsibility here might most convincingly point to the compositor. Although responsibility cannot with certainty be pinned on the scribe or compositor, Q has been emended to follow F.

3.4.26 not you Q inverts F's 'you not'; see also 85n.

3.4.30–4 well . . . When F simply has 'well. / My Lord of Ely, when'; in Q, Hastings and Ely both break into Richard's lines in a good example of ensemble playing; see Introduction, p. 24.

3.4.57 livelihood Q's 'likelihood' is probably a compositorial misreading of an overlarge secretary-hand 'v' as 'k'.

3.4.59 if . . . have Q expands F's 'he, he had', making the line hypermetric.

3.4.60 Derby's line is not found in F; it could be an actor's improvement; 'I say' and 'I pray' in an eight-syllable line hardly sound authorial.

3.4.67 whatsoever, 70 See F has 'whoso'ere' and 'Looke'. Hammond points out that Q is closer to More and Holinshed here than to Halle.

3.4.78–80 Now . . . done Q omits reference to Lovell and Ratcliffe, who in F oversee Hastings's execution. This revision has affected the whole passage, which in Q is, perhaps, more taut than F. F, however, is metrical whereas Q is not and the placement of 'I swear' after 'today' smacks of the actor not the author.

3.4.84 raze his helm Q correctly revises F's 'rowse our Helmes'. Stanley only dreamt that his own helm was razed. This correction would not have been beyond the bookkeeper for he would only have had to follow 3.2.9.

3.4.85 But . . . fly Q inverts F's 'scorne' and 'disdaine', making a preterite of the latter; this is easier on the listener than F and the adversative, 'But' for 'And', is more effective. However, the final letter of F's 'disdaine' may have been read as 'd' (in secretary hand the letters can be very similar) so Q may in this be no more than a fortuitously effective instance of memorial approximation.

3.4.87 started Q's 'startled' is just about possible but probably derives from a compositorial misreading.

3.4.91–2 As 'twere . . . at Pomfret Although the actor's recall of F's 'As too triumphing, how mine Enemies' is faulty, F's 'To day' may have been deliberately changed to 'How they' because the former stretched credulity beyond the limit: news of the executions could not have been conveyed from Yorkshire to London within the day.

3.4.98–9 state of worldly men . . . grace of heaven The antithesis in F is between the 'grace of mortall men' and 'grace of God' – i.e. between the human and divine. Q is a little more subtle; it contrasts the pursuit of worldly status with that for divine grace. Q could – especially if Shakespeare did play Hastings – be authorial.

3.4.103–4 deep. / Come Four lines of F are omitted in Q between 104 and 105. The first, by Lovell, was omitted because he did not appear in the touring version. The omission of three lines by Hastings may also have been deliberate. Hastings had already bewailed his unfortunate state and his further exclamations may have been cut on aesthetic grounds. Had Shakespeare left in these lines it would have been surprising (especially if that actor were Shakespeare) if nothing had been recalled, not even 'O bloody *Richard*'. Thus, Hastings's lines may have been cut for the production in London but Lovell's line cut for the tour.

3.5.0 SD Enter . . . armour Q's entry provides what is necessary but F's remarkable description perfectly sets the scene for Richard's charade.

3.5.3 begin again Q inverts F's 'againe begin'; see 98–9n and Collation 36, 50, 62, 66, 91, 103.

3.5.5 Tut . . . me In Q, the actor 'improves' his part, necessitating an extra, unmetrical, line of text.

3.5.7 Buckingham forgets the next line in F, 'Tremble and start at wagging of a Straw', and 'At any time' at the start of 11.

3.5.11 SD Enter MAYOR In F the Mayor is accompanied by Catesby but in Q it is Catesby, not Ratcliffe and Lovell, who oversees Hastings's execution at the end of 3.4, and Catesby must therefore enter later in 3.5 with Hastings's head. The text in Q is modified accordingly – and perhaps further modified by the actors; see 15n, 16n; and Collation 11–12, 14, 18 SD, 19. For the replacement of Ratcliffe by Catesby see 3.4.0 SDn. Lovell was completely cut from Q to save a part on tour.

3.5.15 Buckingham In Q and F this instruction is given to Catesby. In F this makes sense but in Q Catesby does not enter for another three lines (with Hastings's head). On stage the only actor available is the man playing Buckingham. By amending the text from Catesby to Buckingham the incident, as re-arranged in Q, falls neatly into place. See Introduction, p. 28.

3.5.16 Hark! I hear a drum Q places this line after and not before 15 as in F. F's order seems more logical and would be unlikely to be mistaken by both actors. Q might thus represent a production change. Burbage approximates his line in F; for further substitutions, see 54n, 60n, 80–1n, and Collation 18, 19, 24, 31, 33, 34, 35, 38, 41, 46, 51, 52, 53, 56, 61, 63, 64, 67, 68, 69, 71, 79, 86, 90, 92, 98–9, 100, and 102.

3.5.23 man Gloucester repeats 'man' from the previous line for F's 'Creature'. See also 102n.

3.5.25 Look . . . Mayor This line is not found in F and may have been added in course of production in London or on tour (perhaps as an 'improvement' by Burbage) in order to involve the much-bewildered Mayor, who is otherwise but a bystander to all the simulated disturbance.

3.5.31 lived Q's 'laid' is probably a compositorial misreading of the manuscript.

3.5.48–9 I never . . . Shore For the transfer of these lines from Buckingham to the Lord Mayor, see Introduction, pp. 32–3 and figure 4.

3.5.54 we Q's plural is more appropriate than F's 'I'. The change could be deliberate (and authorial) but might have sprung automatically to the actor.

3.5.60 Grace's word Q's 'graces word' suggests a singular 'Grace' – His Grace the Duke of Buckingham who alone has spoken to him – as opposed to F's 'Graces words' which might imply the plural, 'Graces'. Contrast 3.4.17n.

3.5.68 SD and Catesby In F, Ratcliffe and Lovell are given minor tasks to perform to get them off the stage after Buckingham exits at the end of the scene. These instructions are cut from Q so Catesby, who has replaced Ratcliffe, has no exit. It is better to have him leave with the Lord Mayor than later, with Buckingham.

3.5.80–1 lustful . . . listed Q produces interesting memorial substitutions for F's 'raging . . . lusted'. Presumably one word suggested the other, making perfectly good sense; listed = desired.

3.5.98–9 About . . . farewell Buckingham approximates, inverts ('news' and 'Guildhall'), and transfers his farewell in F that followed 'myself' in 68 to 99 (substituting 'farewell' for 'adue').

3.5.100 Now will I F has three lines preceding addressed to Lovell and Ratcliffe who are despatched to Dr Shaw and Friar Penker respectively. As the two former have been omitted from the scene in Q, these instructions are omitted. (These instructions are an example of the technique of clearing the stage of unwanted characters. Their tasks have no narrative significance.) See 68 SDn.

3.5.102 notice F here repeats 'order' of two lines earlier; Q's 'notice' could be authorial.

3.6.6 brought Substitution for F's 'sent'. The speech has a relatively high proportion of minor substitutions and memorial slips. The actor had probably taken on the part for the tour and was unfamiliar with it. See 12n and Collation 1, 3, 5, 14.

3.6.8 lived Lord Hastings Q inverts F 'Hastings liu'd'; see Collation 11.

3.6.10 Why Actor's improvement?

3.6.12 blind Substitution for F's 'bold', prompted by 'sees' in 11 and 12 and 'seen' in 14.

3.6.14 bad Repetition of 'bad' from 13 (for F's 'ill'), making Q more obviously platitudinous.

3.7.1 How now, my lord Q substitutes F's 'How now, how now'; see also 46n, 50n, 53n, 67n, 131n, 178n, 199n, 207n, 222n, 225n; and Collation 3, 14, 16, 22, 25, 29, 34, 35, 36, 41, 43, 44, 45, 49, 51, 58, 60, 61, 62, 65, 73, 74, 75, 76, 77–8, 80, 85, 88, 90, 94, 98, 105, 107, 108, 115, 117, 118, 120, 130, 138, 141, 151, 160, 163, 164, 167, 171, 179, 184, 185, 192, 194, 201, 203, 205, 209, 215, 220, 223, and 226.

3.7.5–8 I did . . . lineaments Q cuts four lines within this passage, possibly authorially, so avoiding repetition.

3.7.19 Ah In Q, Burbage slightly improves his part.

3.7.20 No . . . me In F followed by 'they spake not a word', which Buckingham had used at 3 for F's 'say not a word'.

3.7.31 the lower The sense seems to demand 'the' (not found in F), but it makes an already inelegant line distinctly prosaic.

3.7.32 God save King Richard! F follows with 'And thus I tooke the vantage of those few.' The actor may have failed to recall this but Buckingham's immediate expression of thanks in Q is very effective and the omission could be deliberate.

3.7.33 loving The actor anticipates 'loving' in the next line for F's 'gentle'; Q7, followed by Q8, spotted the error and emended to 'noble'.

3.7.38 No . . . lord Actor's improvement.

3.7.40 hand. Intend Q has 'hand, and intend' for F's 'hand: intend'. The error is almost certainly the compositor's; he has repeated the 'and' sound of 'hand' when memorising the line for setting.

3.7.46 say . . . it Q is much crisper than F ('still answer nay, and take it'). This may derive from production rather than be a 'fault' of the actor's recall.

3.7.47 Fear not . . . plead In Q, Gloucester improves his part by picking up Buckingham's ad-lib, 'fear not me' from 3.5.5 and 'Fear not' from 3.5.92. F has 'I goe: and if you plead'.

3.7.50 You . . . leads Buckingham recalls F's 'Go, go vp to the Leads, the Lord Maior knocks' only roughly. Possibly there was no knocking on tour (compare 3.2.0 SDn) and this led to the disturbance in this line.

3.7.50 SD Enter . . . CITIZENS There is no entry for Citizens in Q but obviously the Mayor is required here.

3.7.53 Here . . . says he? Buckingham's recall of F's 'Now *Catesby*, what sayes your Lord to my request?' is again only approximate but the reference to Catesby as Richard's servant is significant: see 3.2.5 ff. n.

3.7.54 My . . . Grace Q inverts F's order of 'entreat . . . Grace . . . Lord'; see Collation 82, 85, 110, 146, 159.

3.7.67 day-bed Q weakens F's 'Loue-Bed'; compare 1.1.13n. See 219–20n, 222n; and Collation 61, 90, 100, 168.

3.7.79 My lord Catesby picks up Buckingham's last two words: an actor's improvement?

3.7.89 SD aloft Q has *a loste*, making it apparent that, despite the misprint (a ligature small 's' with 't', not a long 's'), the touring company expected to be able to act on two levels.

3.7.92–3 vanity. / Famous Q omits the first two of seventeen lines cut from here to the end of the scene. See below 182n, Collation 112–13, 118–19, 122–3, 133–4, 224–5, and Introduction, p. 32.

3.7.131 know not whether Gloucester begins with an approximation of the equally insignificant opening words of F – 'I cannot tell' – but, apart from the ten lines cut after 133, the speech is very accurately reported. D. L. Patrick considered the lines 'complicated and difficult and do not forward the action in any way. There is not much in them to attract an actor.' He also noted that Irving cut these lines 'and so probably did Shakespeare' (p. 127). If the cut was deliberate it might have been made for London rather than particularly for the tour.

3.7.178 draw out . . . stock Substitution for F's 'draw forth your Noble Ancestrie'; Buckingham here draws on the line he omitted after 118, F's 'His Royall Stock grafft with ignoble Plants'.

3.7.182 Refuse not . . . love! Q's omission could be Buckingham's oversight but he would surely have been prompted by the Mayor or Catesby (especially the latter whose cue the line was). The error looks like the compositor's (which is why the line has been restored here). The compositor may have been deceived by the repetition of 'my lord' (and even by the memory of 'proffered' six lines earlier) into imagining he had set this line. If setting was by formes here, it is possible that the line was deliberately omitted by the compositor in order to get his copy into H2ᵛ.

3.7.193 equally Q sets the archaic form, 'egallie'.

3.7.199 Zounds, I'll Either Buckingham improves his part in Q for F's 'we will' or this is what Shakespeare originally wrote and the swearword was eliminated when F was set following the passing of the Statute to Restrain Abuses, 1606. But see 200n.

3.7.200 O do . . . Buckingham! This delightfully ironic line is not found in F though editors following F find it difficult to refrain from taking it in. It could be that the line was cut from F because 'Zounds' was dropped (see 199n). However, it was surely possible for a milder imprecation to have been substituted – 'God' and 'Heaven' survive elsewhere – in order to retain Gloucester's response. Surely Shakespeare would not so readily and unimaginatively have sacrificed such a line? It is more probable that 'Zounds' and this line were worked in when the play was produced in London.

3.7.200 SD *Buckingham . . . at 206* It may be that no directions are marked in Q because such toing and froing was awkward to manage on a cramped tour stage. On the large London stage there would be no difficulty in getting everyone off and then have them make a new entry, as indicated, after 206. Only one Citizen has anything to say, at 202, and, significantly this is a line given to Catesby, on-stage, in F. Looking at the touring circumstances, it is necessary to get four citizens off the stage in order that they can appear at the start of the next scene. If all except Gloucester and Catesby moved to exit, but only the four required at the start of 4.1 completely cleared the stage, the needs of the rest of 3.7 and of 4.1 could be met without recourse to the use of backstage staff. The entry at 4.1.0 requires Anne to enter at a different door from the others (implicit in the first line of dialogue in F but specified in the actual entry in Q). It would be effective on tour, therefore, if the actor playing Anne left the stage first and at a different side from that taken by the other three at 200; then, at 202, appealed to Gloucester virtually off-stage as if from the audience (who are also, in effect, the citizenry); see also 202 SHn.

3.7.202 SH A CITIZEN [*Off*] This line is Catesby's in F (as 'If you denie them, all the Land will rue it.') It does not necessarily have to be given off-stage – see 200 SDn.

3.7.204 Well An actor's improvement.

3.7.207 you Not found in F; another example of an actor adapting a line, regardless of the strict count of syllables, for greater effect. The stress falls on 'you' and the ensuing 'sage grave men' becomes patently ironic.

3.7.216 thereof The actor unwittingly repeats 'thereof' of two lines earlier for F's 'of this'.

3.7.219–20 kingly . . . royal In Q the actor confuses the epithets for F's 'Royal' and 'worthie' respectively, so weakening the effect.

3.7.221 Amen In Q only the Mayor is directed to respond (*All* in F). This may be because only he remained on stage after 201, or it may be a scribal error indicating that it was the actor playing the Mayor who recalled the response that he and others would utter.

3.7.222 will Q, typically in memorial recall, confuses 'will' and 'may' (found in F); compare 3.1.185n.

3.7.225 task Probably a memorial rather than an authorial substitution. F has 'Worke', which Shakespeare uses far more frequently than he does 'task'.

4.1.0 SD *Enter . . . another door* Q (which has *Quee. mother* for Elizabeth and, unlike F, omits Anne's name) specifies entry at two opposing doors. Such an entry is implicit in the first line of Q and F.

4.1.1–2 niece . . . fast Six lines of F are cut in Q making 'niece' refer to Anne (a niece by marriage) instead of Clarence's daughter. Anne has by this stage married Gloucester – hence her description at o SD – and she thus becomes Queen Elizabeth's sister. The excision in this way of a niece (Clarence's daughter) to be led in by Anne shows how neatly the prompt-book was adapted for touring. See Collation 1–3.

4.1.5 tender A substitution for F's 'gentle'. There are many memorial substitutions in this scene but this could be deliberate (and see notes to 9, 64, and 91); 'tender Prince' was lost when the Duchess of York's speech was cut (line 5 in F; 4 in Arden), and it might have been restored here.

4.1.9 Prince F follows with 'and my young Sonne of *Yorke*'. The omission from Q seems to be deliberate for the Lieutenant responds in 11 by saying Elizabeth may not visit 'him' rather than 'them', as in F.

4.1.10 Well . . . leave An approximation of F's 'Right well, deare Madame: by your patience'; see also 5n, 20n, 22–3n, 64n, 70n, 87n; and Collation 11, 12, 16, 17, 24, 27, 29, 30, 32, 33, 34, 43, 51, 52 SH, 52, 53, 55, 56, 58, 60, 71, 73, 75, 76, 78, 82, 83, 84 SH, 85, and 88 for further substitutions.

4.1.13, 14 Why, I cry you mercy Actors' improvements; they make the Lieutenant's error in referring to Gloucester as King the more dramatically pointed.

4.1.20 fear not thou In Q the actor weakly pads out the line to make up what has been forgotten – F's 'bring me to their sights'.

4.1.22–3 I do beseech . . . not do it The Lieutenant roughly summarises F, recalling in the process a line twice used earlier by Brakenbury at 1.1.84 and 103. Both parts were almost certainly played by the same actor.

4.1.45 To meet . . . you The actor inverts and extemporises for F's 'In your behalfe, to meet you on the way'; see Collation 79.

4.1.61 corse F has 'Corse' and that may be what is intended for Q's 'course' (which would make sense). As 'corse' appears at 1.2.30, 31, 34, and 35, and at 2.1.78, this differently spelt form might be intended *if* the compositor followed copy. Alternatively Q's spelling may derive from Short's compositor (Simmes's house having set the earlier passages).

4.1.64 dead Q's reading (for F's 'deare') makes good sense; it could be authorial, an actor's substitution, or even a compositorial error (see Introduction, p. 7).

4.1.70 As ... thee The actor playing Anne has recalled his/her line at 1.2.25, 'As miserable by the death of him' for F's line here, 'More miserable, by the Life of thee', perhaps prompted by anticipating 'death' in the next line.

4.1.82 Alas, poor soul The actor repeats these words from 58 for F's 'Poore heart adieu'. Anne has 'poor soul' three lines on (in Q and F).

4.1.87 guard Q's substitution for F's 'tend' shows increased alliteration.

4.1.91 week of teen. F follows with seven lines which may have been cut from Q; even without them the scene ends with a concluding couplet – seen/teen. The subject matter of the Babes in the Tower is found in Elizabeth's speech at 4.4.301–5, directed at Richard, and it might have been thought best not to undercut the effectiveness of that speech by anticipation here.

4.2.0 SD F's entry includes Ratcliffe and Lovell but they do not speak in this scene in F and could therefore be conveniently excluded on tour, as in Q. Lovell has thus been completely excised from Q. The Page is so described in speech heads in F; in Q he is simply *Boy*. He is given no entry later in the scene; he probably entered with Richard, carrying his train. Only in F is his exit marked. He is described in this edition as a page. The doubling pattern conjectured for this edition could readily allow three attendant lords (all mute and in whom Catesby could confide at 26) without drawing on back-stage staff.

4.2.1 SH RICHARD F calls Richard so throughout; Q distinguishes him by referring to him as *Gloucester* to this point and from here as *King*. The dual designation is used in this edition but with *Richard* for *King*.

4.2.1–2 Buckingham! / Give Q omits Buckingham's response, 'My gracious Soueraigne'; see Collation for omissions at 41 and 45.

4.2.4 honours Q substitutes for F's 'Glories'; see 24–5n, 26n, 47–8n, 49–50n, 80n, 84n, 94n, 118n; and Collation 6, 9, 10, 12, 16, 19, 21, 34, 36, 41, 43, 46, 47, 49, 52, 56, 63, 67, 69, 70, 76, 77, 78, 79, 85, 86, 87, 88, 90, 91, 95, and 120.

4.2.21 Tut, tut Although the text of Q sometimes only approximates to F and there are many substitutions, the exactness of the verbal detail, especially for Burbage/ Richard is often remarkable. This is exemplified here by Q's reporting this line, complete with 'Tut, tut', as in F. But see 119n.

4.2.23 breath, some little pause Q inverts F's 'litle breath, some pawse'; see also 30–1n and 78n.

4.2.24–5 herein ... immediately In contrast with Richard, Buckingham's recall is only approximate. He transfers 'herein' to 24 from 25 and substitutes 'immediately' for F's 'presently'. The former means 'at once', as could the latter, but 'presently' tends rather to mean 'soon'. Thus Buckingham has weakened Shakespeare's meaning.

4.2.26 bites the lip F has 'gnawes his Lippe'. In F Richard is never said to bite his lips, so this is doubtless a memorial substitution.

4.2.30–1 Boy! . . . circumspect. These lines are reversed in F. Both arrangements are practicable but Q may represent what happened on stage in London and on tour.

4.2.35 My lord The Page recalls his few lines well but 'improves' his part by this addition.

4.2.47–8 My lord . . . abides Q re-arranges and expands F. Neither version is metrically satisfactory; Q's lineation has been modified here.

4.2.49–50 Catesby . . . die This may be no more than a memorial anticipation of 56 but Burbage is generally accurate and Q is more effective than F's simple 'Come hither *Catesby*, rumor it abroad, / That *Anne* my Wife is very grieuous sicke', so Q may represent how the play was modified in production. The repetition in Q of this line at 56, following 'I say again, give out', would then be deliberate, even 'wife' being repeated instead of varied to 'Queene' as in F. Catesby's interjection, 'my lord' (not found in F), is another example of ensemble playing; see Introduction, p. 24 and 98n below.

4.2.69 enemies Q and F have the same reading but the compositor of Q2 anticipated the next line and set 'deepe enemies'; later Qs followed.

4.2.71 disturbers Q's 'disturbs' is almost certainly a compositorial error.

4.2.78 is it F has 'it is', which makes more obvious sense but Q does suggest Richard's developing uneasiness and just could be a deliberate change rather than a memorial slip.

4.2.80 'Tis done . . . lord Presumably a memorial approximation for F's 'I will dispatch it straight'; in the light of the possibility of a deliberate change at 78 (see note), it might be intentional.

4.2.81–2 Shall we . . . lord Richard's question is asked of Catesby at 3.1.186 and Tyrrel replies as did Catesby then; neither line appears in F in 4.2. This repetition is almost certainly an addition by the actors and might have been Burbage's work.

4.2.84, 94 demand F has 'request' here. Buckingham is not reliable in recalling his part so this double substitution may be a memorial slip. However, 'demand' is apt here and the change could be authorial.

4.2.98 perhaps F does not repeat 'perhaps'. The repetition in Q is almost certainly Burbage's improvement and is surely justifiable. Buckingham's 'My lord!' that follows is also peculiar to Q and indicates how the play was worked up in performance. See 49–50n above and compare 3.2.58 and 3.4.30–4 and notes.

4.2.98–117 See Introduction, p. 26, for this Rougemont addition.

4.2.118 Why . . . or no! Buckingham is an unreliable witness so this may be a memorial approximation of F, but Q much better dramatises Buckingham's frustration after he has been toyed with in the Rougemont sequence and this line may have been changed when 98–117 was added.

4.2.119 Tut, tut Burbage again improves his part, repeating the 'Tut, tut' given him at 21. Q also repeats 'I am not in the vein' here, the sentiment that concludes the Rougemont addition (117).

4.2.121 deep contempt Buckingham exaggerates F's 'contempt'.

4.3.0 SD JAMES Q gives Tyrrel's first name as Francis although he is called James at 4.2.66. Halle and Holinshed call him James (and his brother, Thomas). Possibly a scribal error?

4.3.1 deed 4.3.2 act Transposition of F's 'Act' and 'deed'. See Collation 5, 11, 43, 45.

4.3.4 whom Q substitutes the grammatically correct form for F's 'who'; for further substitutions see also 1.3.54n and, below, 19n, 30n, 35n, 46n; and Collation 6, 7, 8, 9, 10, 13, 15, 16, 17, 20, 22, 23, 31, 32, 33, 39, 42, 50, 51, 56.

4.3.19 she F has the traditional 'she' for Q's 'he'; possibly a scribal or compositorial slip; see 25n and 31n.

4.3.25 gave Q's 'give' is almost certainly a compositorial error.

4.3.27 my lord Tyrrel anticipates from 28, throwing out the metre.

4.3.30 But how . . . place Q's expression of doubt is much more precise than F's 'But where (to say the truth)'; given the inaccuracy of Tyrrel's reporting this may have to be put down to the actor rather than Shakespeare.

4.3.31 SH RICHARD Q erroneously gives this the speech head *Tir.*; a compositorial error.

4.3.35 till soon Q's farewell is a Midlands dialect variant of F's 'till then'. It is used by Thomas Heywood (born in Lincolnshire) in *The Captives* (performed 1624) and *The Wise Woman of Hogsdon* (published 1638).

4.3.35 SD *Exit Tyrrel* Tyrrel's exit is in the right margin of 34 in Q; it is not found in F. F gives Tyrrel a final line after 35, 'I humbly take my leaue'; as the exit is placed so much earlier it was presumably a cut rather than the actor's oversight.

4.3.43 SD *Enter CATESBY* In F this is played by Ratcliffe but the doubling evidently dictated that Catesby took over this rôle, implying that Tyrrel and Ratcliffe were played by the same actor on tour.

4.3.46 Ely It is unlikely that Ely's name was accidentally introduced in Q for F's 'Mourton'. There is nothing in either Q or F to identify the Bishop of Ely with John Morton (though doubtless a few of the better informed of the audience would know the originator of Morton's Fork); in 3.4 Richard calls him Ely. The substitution makes clear the relationship between the obsequious, strawberry-growing Bishop and the man whose flight to Richmond so troubles Richard. This brings home how uneasy Richard has become that such a one should cause him anxiety. Richard refers to the Bishop as Ely at 49 in Q and F. 'Ely' is also substituted for F's 'Morton' at 4.4.381.

4.4.4 adversaries Q substitutes for F's 'enemies'; for further substitutions see also 38n, 63n, 71n, 129n, 153n, 164n, 229n, 238n, 250–3n, 266n, 273n, 287n, 310n, 312n, 320n, 324–5n, 348n, 361n, 381n, 404–5n, 414n, 415n, 423–4n, 435–6n; and Collation 9, 10, 24, 25, 28, 41, 42, 47, 54, 59, 61, 68, 73, 82, 88, 89, 98, 99, 101, 109, 112, 114, 124, 125, 128, 130, 135, 137, 152, 156, 166, 169, 176, 177, 187, 188, 190, 199, 201, 205, 206, 216, 218, 220, 239, 242, 244, 249, 252, 253, 257, 263, 271, 272, 277, 281, 282, 287, 288, 289, 290, 293, 294, 295, 296, 298, 300, 303, 304, 308, 316, 320, 326, 329, 332, 336, 339, 341, 349, 357, 360, 362, 364, 365, 366, 371, 372, 374, 375, 380, 382, 387, 392, 394, 398, 400, 401, 408, 409, 419, 420, 422, 424, 425, 429, 430, 431, 433, 434, 440, 445, and 447.

4.4.21 Blind sight, dead life Q inverts F's order. See also 29–31n, 58n, 62n, 282–3n, 292–5n, 324–5n, 417n; and Collation 30, 164, 203, 240, 243, and 248.

4.4.22 F follows with 'Breefe abstract and record of tedious dayes'. This was presumably omitted by oversight but its omission does not invalidate the sense. See also 29–31n, 48–9n, 95–8n, 141n, 153n, 164n, 170n, 171–2n, 210–11n, 260–1n, 305n, 317–18n, 345–6n; and Collation 152–3, 347–8, and 365.

4.4.29–31 So many . . . dead? These three lines follow 16 in F and F follows them with Margaret's '*Plantagenet* doth quit *Plantagenet*, / *Edward* for *Edward*, payes a dying debt.' It is fairly easy to imagine that the lines have been accidentally misplaced (though difficult to explain why) and then Margaret's lines accidentally omitted (and see 22n). This would be reasonably acceptable were it not that the sequence of Margaret's comments is pretty faithfully reproduced, although Margaret, it is true, fails to recall precisely some of the more involved lines at 83–5 and 95–8. Some F-preferring editors actually select Q's order. Margaret rehearses her Edward-for-Edward sequence more fully later (see 37 ff and 58 ff) and the scene has some deliberate and extensive cuts. Thus it might be that the transposition and the cut are not accidental.

4.4.34 woes Anticipation of 'woes' in 36 for F's 'greefes'. See 238n and 266n; and 'parents' in Collation at 309 (of 311).

4.4.36 Tell . . . mine Omitted from F but essential to the sense.

4.4.38 husband Q's reading, 'Richard', has sometimes been preferred by F-inclined editors. The balance of names is attractive but it may owe more to Q's actor than to fact. Margaret's husband was Henry VI (see 54). The actor has probably anticipated the Richard–Richard pairing of two lines later. Riverside amends to 'Harry'.

4.4.48–9 handiwork, / Thy Between these lines F has two lines with which editors have difficulty: Arden, for example, inserted the lines after 47 (not 48, where they come in F) and printed the second line before the first. The error in F may go back to copy and it looks very much as if the uncertainty was such that, in production, and certainly on tour, they were cut to produce simple, direct sense.

4.4.54 wife Q's error may be compositorial, a carrying on of the 's' of 'Harries'.

4.4.58 stabbed, 62 killed Q transposes F's 'kill'd' and 'stab'd'.

4.4.63 tragic Q substitutes for F's 'franticke'. This is not quite the synonym Patrick believes it to be (p. 87) for Elizabeth is recalling 'tragical' of line 7 of the opening monologue. The Duchess has 'frantic outrage' at 2.4.67 and Queen Elizabeth has 'tragic violence' at 2.2.38, in both Q and F.

4.4.71 away Q's substitution for 'from hence' may have been influenced by the rhyme of 'pray' at the ends of 70 and 72.

4.4.83–5 A dream . . . shot Margaret recalls remarkably accurately the complex lines of this speech but slightly disorders F here and at 95–8.

4.4.95–8 For Queen . . . scorned of me Q re-orders and cuts.

4.4.106 neck Q repeats 'neck' from the preceding line for F's 'head'.

4.4.121 your client-woes There are many interpretations of this passage and many amendments are offered. As Q has it, words that express calamities are but windy advocates (expressions) of the woes you (your clients) experience.

4.4.122 intestate F's 'intestine' could, possibly, imply deep-seated feeling (compare 'gut-reaction'), but the word in F is probably a compositorial error, perhaps from a misreading of the manuscript.

4.4.129 I hear his drum F's SD omits reference to the drums and trumpets found in Q's entry. At 142 Richard orders the trumpets and drums to sound in Q and F in order to drown out the women's complaints but whereas F follows with the direction *Flourish. Alarums.*, Q has only *The trumpets* in the right margin of 144. The explanation could lie in the exigencies of touring, that is, that the company had lost its drums. But were that so, no instrument can be more easily simulated (or, indeed, borrowed, especially in the then well-garrisoned south-east). The existing direction, *The trumpets*, looks incomplete and it is likely that the compositor has simply failed to continue the direction in the right margin of the following line (perhaps following an interruption). Drums and trumpets are specified for Q at 5.2.0 SD (F has *with drum and colours*).

4.4.141 ELIZABETH . . . Grey? As it is unlikely both Q actors would forget the lines present in F, this could be an intentional change.

4.4.153 speech Q's substitution (as 'speach') for F's 'words' suggested to Patrick that the preceding two-and-a-half lines in F (the Duchess's 'O let me speake' and Richard's 'Do then, but Ile not heare') were omitted by accident (pp. 177–8). If 'speake' was in the copy it would have been possible for the compositor to have made such an omission, though for an omission of this kind the duplicated word is better at the start of the lines; if a jump were dependent upon the Duchess's 'speake' it is more likely that Richard's response and her next line – the one that survives – would be missed. A cut on artistic grounds is more likely. Stichomythic exchanges are a very frequent, perhaps a too-frequent, characteristic of this play. See also 171–2n.

4.4.164 bloody, treacherous Substitution for F's 'slye, and bloody'. Q omits the next line in F. This is probably an oversight by the actor but it could be a cut on the grounds of difficulty for the audience.

4.4.170 Let me march on In F Richard follows this with 'Strike vp the Drumme.' There is no stage direction accompanying this to indicate that a drum was to be beaten. Q's omission may be deliberate as being out of place at this point.

4.4.171–2 O hear . . . bitter F has another quasi-stichomythic effect of five lines here. It is unlikely that the two actors, who have recalled their parts well, should forget this exchange and the cut may be like that at 153: to reduce this effect here, because it is being deployed in another minor exchange, in order to save it for a more important occasion later in the scene.

4.4.210–11 life. / Madam Between these lines two F speeches are cut in Q, one line of Richard's and thirteen of Elizabeth's. In shortening the scene – especially the fifty-five lines between 260 and 261 – an opportunity may have been taken to make this slighter cut, perhaps because its tone is too like Margaret's. These lines could have been cut for the London production.

4.4.211 so thrive I . . . arms It looks as if Burbage has confused this passage with 315–16: 'So thrive I in my dangerous attempt / Of hostile arms.'

4.4.229 do A weakened substitution for F's 'date'; see also 266n; and Collation 303, 415, 426, and 430.

4.4.238 mean Substitution for F's 'intend', by attraction to 'mean' in the preceding and next lines.

4.4.250–3 Did to thy father . . . noble acts The actor playing Elizabeth suffers a comprehensive loss of memory here; see Collation.

4.4.257 Come, come Burbage once again 'improves' his part but keeps the metre by omitting 'Madam' after 'me'.

4.4.260–1 done all this. / Infer Between these lines Q cuts fifty-five lines, all but eight of which are Richard's. The stichomythic passage that follows is well recalled and it is inconceivable that none of this passage would have been remembered. It is also extremely unlikely that F represents an addition to what is already a lengthy scene (and play). These lines could have been cut for the London production. See Introduction, p. 32.

4.4.266 wail The actor may have substituted a weaker word for F's 'vail', or anticipated 'wail' at 310 and 312. A compositorial error is possible though secretary-hand 'v' and 'w' are usually quite distinct.

4.4.273 love Like 266, Q's reading (for F's 'low') could stem from the actor or the compositor. In this case the balance is in favour of a compositorial error as 'love' and 'low' may easily be confused in secretary hand.

4.4.279 Madam Burbage again 'improves' his part.

4.4.282–3 Harp not . . . break F reverses the order of these two lines giving Elizabeth three successive lines and then Richard two. Q's arrangement is more convincing. It is possible that when F was set the line, 'Harp not . . .' was omitted and, when corrected, inserted in the wrong place.

4.4.286 I swear by nothing F omits Richard's 'by nothing' and this is taken as 'obviously a copyist's mistake' by Arden, which it could be. The omission of Richard's 'by nothing' ensures a five-foot line, but there are enough hypermetric lines for this to be intentional. Q probably shows what was acted and it is an instance of ensemble playing (see Introduction, p. 24), and the duplication of 'by nothing' enables Elizabeth to turn Richard's oath against himself more effectively. This stress on 'nothing' drives home Elizabeth's 'something' at 290 and 291.

4.4.287 holy Q may be an authorial amendment to match 'profaned' earlier in the line (so Smidt, p. 92); contrast the addition of 'holy', 1.4.179n.

4.4.292–5 Now, by the world . . . most of all Hammond argues that Q 'forms a clear rhetorical hierarchy which F's order lacks' and suggests that the change in Q is authorial. However, F can be said to show a rhetorical pattern of self-in-the-world as opposed to father-in-heaven (with God).

4.4.297 husband Q's error, 'brother', was probably caused by the compositor's eye catching 'brother' in the next line of his copy. The actor (playing the Queen) must have known that it was the King who was her husband.

4.4.305 What canst . . . now? Supplied from F. Richard's answer to this question forms the second part of this line and it is essential he has a question to answer. The actors between them would have cobbled up something so the omission looks like a compositorial error.

4.4.310 in their This reading, also in Q2–4, is correct as against Q5's 'with their', Q6–8's 'with her', and F's 'with their'.

4.4.312 withered Memorial substitution for F's 'barren'; 309–12 are carefully patterned and Q's slight variation of 'it in' / 'it with' (F has 'it with' both times) may be authorial; Q is preferred by some editors.

4.4.314 time misused o'erpast It is not surprising that the actor stumbled here; the first two words of F's 'times ill-vs'd repast' may be correct but hardly 'repast'.

4.4.317–18 confound. / Day Q's omission of F's intervening line is either an actor's or compositor's oversight; its absence does not undermine the sense.

4.4.320 pure Substitution for F's conventional 'deere', possibly prompted by 'Immaculate' three words later. F repeats 'deare' at 329 where Q has 'good'.

4.4.324–5 to this land . . . herself Q does not recall F's word order precisely but the sense is conveyed.

4.4.328 by this Q omits 'by' – probably, a compositorial slip.

4.4.334 peevish, fond Q makes sense (though Malone suggested hyphenation): Richard begs her not to be petty, perversely resisting Richard's plans for her daughter. Arden prefers F's 'peeuish found'.

4.4.345–6 shortly. / Bear Q's omission may be an oversight but it could be that in production the cut made for a more dramatic exit.

4.4.346 SD *Kisses her* Johnson's addition. This seal of a kiss is the more significant because it is public, Richard's 'train' being on-stage throughout the scene.

4.4.348 gracious This could be a deliberate change for F's 'mightie'. The adjective 'mighty' is much used in this part of the scene: at 361 Catesby has 'mighty Soueraigne' in Q for F's 'mighty Liege'; at 379, Derby has 'mighty soveraign' in Q and F; at 392 'mighty liege' appears in Q for F's 'my good Lord'; and 'mighty' appears in Q and F at 400 and 405.

4.4.358–9 Fly . . . villain F's second command to Catesby should be addressed to Ratcliffe (and editors since Rowe have so emended). Evidently Richard's confusion communicated itself to those who prepared and set F. Q, with the added editorial direction implied by the text, works perfectly well.

4.4.361 let me know your mind Paraphrase of F's 'tell me your Highnesse pleasure'.

4.4.362 him Editorial amendment following Q3–6 for Q1–2's 'them' and F's 'to him'.

4.4.369 My mind . . . changed Burbage once more 'improves' his part, repeating 'my mind is changed'; at 380 he repeats 'as you guess'.

4.4.370 How now . . . you Richard asked Ratcliffe 'How now, what newes' at his entry at 347 in F as well as here of Derby in Q and F. The earlier question might have been authorially cut (for the London production?) to avoid too-obvious repetition. In Q (unlike F) Richard's question precedes Derby's entry. This could be a mistake, but it may well be that question and entry were intended to overlap on tour. And see 1.4.86n and 3.7.200 SD regarding the effect of small touring stages.

4.4.374 miles Erroneously set as 'mile' in Q.

4.4.380 Burbage improves by adding 'sir' to F and repeating 'as you guess'.

4.4.381 Ely F has the Bishop's personal name, Morton, as at 4.3.46.

4.4.404–5 Ay, ay . . . sir The changes in Q are slight but they intensify the tension between Richard and Derby and may derive from Burbage.

4.4.412 SH 1 MESSENGER The Messengers are not distinguished one from another in Q/F; for convenience they have been numbered here.

4.4.414 William F's '*Edward*' is correct (as Halle). The scribe or actor may have been influenced by 'William, Lord Hastings' at 3.1.190 (Buckingham adding 'William' in Q), and 3.4.27; also, perhaps, Sir William Brandon, 5.3.22 and 5.5.14.

4.4.415 brother there Substitution for F's 'elder Brother'. Halle and Holinshed refer to Courtney's brother, Peter, Bishop of Exeter; he was in fact a cousin.

4.4.417 ff. Only the First Messenger knows his part reasonably accurately. The Second inverts F's 'In Kent, my Liege' and paraphrases F's 'Flocke to the Rebels, and their power growes strong'. The Third Messenger is especially weak but the Fourth rather better.

4.4.421 SD *Richard strikes him* *He striketh him* Q (following 420); F (following 421); Q presumably indicates what happened in production.

4.4.423–4 Your Grace . . . that Q's approximation for F.

4.4.427–8 O . . . gave him Burbage in Q 'improves' his part and there is a change in stage business, presumably derived from practice in London as well as on tour. A King would not normally carry a purse. Compare *H5*, 4.8.57–60, where Henry bids Exeter to fill a glove with crowns to give to Williams.

4.4.435–6 Richmond . . . shore Q paraphrases and introduces the unusual 'Dorshire' to avoid an exceedingly long line (emended here to 'Dorset').

4.5.2 bloody boar Derby may have slipped in substituting 'bloody' for F's 'deadly', but it is possible that 'most deadly Bore' sounded more tedious than threatening and that this is an authorial change. For further substitutions, see 16–18n and Collation 5, 12, 13, 14, 18, and 19.

4.5.15 withal F follows with Derby's 'Well hye thee to thy Lord: I kisse his hand', a second dismissal for Urswick (the first was at line 6 in F), which Q evidently cuts.

4.5.16–18 Return . . . daughter This passage, modified (see Collation), follows 'aid' (line 5) in F. Derby is a fairly reliable reporter and Q's re-arrangement may well be authorial. In F, the offer of espousal comes almost as an afterthought.

5.1.0 SD *Enter . . . a guard* See Introduction, p. 28.

5.1.2 lord Q reduces F's 'good Lord'. For substitutions see 10n, 25n, 28n; and Collation 11, 13, 15, 20, 23, 24, 25.

5.1.3 Rivers, Grey Q inverts F's *Gray & Riuers*; see Collation 17, 28.

5.1.10 fellows F has 'Fellow' although the Sheriff has a guard with him, so suggesting that Burbage only addresses Ratcliffe. The plural form in Q may be a compositorial error prompted by the abundance of s's in the line.

5.1.15 or F's 'and' makes easier sense and as Q stands a dash is called for and is provided here. At 2.1.28–9 Buckingham was asked to seal a league with Edward's wife's allies. Buckingham has not been involved in the murder of the children; indeed, his reluctance to assist has led to his falling out with Richard. This might not, therefore, be an error, even though occurring in a speech by the often unreliable Buckingham.

5.1.25 is . . . head Despite the weakness of Buckingham's recall, he remembers this scene well. This is the most significant change, a paraphrase of F's 'falles heauy on my necke'; surprising as 'neck' might be expected to be prompted by the character's impending execution.

5.1.28 Come . . . me Paraphrase of F. The plural 'sirs' in Q indicates that Ratcliffe was accompanied by at least one guard.

5.2.0 SD Enter . . . trumpets Q's entry gives no indication that three lords attend Richmond but each is given lines to speak, the speech headings for the three lords being numbered sequentially; the lords are not individualised. In F their lines are given to Oxford, Herbert, and Blunt. Blunt will reappear in 5.3 and is named in that scene in Q and F. None of the three lords gets his brief part precisely correct, unlike Richmond, who is very accurate throughout. Perhaps he was played by Shakespeare, doubling with Hastings.

5.2.11 Lies . . . centre Q substitutes for F's 'Is . . . Centry'; see also Collation 17 SH, 17, 18, 19 SH, 19, 20 SH, 20, 21.

5.2.24 makes From F; Q's 'make' is possibly a compositorial error.

5.3.0 SD Enter . . . soldiers F is more specific: See Introduction, p. 27.

5.3.1 tents Q substitutes for F's 'Tent'; see also 2n, 9n, 10n, 11n, 34n, 45n; and Collation 6, 7, 13, 14, 15, 17, 19, 20, 21, 22, 23, 27, 28, 35, 41, 42, and 43.

5.3.2 Why . . . Catesby? On tour, Surrey was replaced by Catesby. Burbage approximates and, again, improves his part.

5.3.4–5 hither. / Norfolk Q omits Norfolk's 'Heere most gracious Liege', which precedes 'Norfolk'. See also Collation 36–7.

5.3.9 foe Q's substitution for F's 'Traitors' may be deliberate. It is one thing for Richmond as Henry VII to speak of traitors in the final scene (lines 22 and 35) but Richard's foes are here the founders of the Tudor dynasty and its supporters. Compare 13, Q's 'party' for F's 'Faction'.

5.3.10 utmost number One copy of Q1 has 'greatest' for 'vtmost' showing that a) Peter Short's compositor Y initially set the wrong word; and b) that copy must have been consulted when proofs were read. Y's setting of 'greatest' may indicate how powerful is association when setting type (or copying or typing). Y had set 'greatest neede' at 5.2.21 on this page fifteen lines earlier; and at 4.4.364 (K3ᵛ 37) 'greatest strength' – not as much as 200 lines earlier if setting were by formes but a little more than one hundred. That proof was, at least occasionally, checked against copy indicates that some care was taken in printing Q1. See also 2.1.5n.

5.3.11 battalia F's unusual word (for Q's 'battalion') was doubtless misunderstood by scribe or compositor. It means a whole battle-line.

5.3.18 SD Enter . . . tent Q's entry is unspecific, unlike F's from which Blunt is omitted, and Dorset is an error for Herbert. In Q and F only Richmond and Blunt speak in this section but in F Oxford, Brandon, and Herbert are addressed by Richmond; in Q they are referred to indirectly. The '&c.' in Q's direction after 18 presumably indicates that Richmond's tent should be erected on the side opposite Richard's tent. Allowance has been made in the doubling pattern for two soldiers to erect the tent without the need to call on backstage staff.

5.3.34 Good . . . to him Richmond repeats 'bear my good night to him' from 24 for F's 'make some good meanes to speak with him'. In Q, Richmond's repeated calls to Blunt in this section vary from those in F.

5.3.38–41 Give me . . . small strength These lines are placed after 21 in F. They may have been shifted in production to allow for the tent to be erected before ink and paper were called for, for use inside the tent. It is also preferable that Richmond's sequence of dispositions should not be interrupted by the request for paper and ink.

5.3.43 SD Enter . . . soldiers Q again has '&c.' Allowance has been made in the doubling pattern for two soldiers. From hereon copy for *R3* is dependent on Q (especially Q3), F being derived therefrom, so losing its independent status. Whereas up to this point Richard has been so described in SHs in F, from 46 *King* (as in Q) is used intermittently and, from 205, continuously except for Richard's last two speeches, 5.4.7 and 9.

5.3.45 It is . . . time F has 'It's Supper time my Lord, it's nine a clocke', but Q gives the time as 6 o'clock. There has been much debate as to the appropriate time for supper in Tudor England in the summer. Shakespeare makes us very aware of the passage of time in this scene: sunset (19), 'mid of night' (74), 'dark night' (77), 'flaky darkness breaks within the east' (83), 'early in the morning' (85), 'now dead midnight' (177), 'The early village cock' (206), and 'Upon the stroke of four' (232). This progression is temporally imprecise.

5.3.55 Catesby F mistakenly has *Ratcliffe*; this may have been caused because the next speech heading in Q and F, after Richard's at 56, is *Rat.*

5.3.76 sit Q has 'set', a variant spelling; also at 128. For 'e' for 'i', compare Q1's 'Wel' for Q2's 'Will' at 142.

5.3.143–50 Dream on . . . flourish The ghosts appear in F in the order that their material forms were killed but in Q the ghosts of the two young princes precede the ghost of Hastings. See Introduction, p. 29.

5.3.159–60 Tomorrow . . . and die! These lines repeat those of Clarence's Ghost at 131–2 above in Q and F.

5.3.177 now F has 'not', introduced via Q2 and reprinted thereafter.

5.3.179 What . . . Myself? Q's punctuation, reproduced here (for F's 'What? do I feare my Selfe?') may represent Burbage's delivery.

5.3.205 Zounds . . . there? F's 'Who's there?' omits the oath in conformity with the Statute to Restrain Abuses of 1606. 'Zounds' was particularly affected and all its appearances in Q were omitted from F.

5.3.219 SD Enter . . . RICHMOND F adds *sitting in his Tent*; this direction may have been overlooked when the manuscript for Q was prepared but it may be that in the cramped conditions on tour it was not practicable to set this scene within a tent.

5.3.220 SH LORDS Q1's speech heading is *Lo.* and Q2's *Lor.*; these can be singular or plural. Q3–8 have *Lords* and F mistakenly has *Richm.* and then *Rich.* at 221.

5.3.223 SH 1 LORD Q has *Lo.* here and at 232. F has *Lords.* at 223 and *Lor.* at 232. Allocating the speeches to a first or second lord is arbitrary.

5.3.233 SD *His oration to his soldiers* and **309** SD *His oration to his army* These are strange 'directions' for a play though not unique. They are not announcements to be spoken, they do not indicate action, and what they describe is self-evident. Marston's *The Dutch Courtesan*, 1605, has a Latin tag, *Turpe est difficiles habere nugas*, alongside the heading, Act 1 and Scene 1, an indication which forms no part of the text proper but seems to be self-directed at the author. In *The True Tragedy of Richard the Third*, 1594, there is at the end of Scene 16 (very roughly equivalent to Act 5 of Shakespeare's play but a little before the battle), a Latin tag, *Quisquam regna gaudit, ô fallex bonum*, for which there can be no speaker. Both the 'directions' in *R3* appear in the sources (where they are appropriate), though Richard's oration comes first. The titles are slightly closer to those in Holinshed than those in Halle. Whereas the heading for Richmond's oration appears in Q and F, that for Richard's appears only in Q. As F's copy here derives from Qq and is not independent, there is no ground for believing the 'directions' appeared in the original manuscript for the London production. A possible explanation for their appearance, in effect in the touring manuscript, is that in checking the memorial reconstruction against a source (and that source was probably Holinshed, a main source for Shakespeare's later histories), he marked into the manuscript these 'directions' to denote the passages to be checked. Both orations show close verbal similarities to this source. Both are singularly well reported and it may be that rather than merely checking the reconstruction, Shakespeare prepared the orations afresh from Holinshed. See 255n and 320n. More's account was not continued beyond the murder of the princes and its aftermath, Hardyng's *Chronicle*, 1543, has only, 'Afore he went to bed, he made an oration to his company with great vehemency, persuading and exhorting them manfully to fight. And afterwards, as it was said, he had a terrible dream in his sleep.' There is no mention of an oration by Richmond in Hardyng.

5.3.240 Richard except, This is a good example of the substantival effect of punctuation. Q has 'Richard, except those whome we fight against, / Had rather haue vs winne,'; F has '(*Richard* except)', so clearly marking him off from the bulk of his army.

5.3.255 your pains As Holinshed; Halle has 'your payne'.

5.3.267 SD *Exeunt . . . lords* Neither Q nor F has an *Exeunt*. F includes Ratcliffe and Catesby in the ensuing entry but Q refers only to Ratcliffe and the familiar but elusive '&c.' Catesby has no lines in the remainder of this scene. (He next speaks in 5.4.)

5.3.285 SD RICHARD *arms* Neither Q nor F has an indication that Richmond and Richard arm. Richmond can do so off-stage at the exit provided for him at 267.

5.3.298 SD *He shews him a paper* Appears (with *sheweth*) in Q only in right margin of 298.

5.3.300–1 *Jockey of Norfolk . . . sold* These lines follow Norfolk's second line in Q and F but Norfolk could hardly read out such an insult to his monarch.

5.3.320 brother's Q/F have 'mothers'. This indicates that Shakespeare relied here on the 1587 edition of Holinshed for this erroneously prints 'mothers'; the earlier edition and Halle have 'brothers'. The brother-in-law in question was the Duke of Burgundy, who supported Richmond. There is so much historically wrong with Shakespeare's *R3* that it is beyond correction, but this mistake is a fortuitous error of a particular edition of a source and correction is therefore appropriate.

5.3.340 Off with his . . . head! Cibber took in this order after 4.4.444 as 'Off with his head! So much for Buckingham' and 250 years later it was still being incorporated into productions (e.g. Olivier's 1955 film version).

5.4.0 SD No entry is given for Norfolk in Q/F and it may not have been intended that he should appear even in the London production. On tour, at least, the Battle of Bosworth is represented by no more than this brief scene with its trumpet calls (alarums) and the toing and froing of unidentified soldiers (excursions). As F's text here derives from Q it may be that the original version presented in London was fuller.

5.5.0 SD *with other lords* [*and soldiers*] Only Richmond and Derby speak in the last scene of the play. All the cast, except Burbage, could assemble as lords and soldiers (represented by Q's ubiquitous '&c.').

5.5.7 enjoy it Omitted from F – an omission that stems from Q3–8.

5.5.12 SD *A document . . .* RICHMOND Q gives no indication as to who reads out the list of fallen but F assigns these lines to Derby. F has no authority here and there is much to be said for Richmond – Henry VII – reading out the names as does Henry V after Agincourt.

5.5.13 *Ferrers* Q/F have Ferris. Hammond notes 'The odd form "Water Lord Ferri[s]" derives from Hall' – the 1548 edition. The 1550 edition of Halle has 'Water [*sic*] Lorde Ferrers of Chartley' (2f4ʼ); Holinshed also has Ferrers. Hardyng's *Chronicle*, 1543, has 'Walter Feris'.